Bernard P. Cohen and Hans Lee
CONFLICT, CONFORMITY AND SOCIAL STATUS

ERRATA

...ne 3: *For* 97 *read* 98

...ne 32: *For* Kemeny-Shell *read* Kemeny-Snell

...e 7: *For* homogenous *read* homogeneous

...ne 39: *For* and equilibrium *read* and in equilibrium

...ne 6: *For* parameters of Conflict Model *read* parameters of the Conflict Model

...ne 1: *For* n_{ij} *read* n_{ij}

...ne 19: *For* The product of *read* The product for

...ne 31: *For* $\frac{\gamma}{\epsilon}$ *read* $\frac{\gamma}{\epsilon}$

line 32: *For* on Trial with *read* on Trial 1 with

line 10: *For* E(A) vector for *read* E(A) for

line 23: *For* hypotheses *read* hypothesis

line 1: *For* laternation *read* alternation

line 28: *For* Connor *read* Conner

...line 28: *For* Expectation States Theory *read* "Expectation States Theory"

...line 31: *For* 115–177 *read* 115–117

...ACKET

...*or* Bernhard P. Cohen *read* Bernard P. Cohen

...nel, line 7: *For* Hans Lee, Department of Computer Service *read* Hans Lee, Department of Computer Science

Progress in
Mathematical Social Sciences

Volume 7

DUST

Front:

Front

CONFLICT, CONFORMITY AND SOCIAL STATUS

BERNARD P. COHEN

Department of Sociology,
Stanford University,
Stanford, California 94305

and

HANS LEE

Departments of Computer
Science and Sociology,
Michigan State University,
East Lansing, Michigan 48824

ELSEVIER
Amsterdam — Oxford — New York 1975

For the U.S.A. and Canada
ELSEVIER SCIENTIFIC PUBLISHING COMPANY, INC.
52 VANDERBILT AVENUE
NEW YORK, NEW YORK 10017

For all other areas
ELSEVIER SCIENTIFIC PUBLISHING COMPANY
335 JAN VAN GALENSTRAAT
P.O. BOX 211, AMSTERDAM, THE NETHERLANDS

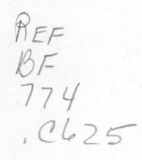
Library of Congress Cataloging in Publication Data

Cohen, Bernard P
  Conflict, conformity, and social status.

  (Progress in mathematical social sciences ; v. 7)
  Bibliography: p.
  1. Conformity—Mathematical models. I. Lee, Hans,
joint author. II. Title.
BF774.C625   301.15'01'84   74-21852
ISBN 0-444-41269-7

With 13 illustrations and 24 tables

Library of Congress Card Number: 74-21852

ISBN 0-444-41269-7

Printed in the United States of America

Progress in Mathematical Social Sciences

Other books included in this series

Dedicated to the memory of
Robert R. Bush

Acknowledgements

In the course of a project that has lasted over ten years, many people have contributed their advice, assistance, and criticism. We wish to express our gratitude to our colleagues and students who have contributed in many significant ways to this research. We are particularly appreciative of the advice and criticism given by Israel Adler, Bo Anderson, Joseph Berger, Frank Camilleri, Elizabeth Cohen, Thomas Conner, Sanford Dornbusch, J. Laurie Snell, and Morris Zelditch, Jr. Several people participated in contributing to the experiments reported here: Patricia Comstock, Judy Young Davidson, Eugene Lehr, Thomas Mayer, Alan Sable, Sheila Ryan, Gary Schulman and John Yellott. We were greatly assisted through the trials and tribulations of the computer by William McKeown, Ann Flood, and Thomas Rundall. In addition to his assistance with the computations, William McKeown made substantial contributions to the development of the equations utilized in the estimation procedures. We thank him for all of his varied contributions to this research program. We are very appreciative of the comments, suggestions and critiques offered by students in our courses through the years, especially the students in Sociology 147 at Stanford, and Sociology 940 at Michigan State University.

No monograph like this one could be developed without the aid of those who typed the various versions of what eventually became the manuscript. For these sometimes very painful tasks we thank the following: Mrs. Marion Aylesworth, Mrs. Lynda Barnhouse, Miss Ann Black, Mrs. Ruth Graham, Mrs. Jane Henley, Mrs. Mariam Shaffer, Mrs. Dawn Thelen, and Miss Gwendolyn Weaver.

At times we became so frustrated with using the English language as a vehicle for precise expression that we were temporarily incapable of writing anything. On the basis of this experience, we are convinced of the treachery of English for the statement of ideas for empirical verification. Yet somehow we continued the struggle. In a large part, any successes we may have achieved were due to Mrs. Nancy Hammond who as Editor for the College of Social Science (MSU) so freely gave her time.

In the development of this monograph, Mrs. Theresa Roberts patiently Xeroxed and collated several versions of this manuscript. Mrs. Marilyn Lovall, Executive Secretary of the MSU Department of Sociology, merits special thanks for so many "little things" (and some not so little!) which eased the task of manuscript preparation.

The research reported in this volume was begun under NSF Grant G 9030, "Probability Models for Conformity Behavior"; and continued with the assistance of NSF GS 23990, "A Study of Authority Structures and Evaluations"; NSF GS 1170, "A Study of Status Conceptions and the Distribution of Power and Prestige"; and NSF GS 01720, "A Comparative Study of Models for Binary Data". We are pleased to acknowledge the generous support of this basic research from the National Science Foundation.

We would like to acknowledge support from Michigan State University and from Stanford University. Both universities assisted by supplying secretarial support. Both universities also contributed computing services beyond those directly funded by the various specific NSF grants supporting this research. We are very pleased to be able to acknowledge this support and we wish to take this opportunity to thank them.

We appreciate receiving permission from Academic Press to reproduce copyrighted material from Vernon L. Allen's review of situational factors in conformity behavior. Also, we wish to acknowledge our debt to John G. Kemeny and J. Laurie Snell. A paraphrase of their original work on the parameter estimation problem appears in our appendix. MIT Press holds the copyright on the original material.

Finally, we will always be indebted to someone who did not live to see the completion of this project, but who was responsible in large measure for its beginning. The late Professor Robert R. Bush provided the stimulus and the training, and most of all, the belief that this is the way social science must go.

CONTENTS

CONFLICT, CONFORMITY AND SOCIAL STATUS

CHAPTER 1

The Development of a
Researchable Question

1.1 Introduction

The present report is a sequel to a previous research monograph, *Conflict and Conformity* (Cohen, 1963). Both works concern the continuing development, modification and empirical testing of a probability model for conformity behavior. Here we also present for the first time several experiments dealing with the effect of status in a group on susceptibility to social influence.

We present this study as a case history of the successes and failures along the road to rigorous, empirically supported sociological theory. It represents a stage in theory construction focused on the substantive problem of group determination of individual behavior. We have been guided by two fundamental assumptions in attempting to understand key features of group determination of individual behavior. Our first assumption is that the understanding which we seek requires both adequate conceptual tools and coordinated standardized empirical data gathering situations. The second assumption is that there is an intimate connection between the process of constructing formal models and the process of studying the sociological ideas these models attempt to illustrate.

When we began the series of experiments to be reported here, we aimed our work at the formulation of a theory of influence processes. The conception of theory with which we began, however, was inadequate to our objective. Now we have a much better understanding of fruitful strategies, of promising substantive ideas, and of useful ways to treat these ideas. We have developed a "systemic" approach which enables us to deal with a system of variables through time and to relate this system to significant so-

1

ciological ideas. It is our hope that this systemic approach provides a strategy that will promote the development of adequate theories of social influence processes.

In writing this monograph, we have several objectives in addition to the presentation of research results. The additional objectives are: (1) to delineate our research strategy and the substantive and methodological issues which motivated the development of this strategy, (2) to demonstrate the necessity for the utilization of technical skills, and (3) to provide researchers with a new set of strategic options with which to pursue their own problems. Let us discuss these briefly.

A research strategy aimed at generating cumulative knowledge through the development of rigorous, empirically supported theory requires a sustained commitment over a long period of time to a series of related problems. In short, our strategy is a long term strategy and the work we report has continued over many years. The development of formal models, the testing of these models, the revision of models in the light of empirical experience, and the application of these models is itself a process, the units of which are years, particularly when one comes up against intractable problems. In this monograph, we will document our step-by-step efforts in the process of theory construction so as to indicate the substantive and methodological issues that motivated us.

Our second objective is to demonstrate that the pursuit of cumulative knowledge demands not only perseverance, but a high level of technical skills. One may begin with vague intuitions and crude observations, but success demands the constant challenging of our intuitions and the continual refining of our observations. We maintain that progress beyond the level of interesting insight requires the development of rigorous conceptual tools and the mastery of a battery of technical tools. In this monograph, we intend to demonstrate that the process of developing such tools is directed by our understanding of our substantive concerns.

Our third objective of providing researchers with a new set of strategic options for the development of cumulative knowledge probably needs the most amplification. We feel that even when social scientists accept formal theory as their goal, they argue about how to move toward that goal. While we would certainly not argue that the strategy we have employed in this work is either optimum or unique, we believe that our experience can help others.

We see two opposing research approaches developing in social sciences. We may call one a holistic strategy and the other an

2

atomistic strategy. What we term the holistic strategy is an attempt to capture all of the important variables of a phenomenon and their relations — either in a vague discursive theoretical description or through multi-variate statistics. The attempt to explain the variance of an individual's behavior in a group by measuring personality variables, attitudes of both the individual and the group members, structural properties of the group, and properties of the culture in which the group operates — to capture the whole phenomenal situation — exemplifies the holistic strategy.

What we call the atomistic strategy is the attempt to deal with two-variable relationships as if the two variables constituted an insulated system unaffected by anything else. For example, studies which investigate the correlation between score on a pencil and paper test and conformity in the Asch situation without considering any other properties of either the individual or the situation represent the atomistic strategy. The knowledge that results from a collection of studies consists of a number of often unrelated, two-variable correlations.

We regard both of these strategies as inadequate for the development of cumulative knowledge; neither strategy provides the material from which one can construct increasingly precise theories. The holistic strategy at its best provides a set of relationships which may conceal the operation of many distinct processes, some of which may be appropriate objects for theorizing, but the collection as a whole could not be the object of a single theory. The set of relationships may describe distinct processes that sometimes interfere with one another or are only accidently related. The holistic strategy avoids the analysis necessary to determine what these processes are and under what circumstances one is related to another. The atomistic strategy, on the other hand, rarely provides any insight into what process or processes are operating and rarely considers what constraints affect these processes. For example, the observation that "dependency" (as an attribute of individuals) is correlated with conformity behavior does not provide any basis for considering why this relationship occurs, how dependency operates in the situation, and the conditions under which one would expect the relationship to obtain.

Neither atomistic nor holistic strategies ask theoretical questions, and so do not provide the foundation on which theories can be built. In the next section we present a list of some theoretical questions that can guide a research strategy.

There is a pragmatic aspect to the choice of strategy at the present stage of development of social science. The researchers' options are in part conditioned by the availability of techniques. On the one hand the explosive development of computer technology has made it as easy to examine multi-variate relations as bi-variate relations; thus the fact that all relationships are not of the same theoretical status gets obscured in the output of a matrix of correlation coefficients or a set of regression weights. On the other hand, the limits of the cost of laboratory experimentation make it extremely difficult to collect observations on many behavioral variables simultaneously. Cost considerations may lead an investigator to focus on a single correlation, but it is neither necessary to treat all variables identically nor to restrict measurements to two variables. In our research program we believe we have successfully avoided both pitfalls.

Our ability to avoid these pitfalls is based on the decision not to restrict ourselves to manifest observable variables. It is our belief that one of the more basic reasons for adopting either the atomistic or the holistic strategy is that investigators deal solely in terms of observable variables. Once this constraint is removed, the strategic options available to the researcher broaden. For once we allow ourselves to postulate underlying and unobservable variables, we have the ability to deal with systemic observations. This represents a key element of our present strategy; the system of variables with which we deal is not directly observable. What we observe are functions of this underlying system.

Formulating a model of a system of underlying variables provides us with a set of conceptual tools that is neither holistic nor atomistic but is systemic. As we see it, there are two key elements of our strategy which open up additional research options; namely, our willingness to postulate hypothetical entities, and our concern with formulating systematic relations among these entities. Before turning to the details of model building, we will consider some of the major substantive and methodological issues dealing with the general problems of sociologists' concern for group effects and the more specific problem of conformity and influence.

1.2 Group determination of individual behavior

It is a basic assumption of sociology that the group determines the behavior of the individual for a wide range of individual behaviors. Indeed, a great deal of research is devoted to documenting this assumption, to isolating the sources of group influence for particular beliefs, attitudes, or behaviors of individuals, or to interpreting a particular situation as an instance of "group effects". That there are group effects and that they occur in the most unexpected places is clear. We should not underestimate the achievement of sociology in making others aware of these group phenomena; yet we must do more than this. A systematic understanding of group effects requires a body of laws relating group characteristics to individual behaviors, a set of general principles specifying how group properties determine individual responses, and conceptualizations of the conditions under which the group affects the individual.

In approaching conformity and social influence one can ask several general questions:

1. What is it about the group that affects individual conformity?
2. What is it about the individual that affects his acceptance of social influence?
3. What kinds of individual behavior can be influenced?
4. How does the relationship between the individual and the group affect his conformity?
5. What properties of the situational context in which the group is interacting affect conformity?
6. How does group influence come about?
7. Under what conditions do individuals conform to groups? [1]

Reviews of the literature (Allen, 1965; Collins and Raven, 1969) summarize the state of our knowledge with respect to these questions. While we do not intend to recapitulate these reviews, we must indicate why we regard the state of our knowledge as an unhappy one. Consider, for example, our first question. Allen has found numerous studies reporting a relationship between such factors as attractiveness of the group, composition of the group, size of the group, and extremeness of the group norm to conformity. Some studies show that conformity is related to attractiveness (Festinger et al., 1952; Gerard, 1954; Schachter, 1951; Berkowitz,

---

[1] One might question whether or not Items 6 and 7 were two different versions of the same question. In our view, Item 6 requires us to formulate theories which describe processes or mechanisms that result in group influence. Item 7 on the other hand requires us to state when these theories are applicable. For a discussion of the issue of conditions, see Cohen (1972).

1954; Lott and Lott, 1961; etc.), and some studies show that conformity is unrelated to the attractiveness of the group (Harper, 1961; and Wilson, 1960). Only *ad hoc* propositions may be advanced to explain the discrepancy. With respect to group composition, Allen presents such factors as: Whether an individual is a member or a non-member of the group, whether the group is homogenous, whether the individual is similar to the group on certain important dimensions. One of Allen's concerns is particularly relevant to our own work, and we quote him:

A highly visible and readily detectable aspect of group composition is sex of the members. Difference in amount of conformity for males and females has been repeatedly demonstrated, with females generally conforming more than males (Crutchfield, 1955; Tuddenham, 1958). The finding holds, it should be noted, for groups composed of like-sex members, but must be qualified when sex composition is varied. Tuddenham *et al.* (1958) formed three types of groups: five men; three men and two women; and two men and three women. The same three types of groups were formed also with females. It was hypothesized that yielding by men would vary directly with the number of men in the group, while yielding by women would vary inversely with the number of women in the group. Results were generally consistent with these predictions. Tuddenham *et al.* (1958) interpreted the data in terms of the cultural sex stereotype which assumes that men are superior to women in cognitive processes such as perceptual judgments. In terms of similarity of the person to the group, the more homogeneous groups produced more conformity for males, but less for females. Results of this study emphasize that the effect of homogeneity of the group depends on the relevance to conformity of the dimension on which the homogeneity is based.

As this quotation illustrates, the attempts to interpret experimental findings, while couched in general terms, are largely *ad hoc* "explanations". Properties such as the sex composition of the group and the size of the group have been frequently investigated, but there has been little attempt to integrate these concrete variables under more abstract notions of group composition. Tuddenham's interpretation, for example, would explain the result that women yield more as there are more men in the group but would not explain why females conform more than males in groups in

6

which all participants are female. It seems to us that for propositions to be useful, to be testable, and to generate additional research, they must at least tie together two or more sets of diverse findings; so that if we are concerned with the effect of sex (as a characteristic of the individual and sex composition as a characteristic of the group), we would like to formulate principles that deal with sex both as an individual and a collective property.

One could, however, take a different approach and treat sex as an instance of a more abstract property. Following Tuddenham's lead, we could regard sex as one instance of a class of attributes of individuals about which there are cultural stereotypes such that a person possessing one attribute is believed to have an ability superior to a person possessing another attribute. Indeed, this is the strategy we adopt here and have employed successfully in other work (Berger, Cohen, and Zelditch, 1966).

From the various studies that have been done, it seems that our answer to the question "What is it about the group that affects conformity?" is "Many things". Nor can we be sure when a given property of the group will affect conformity of the individual. In other words, the studies that have been done are fragmented and do not add up to a coherent set of statements even about a limited set of group properties. It is not sufficient, for example, to argue that homogeneous groups are more effective in producing conformity than heterogeneous groups. One needs some guidelines as to those attributes for which homogeneity is relevant to conformity. Certainly homogeneity with respect to eye color would not be the same as homogeneity with respect to race. And we really have not learned much when Allen reminds us that "Results of this study emphasize that the effect of homogeneity of the group depends on the relevance to conformity of the dimension on which the homogeneity is based". A reader may be forgiven if he interprets the comment to require a catalog of dimensions and their relevance to conformity and to reject that suggestion as demanding an infinite program of research.

We could examine each of the questions we have posed earlier and document the fact that we are in the same unhappy state for each of these questions. But we need only consider one additional question: the person-group relationship.

One of the factors discussed in this connection is status in the group. Allen cites evidence that high status people conform to group norms more than lower status people; he also presents evidence that a high status person conforms less than other members

7

of the group; and finally he cites investigators who found no differences in conformity between high and low status group members. In our own work, we were particularly intrigued by two hypotheses regarding the relationship between status and conformity:

(1) The higher the social rank of a person the more closely he will follow the group norms (Homans, 1950).

(2) High status persons will have freedom to deviate from group norms (Hollander, 1958).

Depending upon how these propositions are interpreted, they can be complementary or contradictory. As Allen notes, "Both Homans' and Hollander's hypotheses receive some support; both also run counter to much available empirical data". But this problem cannot be resolved by data. It is clear that the hypotheses need further explication. While there are alternative approaches to studying these ideas, a process conception seemed particularly appropriate. If we could specify that the two propositions apply to different stages of the interaction process, we could reconcile any apparent conflict between them. Furthermore, such a conceptualization might enable us to integrate the diverse findings that Allen cites. It may be possible to identify the operation of such things as the nature of the task, the popularity of the high status individual, his security, with different stages of such a process.

Thus in attempting to answer our fourth question we are again in the same position as before. Although the literature indicates that there are conflicting positions concerning the effect of status in the group, there is no cumulative body of research designed to resolve this conflict. On the other hand, our speculations lead us to attempt to ask the prior question of how group influence comes about. That is, our speculations lead us to seek conceptualization of the process of group influence.

We will return to the issue of process conceptions in the next section. Here we should summarize our reaction to the empirical literature. There are many *ad hoc* interpretations of empirical results. Most of the studies report that there was conformity behavior exhibited in the experiments, but the empirical literature provides no sense of direction for the theoretical integration of even some of the numerous factors thought by different authors to be relevant to the understanding of influence phenomena. In short, the empirical literature does not provide a foundation of knowledge of conformity and social influence for the next generation of investigators to extend. Furthermore, this literature offers no

8

guidelines for a research strategy other than the individual researcher's taste.

In addition to the large body of empirical studies, there are theoretical essays which consider the effects of groups on individuals. Does this theoretical work provide a foundation of knowledge or guidelines for research strategy? Unfortunately, we have concluded that the answer must be "No". Some theoretical papers have been primarily definitional and classificatory, but others have advanced sets of related propositions. The classificatory efforts generated typologies dealing with various aspects of the group or various dimensions of the effects on individuals. Thus we have typologies of power (French and Raven, 1959), compliant behavior (Festinger, 1953), tasks (Roby and Lanzetta, 1958), and reference groups (Merton, 1957).

Of particular interest to us was the idea of a reference group. Basically this notion is that an individual compares himself to various groups either for the purposes of arriving at a self-evaluation or for the purposes of validating a belief or opinion. The concept seemed to hold within it the possibility of formulating statements about the conditions under which the group would and would not affect the individual. But applying the concept proved a disappointment for reasons which have been analyzed elsewhere (Cohen, 1962). Indeed, although Merton (1957) lists 26 properties of groups which he feels should be taken into account in work on reference groups, his analysis has not led to theoretical progress. Even those theories which assert propositions have been disappointing. As Collins and Raven (1969) put it, "We often could not discuss the empirical studies under the same organizational framework used to discuss the theoretical models!" In other words, the gap between theorizing and empirical investigation has been so great that neither has had much impact upon the other.

We have long been intrigued by this gap. Throughout our work we have tried to guide our theorizing by empirical investigation and direct our empirical investigation to complement theorizing. At this point, we believe we understand some of the key reasons for the gap between theory and empirical study and some of the necessary conditions for the production of general theory based on and buttressed by empirical evidence. Let us turn to general issues of strategy, a discussion of which should help to explain the present state of affairs and also to provide direction for what can be done to promote the development of a cumulative understanding of social influence and conformity.

9

1.3 Problems of strategy

The development of cumulative knowledge is the development of general theoretical knowledge supported by a range of diverse and high-quality evidence. The formulation and testing of such theory implies a close connection between theorizing and empirical investigation. Why then does the present gap exist? What are some of its consequences? By examining these consequences, we can isolate what we believe to be some key elements of a fruitful strategy.

The holistic orientation, mentioned earlier, contributes to the failure to understand the role of general theory. Those who work in this vein aim to capture the whole of group structure or to formulate the entire range of individual behaviors affected by the group. While no one attempts to capture all properties, the objective is to come as close as possible to studying all the important properties. Studies conducted with this objective often take the form of multi-variate research which maximizes the number of properties taken as independent variables and correlated with a large number of measures of individual behavior as dependent variables. But the collection of investigators who study two variable relationships also reflects the holistic orientation. For when we look at a series of bi-variate studies, we see a number of investigators each of which is either trying to find a new independent variable that will correlate with a previous measure of individual behavior or is trying to locate a new dependent variable that will be affected by a previous isolated "causal" factor. Although no one asserts it explicitly, apparently the objective is to draw a map of a particular phenomenon showing all the independent variables which may produce effects and all the dependent variables that may be affected.

But such maps are not theories nor are they the ingredients out of which theories are produced. Listing all the independent and dependent variables represents an attempt to capture the whole of the phenomenal situation — in effect to hold up a mirror to reality. The holistic orientation has as a consequence a focus on the phenomenal situation. But one cannot theorize about a situation. If one is concerned with explaining the total situation one is bound to reject any abstractly formulated theory. By its nature, general theory forces the theorist to select, to omit and to make judgements of importance.

In short, to incorporate a large number of relationships and to deal with them as if every relationship were equivalent to every other relationship is antithetical to theory construction. Some relationships are invariant and others are not; some relationships are important, others are not; some relationships are spurious, others are not; the theorist must make these judgments and the holistic orientation prevents him from doing so.

The lack of understanding of the necessity for theory and the issues to be addressed in theorizing has lead to empirical studies that are not comparable, research findings that are not invariant, analyses that are not dynamic, and empirical generalizations that are not conditional.

Cumulative knowledge, by definition, requires comparable studies. While we in social science have many studies, in general it is not possible to compare one with another. It is very rare that a researcher can use the results of several previous studies in planning his own research. These studies involve many different variables and it is impossible to associate results with changes in a specific variable. Consider, for example, the Asch situation (Asch, 1956). Can we compare the results of Asch's studies with the results of Blake and Brehm's (1954) tape recorder simulation? The tasks were different; the settings were different; the manipulations were different. At a concrete level, the studies are not comparable. However, at an abstract level, by making some explicit assumptions, we can compare these studies; that is precisely the function of, and the necessity for, general theory.

A second issue which empirical research rarely addresses but which must be considered if knowledge is to be cumulative is the question of the invariance of empirical findings. But this question also is difficult to answer in the absence of a theory. Consider, for example, the finding that some group property such as cohesiveness is related to the conformity behavior of the individual. When is this relationship invariant? To begin to answer this question requires some idea of the invariance properties of each of the variables. Suppose we measure an individual's conformity behavior by taking his conformity score in the Asch experiment, a score that is usually computed as the number or proportion of times he yielded to the group of confederates. Over what set of conditions is this score invariant? If we had two experiments identical except for the stimuli the group judged, would we expect an individual to attain the same score? This question is impossible to answer empirically because the range of conditions over which we could take that score is infinite. The only reasonable way to approach this particular problem of invariance is to formulate a model that contains assumptions concerning invariance properties and test the consequences of the model.

Perhaps the strongest argument for research designed to assist in the development of explicit theory is to point out that implicit assumptions about invariance properties underlie nearly all empirical studies, that these implicit assumptions vary from investigator to investigator, and that, as they are implicit, they are rarely evaluated. When an investigator computes a conformity score in the Asch situation by summing trials of the experiment, he implicitly assumes that a conformity response at the beginning of the experiment is equivalent to a conformity response at the end of the experiment. Making such assumptions explicit would result in a model with testable consequences. If he then tested the consequences of the model, he would find a difference between subjects whose scores were based on early conformity and those whose scores were based on later conformity — a result that would seriously challenge the implicit assumption behind summing responses over trials. Yet there have been countless studies unselfconsciously relating the conformity score to the score on some other measure.

Our concern that previous analyses have not been dynamic points to another class of implicit assumptions. Investigators have not been concerned explicitly with changes over time in their independent variable or variables, but this lack of concern assumes something about process. We have previously discussed the implications of this issue (Cohen, 1963), but let us briefly summarize the argument. In studies of problems like the relationship of cohesiveness of the group to the conformity of the individual, the experiments are typically "cross-sectional" rather than "longitudinal". The experimenter performs a manipulation of cohesiveness, allows the group to behave for some period of time, and then obtains a measure of individual conformity. The measure typically is summed over the time period or taken at the end point as a cross section of behavior.

An implicit assumption underlies this mode of analysis, namely that the measure of conformity represents behavior in a stable state. It is assumed that if the group were allowed to interact for a longer period, the individual's conformity would neither increase nor decrease so that the relationship between cohesiveness and conformity would not vary over the length of the group interaction. Correlational studies by their nature depend upon equilibrium assumptions. If the dependent variable is fluctuating marked-

12

ly over time, the magnitude of the correlation would also be fluctuating; hence, in the absence of an assumed equilibrium, it really would not make much sense to correlate the variables. Yet what justifies the assumption of equilibrium? Here again an empirical justification is impossible. What is required is a conceptualization which defines the equilibrium state of a system and posits the conditions under which equilibrium is reached. Given a conceptualization of equilibrium and a rationale for deciding when a system is in equilibrium, we have every reason to expect that our correlations will have desired invariance properties, and we should be better able to interpret these correlations.

A conceptualization of equilibrium, however, depends upon a conceptualization of what kind of process is occurring and how it works. In social sciences, there have been very few efforts to conceptualize what is occurring through time, that is to posit a moving system of relationships that account for changes in the dependent variables and even where such models have been developed they have had little impact. As Collins and Raven (1969) comment, "The process models ... appear to have had little, if any, effect on empirical investigations of social structure". They note that "the process models do seem to contain a number of interaction propositions and hypotheses". From our point of view, however, they appear to draw the wrong conclusion, for they continue "Nevertheless, the fact that these process models have stimulated so little research raises an interesting point: Why not keep the relatively simple hypotheses and discard the models?" Our answer to Collins and Raven is that you cannot keep the hypotheses without addressing yourself to the equilibrium and process issues involved in testing these hypotheses. For example, consider one almost trivial implication of our argument. To test a relatively simple hypothesis requires running an experiment through time. Will the results of the test vary over the time of the experiment? If so, how long should the experiment be run to obtain the invariance property? Our discussion suggests that what is on the surface a simple problem — that of deciding how long to run the experiment — has a complex answer. Furthermore, we argue that the question has no answer in the absence of a theoretical formulation.

Although the justification of any cross-sectional empirical study depends upon a conception of equilibrium, there are a number of possible equilibrium assumptions and any one of these can only be justified by its place in a model of the process. The experience of the present research underscored this point. The model presented in Cohen (1963) conceptualized a particular process and defined equilibrium states, but investigating various models demonstrated how dependent the nature of equilibrium was on the type of processes postulated. Even fitting these models to the same set of experimental data generated quite different interpretations of when equilibrium occurred. That is, the same set of observations was consistent with a number of different equilibrium postulates, even though the observations may have been inconsistent with other features of these different models. While it was not possible to choose one equilibrium assumption over another on the basis of the data, it was possible to choose one model over another on the basis of other predictions and the equilibrium assumption we settled on was that contained in the model preferred on other grounds.

The final consideration in understanding the gap between theory and research, as well as the properties of general theory, is what we have termed the non-conditional nature of both theoretical statements and empirical generalizations. Many social scientists believe that scientific laws must be universal and without exception. We claim that this belief represents a profound misunderstanding of what science can accomplish. Furthermore, in our view, this belief is in considerable measure responsible for the present state of the social sciences. The search for universally true laws and the failure to find them inhibits the formulation of any law-like statements. But scientific laws need not be universally true. The famous law of falling bodies is not universally true. It is true only under a specified set of given conditions which include such assertions as "in the absence of friction". In general, once science is given the initial state of a system, it can, through its statement of laws, predict the state of the system at a later point in time. In other words, its laws presuppose statements of initial conditions.

We find it strange that despite its obviousness, the conditional nature of science is widely neglected, particularly in the social sciences. At times, writers attempt to address some of the issues by claiming that social science laws will always be probabilistic rather than deterministic. But they evidently believe that by making such a statement they are absolved of the necessity of asserting the conditions under which their generalizations hold. However, probability statements must be conditional as well, for in the absence of statements of initial conditions, the probabilities can vary

14

from zero to one, in which case the generalizations are trivially true and say nothing.

In our thinking about the conditional nature of scientific assertions, we have distinguished two types of conditions. We term these "scope conditions" and "initial conditions". Scope conditions are assertions which determine the applicability of a theory or a model; they are general statements which describe the conditions under which it is appropriate either to test the theory or to employ it as an explanation of empirical phenomena. The statement "the theory applies to 'task-oriented groups' ", is a statement of a scope condition.

On the other hand, statements of initial conditions are descriptions of a particular system at a particular time and place. Thus, for example, the statement that "at the beginning of the Asch experiment the probability of an individual's conforming to the group is close to zero", is a statement of an initial condition. Notice that scope conditions are abstract in form and are non-singular. (By non-singular, we mean they are independent of time, place and historical circumstances.) Statements of initial conditions, however, are particular and contain references to specific (or "particular") times and places, at least implicitly. Most frequently initial conditions will involve numerical values for a set of variables. Our work with Markov chain models brought home to us the importance of formulating both types of conditions and the necessity for determining values of the initial state of the system.

While we began our work with a series of substantive concerns, the purpose of this discussion has been to show the methodological issues that must be confronted before one can reasonably pursue substantive concerns. We conclude this discussion of general issues of strategy with the claim that the answers to our substantive questions must involve statements of relations which have the invariance property, which are conditional and which specify the dynamics operating in the process. Finally, our statements must allow us to conduct a large number of comparable studies that enable us to evaluate empirically the assertions we make. In the next section we will tie together our substantive questions and our strategic constraints and apply them to the present series of investigations.

1.4 The development of strategy

Although we listed seven substantive questions and several issues of research strategy, we were not concerned with all of these at the outset of our research. From the very beginning we were concerned with comparability of experimental results and dynamic formulations of theory; other concerns developed as we proceeded with our research. It appears appropriate to present a brief overview of these developments as background for a detailed consideration of the various aspects of our research in the following chapter.

Our first objective was an apparatus that would allow us to deal with our principal substantive concern, namely, "How does the relationship between the individual and the group affect his conformity to the group?" We sought an apparatus that would allow us to develop cumulative knowledge with respect to this question. We say apparatus rather than theory because what we now believe to be required is both more and less than a theory. It is more in that a repeatable empirical situation, designed to allow comparability, is a necessity if our accumulating knowledge is to be empirically responsible. It is less than a theory in that what is required is a conceptualization that allows the design and analysis of experiments but does not incorporate the law-like assertions connecting substantive concepts. In a sense this apparatus could be the explication of a concept that enters into such law-like assertions. Indeed, from one perspective, the model that we have developed can be considered an explication of a system of dependent variables. From this point of view, our substantive question can be rephrased as: "How does the relationship between the individual and the group affect the dynamic system of dependent variables that represents the process of conforming to the group?" To illustrate this further, the two propositions advanced by Homans and Hollander (see page 8) can be recast into this framework. If we argue that these two propositions refer to different stages of a process, then we would expect that the state of the system of variables would be related to the status of the individual but not in a simple linear way. Comparing a high status person with a low status person, we would expect a different constellation of the parameters of a model for each status and for different time periods — at the outset of the process, during its course, and equilibrium. Alas, we did not begin with the systemic and non-linear features of our question so clearly formulated.

At the beginning of the present research we were already constrained by decisions made in connection with *Conflict and Conformity* (Cohen, 1963). These constraints clearly indicate the continuity of this study with earlier work and were justified by the success of the model presented in *Conflict and Conformity*. It is, however, appropriate to briefly review the principal assumptions which carry forward from our earlier work.

First of all, we clearly rejected a crude cross-sectional investigation of the relationship between status and conformity. We were committed to employing a conception of process in order to investigate that relationship. Secondly, we were committed to employ an Asch type situation as our standardized experimental setting since we believed that this situation captured the key features of the conformity phenomena. In addition, there was a backlog of experience on which we could build. Thirdly, we continued to use the modified version of the original Asch experiment developed in *Conflict and Conformity*. Cohen (1963) maintained that restricting analysis to manifest observations was unnecessarily constraining. In the present study, we again assumed that the appropriate strategy was to formulate an underlying process and ask if such underlying process could have generated the observed data, that is, if the data were consistent with the predictions produced by the model. Finally, we reaffirmed the objective of representing the process in this modified Asch situation as a process of conflict resolution.

A few comments are necessary about the modifications of the Asch situation. The original Asch experiments had many variables built into the sequence of trials. For example, the nature of the stimulus and of the group behavior varied from trial to trial. These variations could have easily masked temporal process or could have produced process phenomena that were quite unrelated to conformity. This possibility motivated the simplification of the original Asch situation so as to remove what for our purposes are extraneous variables. Thus Cohen (1963) redesigned the experiment so the stimulus to be judged was constant from trial to trial and the response of the unanimous majority was also constant from trial to trial. These simplifications reduced the possibility that the situation contained many interfering processes so the model builder could focus on representing a single central process.

Cohen's Conflict Model which will be described in the next chapter and the constraints we have just discussed were our starting points. When we began we knew that we could isolate a single process, describe that process in relatively simple terms and theorize about it. We also knew that there were points of discrepancy between the model's predictions and the data as well as some technical problems in dealing with the model. Furthermore, the Conflict Model had been used to distinguish between different experimental treatments (Cohen, 1963, pp. 159—168); hence we should be able to apply it to the question of how the relationship between an individual and the group affects his conformity.

The Conflict Model incorporated an assumption about the initial state of the system and a mechanism by which the process of conflict resolution evolved through time. In his work, Cohen did nothing to affect the initial state of the system, but rather put subjects directly into a situation where they were confronted by social pressure from a group of confederates. Given our substantive question and our strategy, the obvious next step was to vary systematically the initial conditions and test whether the model reflected these variations in a substantively reasonable way. In other words, if we manipulated the subject's relationship to the confederates, the parameters of the model, either those parameters that represent the initial state of the system or those that represent rates of movement in the process, should reflect the manipulation.

In retrospect our initial views were somewhat naive. Although we were concerned with manipulating factors which affect the initial state of the system, we expected the effects of these factors to be represented in the process rather than in the starting point of the process. We have always thought of manipulating the relative status of the individual in the group as manipulating initial conditions; yet we sought the effects of these manipulations in the parameters that described the process by which the system moved from its initial state to an equilibrium state rather than in the parameters that describe the initial state of the system. The Conflict Model assumed values to represent the initial state of the system. While the assumption was clearly an oversimplification, the Conflict Model still fits the data from Asch experiments which were not preceded by a status manipulation. Also, we believed that the initial state of the system was related to the unambiguous nature of the task, and we wanted to separate that factor from the relation of the individual to the other members of the group. With hindsight, it is clear that the person's relation to the group is just as much an initial condition as the nature of the task, and therefore manipulating that variable should be represented in the initial

18

state of the system. Our desire to separate these two kinds of variables in one part of our model appears now as both unwarranted and not feasible.

But our naivete and the failure to which it led had a very positive consequence. It allowed us to re-think what we meant by initial conditions and actually led to a formulation of the model which is more closely related to our conception of scientific theories, namely, a set of given initial conditions decribing the initial states of the system and a set of assertions in mathematical form that represent how the system moves from its initial state to another state at a later point in time.

Not only were we fixated in our conception of the initial state of the system, but we were also unrealistically optimistic in formulating a set of independent and essentially linear hypotheses relating the parameters of the conflict resolution process to our status manipulation. The parameters of the process were four and were substantively interpreted as:

The rate of rejection of the group

The rate of acceptance of an influence attempt

The rate of rejection of an influence attempt

The rate of acceptance of the group.

We decided in our experiments to manipulate the relative status of the naive subject, *vis-à-vis* that of the confederates, by manipulating his "ability at the task", as will be described in detail below, through the use of contrived tests and contrived scores. Using this manipulation, we formulated the following hypotheses:

Given a task situation (a) for which an ability is relevant and (b) in which there is a conflict between the individual and the group in the performance of the task:

1. If the individual has greater ability than the group, he is more likely to reject the group than if his ability is less than or equal to the group's.
2. If the individual has less ability than the group, he is less likely to reject the group than if his ability is greater than or equal to the group's.
3. If the individual has greater ability than the group, he is less likely to accept an influence attempt by the group than if his ability is less than or equal to the group's.
4. If the individual has less ability than the group, he is more likely to be influenced by the group than if his ability is greater than the group's.

Since we regarded the situation as symmetric, we formulated

19

parallel hypotheses for the parameters "acceptance of the group" and "rejection of an influence attempt". We also considered the intensity of conflict and the time at which conflict is resolved, that is, the point at which equilibrium is reached through stable conflict resolution. We hypothesized:

5. Where the individual is differentiated from the group, he will experience less conflict than where he is equal in ability to the group.
6. Where the individual is differentiated from the group, he will resolve the conflict earlier than when he is equal in ability to the group.

The results of the work to be reported in this volume indicate how over-simplified these hypotheses were, but before we could deal with the hypotheses, we encountered a series of barriers that had to be overcome.

The most significant barrier was that the original model did not fit the new experiments. The model required that we estimate four parameters from the data. But the estimation of these four parameters was itself a difficult technical problem. This mathematical difficulty was another reason for maintaining our assumption about the initial state of the system. We wished to minimize the number of parameters which had to be estimated from the data, for if we treated the initial state of the system as parameters to be estimated, the model would have seven rather than four parameters. Previous difficulties with technical problems of estimation when only four parameters were involved made us wary of increasing the number of empirically determined quantities. Rather than complicate the model, we chose to conduct new experiments, substantively more interesting and closer to our theoretical concerns; and to apply the original model to them without relaxing any of the model's restrictions.

Armed with the model and with a set of hypotheses dealing with the model's quantities, we conducted our first experiment on status and conformity. To our disappointment, three of the four experimental treatments looked very similar in the data they generated, the fourth treatment differed markedly from the three others, and the model fit none of the four sets of data. This result raised the question of whether our strategy had led us down a blind alley. But even that question did have an immediate answer. We alluded above to technical problems in estimating the parameters of the model. Although we had developed a procedure for estimation, it was crude and inelegant. It made use of a computer search technique that did not have a unique solution for the set of parameters and did not allow us to determine whether we had arrived at an optimum set for a given collection of observations. Hence, when we found that the model did not fit any of the four experimental treatments, we could not decide whether the model was at fault or whether we simply had poor estimates for the model's quantities. This question forced us to take another detour. We had to find an alternative way to estimate the parameters that would generate more confidence in the numerical values obtained and thus allow us to attribute the lack of fit to inadequacies in the model itself.

The first step was to undertake a study of several different estimation procedures. Although we were not able to arrive at an optimum set of estimates, the insights gained from employing two different estimation procedures, each with several modifications, convinced us that there was something fundamentally wrong with the model — the discrepancies between the model's prediction and the observed data were too great to be rectified even if we had obtained optimum estimates. We explored various techniques of estimation and developed computer procedures for both estimating the model's parameters and generating sets of simulated data using these estimates. The results of this study again raised fundamental questions.

The success of the Conflict Model indicated that Asch-type experiments could be modeled by assuming a single central process, but the new set of experiments involved experimental manipulation of the status relationship between the individual and the group. Did this manipulation introduce additional processes that interfered with the process of conflict resolution? If we had introduced interfering processes, could we expect what was occurring in our experiments? In manipulating status relationships, we manipulated a subject's expectations about his ability at the task relative to the confederate's. We assumed that the expectation created at the outset would remain constant throughout the experiment. Although we knew that this assumption was unrealistic, we believed it was a reasonable first approximation, that is, any process of expectation change so introduced would be minor relative to the process of conflict resolution. The failure of the Conflict Model to describe these new experiments raised grave doubts about our assumptions and, more seriously, raised doubts about our entire strategy. If it were not possible to vary the initial conditions under which conflict resolution took place without introducing a multiplicity of interfering processes, the utility of the Asch situation as a standardized experiment would be severely limited.

Fortunately the search for alternative estimation procedures led us to re-examine the key features of the Conflict Model. The result was a reformulation, the Cohen-Lee model. The new model has more parameters to estimate, so in some ways is more complex, but allows us to use analytic methods of estimation so in the long run, it is simpler to use. Also, it provides a much better description of the experimental data. (Later on we will present eight sets of new data and show that this model has a reasonably good fit to seven of them.) Once we had demonstrated the success of the new model, we could return to the substantive questions with which we began. And it turned out that the revised model not only enables us to deal with these questions, but points out the inadequacies of our initial hypotheses and provides a vehicle for reformulating these hypotheses. In other words, using the model to test our substantive ideas clarifies and modifies the substance of our assertions. The model provides a description both of the initial state of the system and of the process. Whereas our hypotheses formerly dealt with the parameters which described the process and dealt with them as independent quantities, we are now able to formulate a set of more sophisticated hypotheses. In other words, our initial formulation consisted of relating four independent variables, one at a time, to the experimental manipulation. We now have the tools to deal with a system of dependent variables, and, as we will show, our experimental treatments have their greatest impact on the initial state of the system; hence, the Cohen-Lee model enables us to capture what had only been intuition before, namely that effects can be partitioned into where the individual starts and what happens to him in the course of the experiment, with the former showing more dramatic variation than the latter.

In this section we have presented an overview of the substantive and strategic issues that have arisen in the course of our work. Although there are many problems that remain to be solved, we believe that the accomplishments to date validate our strategic choices. We have succeeded in developing a significant part of the apparatus that we described at the beginning of this section. Although some questions remain about the utility of our modified version of the Asch experiment as a standardized experimental situation, we have a model that is dynamic, that provides for comparability across studies, that focuses on a process rather than on a total situation, that does not restrict itself to manifest observations but postulates underlying entities, and we have clear evidence of the utility of our approach. Perhaps most significantly, our model deals with both fixed initial conditions and the process by which the initial state of the system is transformed into an equilibrium state. We represent this theoretical process as a system of variables and can show that this system has substantive significance. As we will demonstrate later on, the model's quantities differ for different status treatments, and these differences correspond to our substantive intuitions. Finally, by relating the system that represents conflict resolution to exogenous variables such as the individual's relation to the group, we can formulate assertions which have invariance properties. In these assertions we are able to modify our original ideas on the relationship between status and conformity from simple, independent linear language to statements which consider the interrelation of several variables.

The remainder of this monograph is a detailed documentation of the claims we have made in this chapter. We will present the problems we encountered, how we overcame them, what led to modification of our model, and how this modified model deals with experiments relating the individual's status in the group to his conformity in the group. We will begin with a brief summary of the original Conflict Model as presented in *Conflict and Conformity* (Cohen, 1963).

CHAPTER 2

The Conflict Model

2.1 Introduction

In this chapter we will present the Conflict Model, derive equations for several important quantities, and examine the substantive import of the assumptions we have incorporated in the model. After presenting the model, we will conclude this chapter with a brief discussion of its utility.

The Conflict Model does not formulate any substantive theory of conformity. There are serious questions concerning whether conformity is an appropriate phenomenon for theoretical investigation. Certainly at the time this model was formulated, there were no theories of conformity sufficiently developed to formalize. Hence, the purpose of developing this model was to represent as precisely as possible a specific set of experimental results. The concern was to construct what has been called a representational model to represent the phenomena observed in Asch-type experiments (Berger et al., 1962). A representational model "provides a means for exhibiting and systematically studying the relation of various aspects of the conformity process to each other" (Berger et al., 1962, p. 62). Indeed, it was the desire to describe a process which motivated the development of the Conflict Model, since we felt that a process description of Asch-type experiments would greatly enhance the utility of these experiments.

Although one might distinguish between representational and theoretical construct models in that the latter make use of hypothetical constructs in the development of formal descriptions, the Conflict Model whose purpose is representational also employs unobservable constructs. After a series of attempts to develop a formal model based solely on observable elements of the Asch situation, we found that we could not construct a model which adequately fit the data if we insisted that the model employ only observable elements. Thus, one of the features of the Conflict Model is that it postulates an underlying process and regards the observed response process as a function of the postulated underlying process.

2.2 The Conflict Model

The Conflict Model postulates an underlying process of conflict resolution that is described as an absorbing four-state Markov chain. It should be emphasized that the model does not describe the manifest response process. Indeed, the observed responses are clearly non-Markovian.

The model is defined as follows: on a given trial, an individual can be in any one of four states. On the next trial he can move with specified probability to another state. The probabilities of movement are called transition probabilities. The four states of the Markov chain are defined as follows:

S_1 : If an individual is in this state, he has resolved the conflict between conformity and non-conformity in favor of non-conformity.

S_2 : If an individual is in this state, he is still in conflict between conformity and non-conformity but temporarily favors non-conformity.

S_3 : If an individual is in this state, he is still in conflict between conformity and non-conformity but temporarily favors conformity.

S_4 : If an individual is in this state, he has resolved the conflict between conformity and non-conformity in favor of conformity.

Assumption 1. Once an individual has resolved the conflict, it stays resolved.

To capture this assumption, we formulate a special case of Markov chain called the "absorbing Markov Chain" with two absorbing states. That is, once an individual has entered States 1 or 4, he remains there.

Assumption 2. Before conflict is resolved in a given direction, the individual must favor that direction.

We posit that an individual cannot on one trial be in conflict favoring conformity and on the next trial have resolved the conflict in favor of non-conformity. (Although the purpose of this assumption is to simplify the formal representation by reducing the number of parameters of the model, it is certainly a substantively reasonable assumption.)

These two assumptions give rise to a matrix of transition probabilities, P, for our Markov chain:

$$P = \begin{array}{c} \\ 1 \\ 2 \\ 3 \\ 4 \end{array} \begin{pmatrix} 1 & 2 & 3 & 4 \\ 1 & 0 & 0 & 0 \\ \alpha & 1-\alpha-\beta & \beta & 0 \\ 0 & \gamma & 1-\gamma-\epsilon & \epsilon \\ 0 & 0 & 0 & 1 \end{pmatrix} \qquad (2.1)$$

where each entry, P_{ij}, represents the probability that when the subject is in State S_i, he will move to State S_j on the next trial.

Once we can determine the initial distribution of individuals among the four states, that is, the distribution at Trial 0, this initial distribution together with the matrix of transitional probabilities completely describes the underlying process of conflict resolution.

This initial distribution can be treated in two ways. It can be regarded as a set of parameters to be estimated from observed data, or it can be treated as an additional postulate of the model. In the initial formulation of the Conflict Model, the following assumption was made:

Assumption 3. All individuals initially favor non-conformity. In terms of the model, on Trial 0, all individuals are in State 2.

This assumption arises from several considerations. First it was assumed that when the subject is initially exposed to the conflict — at the time the confederates give their first incorrect response and prior to his own response — he will not instantaneously resolve the conflict; hence, he would not be in States 1 or 4. Furthermore, since the non-conforming response represents what people have learned through long experience is the perceptually correct response, we assumed that individuals would initially favor non-conformity. This assumption could be relaxed or modified for situations where there is not a perceptually correct response alternative (Cohen, 1962). It is even possible to question Assumption 3 for the Asch situation itself; an assumption which asserts that some proportion initially favors conformity on Trial 0 might be more useful in describing the Asch situation.

We relate the manifest response process to the Asch situation to the underlying Markov chain in the following way. Let X_{in} be a

26

random variable which takes on the value 1 if the ith subject gives a nonconforming response on Trial n, and the value 0 if the ith subject makes a conforming response on Trial n:

and let $Y_{in} = \begin{cases} 1 \text{ if the } i^{th} \text{ subject is in State 1 on Trial n} \\ 2 \text{ if the } i^{th} \text{ subject is in State 2 on Trial n} \\ 3 \text{ if the } i^{th} \text{ subject is in State 3 on Trial n} \\ 4 \text{ if the } i^{th} \text{ subject is in State 4 on Trial n} \end{cases}$

We assert that

$X_{in} = \begin{cases} 1 \text{ if } Y_{in} = 1 \text{ or } 2 \\ 0 \text{ if } Y_{in} = 3 \text{ or } 4 \end{cases}$

From the transition matrix and the above definitions it follows that, if a subject is in State 1 on Trial n, he will make a non-conforming response on Trial n and on every subsequent trial. If a subject is in State 2 on Trial n, he will make a non-conforming response on Trial n, but may or may not make non-conforming responses on subsequent trials. If a subject is in State 3 on Trial n, he will make a conforming response on Trial n, and may or may not make conforming responses on subsequent trials. If a subject is in State 4 on Trial n, he will make a conforming response on Trial n and every subsequent trial.

Although we have formulated a description of the underlying process of conflict resolution, one further assumption is necessary to tie this underlying process to the manifest conformity responses. Each experimental trial on which the confederates give incorrect responses has its analogue in the underlying process. Such trials are usually termed "critical" trials in Asch-type experiments. From the first critical trial we assert a one-to-one correspondence between the critical experimental trials and trials in our underlying Markov process.

In Asch-type experiments, the subject is initially presented with two "neutral" trials — trials on which the confederates give correct responses.

Originally, Asch included neutral trials interspersed in the sequence of critical trials, but for the experiments reported in *Conflict and Conformity*, two initial neutral trials were followed by a sequence of uninterrupted critical trials. In *Conflict and Conformity*, Trial 0, identified as the state of affairs prior to the critical sequence, was loosely tied to these two initial neutral trials.

27

We raise the issue of identification of Trial 0 in order to be consistent with certain modifications in our present formulation. Here, our development of the Conflict Model presents more abstract definitions of the states of the underlying process. These more abstract definitions require further constraints on the period representing Trial 0. To be in State 2 on Trial 0, when State 2 is defined in conflict terms, requires that the subject be aware of conflict. But on the initial neutral trials the subject is aware of no conflict between what he sees and what the confederates report. He becomes aware of this conflict at the time the confederates make their first incorrect responses on the first critical trial and prior to his own response on that trial. Hence, Trial 0 now refers to that time period prior to the subject's first response, but subsequent to the confederates' first incorrect response.

In practice, the modifications in our present formulation do not change anything that was done in *Conflict and Conformity*, either with respect to deriving properties of the model or to fitting the model to observed data. In considering future developments or alterations of the Conflict Model, however, one important possibility is to change the initial vector assumption, that is, our assumption about the distribution of subjects among the states on Trial 0. To facilitate constructing alternatives to Assumption 3, we have spelled out much more explicitly our restricted view of Trial 0. For example, substituting as an alternative to Assumption 3 an assertion which places some subjects in State 3 in Trial 0 would be inconsistent with the explication of Trial 0 just presented. It would be tantamount to arguing that subjects would favor conformity even though there is a perceptually correct response and as yet there is no conflict. Hence, should we want to incorporate an assumption that allows subjects to be in State 3 at Trial 0, we would have to change either our conception of Trial 0 or our belief in the effect of the subject's past experience.

Although this discussion of Trial 0 may seem to be an exceedingly fine point, in fact the utility of a conception of Trial 0 becomes an important consideration in our examination of the Cohen-Lee model. We raise the issue since one of the directions we take later on abandons the idea of Trial 0 *and instead assumes that the underlying process begins with the first response of the subject on a critical trial.*

28

2.3 Properties of the Model

Conflict and Conformity examined special cases of the Conflict Model and derived properties of these special cases. It also presented without derivation those properties of the general model.

The properties we derive in this section are not sufficient to allow us to estimate the parameters of Conflict Model since they do not provide us with four independent equations relating the parameters to quantities that can be estimated from the observed data. The derivations we will present here are of those quantities of most intrinsic interest in describing the process. When we come to the task of estimation, it will be necessary to derive additional quantities: either quantities which involve further assumptions concerning the nature of the process, or quantities that are not of interest in themselves but are a means by which to estimate the parameters.

The two properties that are most often considered in studies of this type are the mean number of correct responses and the trial-by-trial curve of the proportion of correct responses. The latter is analogous to the "learning curve" of stimulus acquisition experiments — although it is clear from our description of the underlying process that we do not regard conformity behavior as a learning process. We point to this analogy since the most frequently considered quantity in stochastic learning models is the learning curve. Unfortunately, we are not able to derive analytically either of these two properties. Once we have estimates for the parameters, we can compute numerically the response curve and the mean number of conforming responses and thus can use these quantities to test the fit of the model to the data; but we cannot derive analytic expressions and hence cannot use these quantities in the estimation of the parameters.

Numerical computation makes use of the following equations to compute the proportion of correct responses on Trial n:

$$p(n) = p_1(n-1) + (1-\beta)p_2(n-1) + \gamma p_3(n-1) \qquad (2.2)$$

where $p_j(n)$ equals the probability of being in State j on Trial n. The derivation of (2.2) follows from multiplying the vector of probabilities on Trial $n-1$ by the transition matrix to equal the vector of probabilities on Trial n.

$$(p_1(n-1), p_2(n-1), p_3(n-1), p_4(n-1)) \begin{array}{c} \\ 1 \\ 2 \\ 3 \\ 4 \end{array} \begin{pmatrix} \begin{array}{cccc} 1 & 2 & 3 & 4 \\ 1 & 0 & 0 & 0 \\ \alpha & 1-\alpha-\beta & \beta & 0 \\ 0 & \gamma & 1-\gamma-\epsilon & \epsilon \\ 0 & 0 & 0 & 1 \end{array} \end{pmatrix}$$

$$= (p_1(n), p_2(n), p_3(n), p_4(n))$$

which can be expressed as the following set of difference equations:

$$p_1(n) = p_1(n-1) + \alpha p_2(n-1)$$

$$p_2(n) = (1 - \alpha - \beta)p_2(n-1) + \gamma p_3(n-1)$$

$$p_3(n) = \beta p_2(n-1) + (1 - \gamma - \epsilon)p_3(n-1)$$

$$p_4(n) = \epsilon p_3(n-1) + p_4(n-1)$$

(2.3)

The probability of a correct response is the probability that the random variable $X_{in} = 1$, which is the same as the probability that $Y_{in} = 1$ or 2, that is, the probability of being in State 1 or 2; and, since the states are mutually exclusive, $p(n) = p_1(n) + p_2(n)$. Thus, if we add the right-hand side of the first two transition equations, and simplify, we obtain (2.2).

The expected number of correct responses, μ_c, is the sum over trials of the expected value of a correct response on each trial. But

$$\mu_c = E\left(\sum_n X_{in}\right)$$

$$= \sum_n [E(X_{in})]$$

$$E(X_{in}) = Pr[X_{in} = 0] \cdot 0 + Pr[X_{in} = 1] \cdot 1$$

$$= Pr[X_{in} = 1]$$

$$= p(n)$$

hence,

$$\mu_c = \sum_n p(n)$$

(2.4)

Equations 2.3 and 2.4 can be used for numerical estimation through searching the parameter space. That is, by arbitrarily choosing numerical values for the parameters, computing the mean curve, and testing the computed curve for its goodness of fit to any observed curve, it is possible to find parameter estimates. This search procedure is laborious and expensive even with large computers, although it was used in *Conflict and Conformity*. The criterion of goodness of fit employed was "minimum Chi Square". Apart from the difficulty of systematically searching the parameter space, the estimation procedure in *Conflict and Conformity* did not yield a unique minimum for Chi Square, that is, there were several alternative parameter sets which produced the same minimum Chi Square. As a "brute force" method of estimation, the numerical technique just described can be used as a last resort. It seems preferable, though, to find other means of parameter estimation and use Equations 2.3 and 2.4 for testing the fit of the model to experimental data.

Since the Asch situation is often treated as yielding a conformity score for each subject — the number of times he conforms during the n trials — it would be desirable to derive a theoretical frequency distribution of such scores. We can derive several points of this frequency distribution, but the algebra becomes so tedious that it is a practical impossibility to derive the probability for every point. Of special interest, in view of the repeated empirical result that between a quarter and a third of all subjects never conformed to the group, is the probability that an individual will receive a score of 0, that is, that he will give a sequence of completely correct responses. Let us call this π_0. Such a response sequence is generated by a sequence of states in the underlying process of the form

$$\overbrace{2\ldots\ldots\ldots2}^{i+1}\ 1\ldots\ldots$$

That is, the only sequences in the underlying process which generate sequences of completely correct responses are those in which the subject is in State 2 (S_2) for some number of trials and then moves to State 1 (S_1). There are $i+1$ trials in S_2, $i = 0, 1, 2\ldots$. Now we are interested in the probability of all sequences of this form. Since the transition probability from S_2 to S_1 is α and the transition probability from S_2 to S_2 is $1 - \alpha - \beta$, the probability of any one sequence is given by $\alpha(1 - \alpha - \beta)^i$. (Note that the exponent

31

is i rather than i + 1 because all subjects are assumed to be in S_2 on Trial 0; if there are i + 1 trials in S_2, there are only i transitions.) Assuming experiments with an infinite number of trials, we can calculate the probability of all such sequences; because these sequences are mutually exclusive, the desired quantity is

$$\pi_0 = \sum_{i=0}^{\infty} \alpha(1 - \alpha - \beta)^i \qquad (2.5)$$

Let $(1 - \alpha - \beta) = Z$. Further, as α is a constant, the right-hand side of (2.4) may be rewritten as:

$$\alpha \sum_{i=0}^{\infty} Z^i$$

To evaluate this expression, we shall use the following equality:

$$\sum_{i=0}^{\infty} Z^i = \frac{1}{1 - Z} \qquad (2.6)$$

Hence:

$$\pi_0 = \frac{\alpha}{1 - (1 - \alpha - \beta)}$$

and, finally we have

$$\pi_0 = \frac{\alpha}{\alpha + \beta} \qquad (2.7)$$

In a similar way, we can derive the probability that an individual will receive a score of 1, that is, will make one conforming response in the experimental sequence. Call this quantity π_1. To derive an expression for π_1 we need to sum over all sequences of the type

$$\underbrace{2 \ldots 232}_{i + 1} \underbrace{\ldots 21}_{j + 1} \ldots$$

Since to make one conforming response a subject must enter State

3 (S_3) at some point in the process and must remain there for only one trial, the probability of a sequence of this type is $(1 - \alpha - \beta)^i \times \beta\gamma(1 - \alpha - \beta)^j\alpha$. Again, we are interested in all such sequences so that we sum over i and j. Hence we desire

$$\alpha\beta\gamma \sum_{i=0}^{\infty} (1 - \alpha - \beta)^i \sum_{j=0}^{\infty} (1 - \alpha - \beta)^j .$$

Applying Equation 2.6 to this expression and simplifying, we obtain:

$$\pi_1 = \frac{\alpha\beta\gamma}{(\alpha + \beta)^2} \tag{2.8}$$

When we look at the probability that an individual will receive a score of 2, that is, will make two conforming responses during the experiment, complexities begin to arise. There are two different types of sequences which can lead to exactly two conforming responses. Hence, the probability of precisely two conforming responses, π_2, is the probability of either a sequence of Type 1 or a sequence of Type 2. These two types are mutually exclusive so that the probability is the sum of the probabilities of the respective types. Type 1 is a sequence of the form

$$\underbrace{2 \dots 2}_{i+1}\underbrace{32 \dots 2}_{j+1}\underbrace{32 \dots 2}_{k+1}1 \dots$$

and Type 2 is a sequence of the form

$$\underbrace{2 \dots 2}_{r+1}\underbrace{332 \dots 2}_{s+1}1 \dots$$

Thus an individual can receive a score of 2 either by making two conforming responses that are not consecutive (Type 1) or by making two consecutive conforming responses (Type 2). The probability of any sequence of Type 1 is

$$(1 - \alpha - \beta)^i\beta\gamma(1 - \alpha - \beta)^j\beta\gamma(1 - \alpha - \beta)^k\alpha$$

and applying (2.6) we obtain

$$\frac{\alpha\beta^2\gamma^2}{(\alpha + \beta)^3}$$

33

while the probability of any sequence of Type 2 is

$$(1 - \alpha - \beta)^r \beta (1 - \gamma - \epsilon) \gamma (1 - \alpha - \beta)^s \alpha$$

and applying (2.6):

$$\frac{\alpha \gamma \beta (1 - \gamma - \epsilon)}{(\alpha + \beta)^2}$$

Hence,

$$\pi_2 = \frac{\alpha \beta^2 \gamma^2}{(\alpha + \beta)^3} + \frac{\alpha \beta \gamma (1 - \gamma - \epsilon)}{(\alpha + \beta)^2} \tag{2.9}$$

In order to obtain a score of 3, there are three different kinds of sequences that must be considered (actually 4, but two are formally equivalent) so that the labor becomes increasingly tedious. We can, however, derive expressions for points at the other tail of the distribution. Let N denote the number of critical trials. Then consider π_N, the probability that a person makes conforming responses on every experimental trial. Consequently, the sequences in the underlying process must be of the form

$$\underbrace{23 \ldots 34}_{i + 1} \ldots.$$

(We continue to assume that the subject starts in State 2 on Trial 0.) If he conforms on every trial, he must immediately move to State 3 on the first critical trial and at some point would be absorbed in State 4. The probability of such a sequence is $\beta (1 - \gamma - \epsilon)^i \epsilon$ and the sum of all such sequences, again applying (2.6) is:

$$\pi_N = \frac{\beta \epsilon}{\gamma + \epsilon} \tag{2.10}$$

A score of $N - 1$, obtained when a subject conforms on all trials but one, is generated by sequences of two varieties. Case A is when the subject makes his lone non-conforming response on the first critical trial: 223...34... ; Case B occurs when the subject conforms on the first $i + 1$ critical trials and makes his non-conforming response at some other trial in the sequence

34

$$\underbrace{23 \ldots 32}_{i+1} \underbrace{3 \ldots 34}_{j+1} \ldots$$

The probability of a sequence of Case A is $(1 - \alpha - \beta)\beta(1 - \gamma - \epsilon)^i \epsilon$, and the sum of all such sequences is

$$\frac{\beta\epsilon(1 - \alpha - \beta)}{\gamma + \epsilon}$$

The probability of a sequence of Case B is $\beta(1 - \gamma - \epsilon)^i \gamma\beta(1 - \gamma - \epsilon)^j \epsilon$ and the sum of all such sequences is:

$$\frac{\beta^2(\gamma\epsilon)}{(\gamma + \epsilon)^2}$$

Hence, the probability of $N - 1$ conforming responses is given by

$$\pi_{N-1} = \frac{\beta\epsilon[\gamma + \epsilon - \alpha\gamma - \alpha\epsilon - \beta\epsilon]}{(\gamma + \epsilon)^2} \qquad (2.11)$$

The remaining properties for which we derive expressions are obtained by considering the distributions of alternations. An alternation is a change of response from Trial n to Trial n + 1. In the model, the only changes of state in the underlying process associated with changes of response in the manifest process are changes from S_2 to S_3, or from S_3 to S_2. Let $\Phi_k = \Pr[A=k]$, that is, the probability of precisely k alternations followed by absorption. We will now derive the distribution function Φ_k. In examining the following, the reader should recall that the probability of any sequence of the form 2———2, where the subject is in State 2 for i + 1 trials, is given by

$$\frac{1}{\alpha + \beta}$$

and the probability of any sequence of the form 3———3, is given by

$$\frac{1}{\gamma + \epsilon}$$

TABLE 2.1
The number of occurrences of each transition event in sequences leading to 0,
1, 2, 3 or 4 alternations.

Number of alter- nations k	Sequence	Transition event					
		2–2	2–3	3–2	2–1	3–3	3
	(Probability)	$\frac{1}{(\alpha+\beta)}$	(β)	(γ)	(α)	$\frac{1}{(\gamma+\epsilon)}$	$(\epsilon$
0	2---21------------------	1	0	0	1	0	0
1	2---23---34-------------	1	1	0	0	1	1
2	2---23---32---21---------	2	1	1	1	1	0
3	2---23---32---23---34------	2	2	1	0	2	1
4	2---23---32---23---32----21	3	2	2	1	2	0

We define a transition event as an ordered pair of states on two
consecutive trials. (We ignore 1-1 and 4-4 because these events are
not involved in producing alternations.)

Then we construct a table showing the number of occurrences
of each transition event in sequences leading to k alternations for a
few values of k. The result is Table 2.1.

The probability of any sequence of a given form is the product
of the probabilities of the transition events in that sequence. From
Table 2.1 we can now write the probability of any sequence listed,
and hence the probability that that number of alternations will
occur. For example, for k = 3, the transition event 2———2 occurs
twice. The probability of this event occurring twice is simply

$$\left(\frac{1}{(\alpha + \beta)}\right)\left(\frac{1}{(\alpha + \beta)}\right)$$

Thus, the cell entry in the table is the power to which the probability listed at the top of the column should be raised for the value
of k to which the row refers. Let A denote the number of alternations; then, using the table in this way, we can write:

$$\Pr[A=3] = \left(\frac{1}{\alpha + \beta}\right)^2 \beta^2 \gamma \alpha^0 \left(\frac{1}{\gamma + \epsilon}\right)^2 \epsilon$$

$$= \frac{\beta^2 \gamma \epsilon}{(\alpha + \beta)^2 (\gamma + \epsilon)^2}$$

To find a general expression for the probability of k alternations, we should first note than when k is even, absorption takes place in S_1, and the transition 3-4 does not occur. Similarly, when k is odd, absorption is in S_4, and the transition 2-1 does not occur. In the former case, ϵ will not appear in the numerator of the expression, whereas in the latter α will be absent from the numerator. This implies that there will not be an expression that holds for all values of k, but rather an expression for even values of k and a separate expression when k is odd.

Table 2.1 allows us to generalize each of the cell entries in terms of k. So, for example, writing the cell entries for the row for k = 3 in the table in terms of k, we have:

$$\frac{k+1}{2}, \frac{k+1}{2}, \frac{k-1}{2}, 0, \frac{k+1}{2}, 1$$

Writing the entries in this way enables us to prepare a general table in terms of even and odd values of k. This general table is presented as Table 2.2. The reader can verify the entries in Table 2.2 for the first values of k by substituting the value of k and comparing the results with Table 2.1. To prove that these entries are true in general requires a proof by mathematical induction, which we shall omit. Let Φ_k denote the probability of exactly k alternations: that is,

$$\Phi_k = \Pr[A = k]$$

TABLE 2.2
Number of occurrences of each transition event in sequences leading to k alternations as a function of k.

	Transition event					
	2–2	2–3	3–2	2–1	3–3	3–4
(Probability)	$\frac{1}{(\alpha+\beta)}$	(β)	(γ)	(α)	$\frac{1}{(\gamma+\epsilon)}$	(ϵ)
Even values of k	$\frac{k}{2}+1$	$\frac{k}{2}$	$\frac{k}{2}$	1	$\frac{k}{2}$	0
Odd values of k	$\frac{k+1}{2}$	$\frac{k+1}{2}$	$\frac{k-1}{2}$	0	$\frac{k+1}{2}$	1

We use the entry in Table 2.2 to write the function Φ_k by taking the product of the probabilities of these events, each raised to the power shown in the table.

$$
\Phi_k = \begin{pmatrix}
\dfrac{\alpha \beta^{\frac{k}{2}} \gamma^{\frac{k}{2}}}{(\alpha + \beta)^{\frac{k}{2}+1} (\gamma + \epsilon)^{\frac{k}{2}}} & \text{for k even} \\[2em]
\dfrac{\beta^{\frac{k+1}{2}} \gamma^{\frac{k-1}{2}} \epsilon}{(\alpha + \beta)^{\frac{k+1}{2}} (\gamma + \epsilon)^{\frac{k+1}{2}}} & \text{for k odd}
\end{pmatrix}
\tag{2.12}
$$

The proof that (2.12) is a distribution function, that is, that the right-hand side sums to unity and all values of Φ_k are between zero and one, is an obvious extension of available results (Cohen, 1963, p. 103). We make use of (2.12) to derive two expressions that are of interest. The first quantity is the probability that at the end of an infinite sequence of trials, a subject will be responding correctly. Call this quantity $p(\infty)$. Looking at Table 2.1 immediately gives the clue to the derivation of this expression. For, in order to end the sequence of trials in a non-conforming state, a subject must make an even number of alternations (after an infinite number of trials, all subjects will be in one of the absorbing states; but to be responding correctly, the subject must be in State 1 and therefore must have made an even number of alternations), thus we require the probability of any sequence which has an even number of alternations. This is simply the sum over even values of k of the top expression in (2.12). To derive this sum, let $Z = \beta\gamma/[(\alpha + \beta)(\gamma + \epsilon)]$. Now we re-write the top of (2.12) in terms of Z:

$$
\Phi_k = \frac{\alpha}{\alpha + \beta} Z^{\frac{k}{2}} \qquad \text{for k even}
\tag{2.13}
$$

Summing this over all even values of k,

$$
\sum_k \Phi_k, \, k = 0, 2, 4 \ldots \qquad \sum_k \Phi_k = \sum_k \frac{\alpha}{\alpha + \beta} Z^{\frac{k}{2}} , \, k = 0, 2, 4, \ldots
$$

$$
= \frac{\alpha}{\alpha + \beta} (Z^0 + Z^1 + Z^2 + Z^3 + \ldots)
$$

But, the parenthetical expression is simply the sum of Z^i, which we know from (2.6) is equal to $1/(1 - Z)$. Hence we have

$$p(\infty) = \frac{\alpha}{\alpha + \beta}\ \frac{1}{1 - Z} = \left(\frac{\alpha}{\alpha + \beta}\right)\left(\frac{1}{1 - \dfrac{\beta\gamma}{(\alpha + \beta)(\gamma + \epsilon)}}\right)$$

which may be simplified to produce

$$p(\infty) = \frac{\alpha(\gamma + \epsilon)}{(\alpha + \beta)(\gamma + \epsilon) - \beta\gamma} \qquad (2.14)$$

which, put into more convenient form is:

$$p(\infty) = \frac{1 + \dfrac{\gamma}{\epsilon}}{1 + \dfrac{\beta}{\alpha} + \dfrac{\gamma}{\epsilon}} \qquad (2.15)$$

We can also use (2.12) to derive the expected number of alternations (Cohen, 1963, p. 129):

$$E(A) = \frac{\dfrac{\beta}{\alpha}\left(2\dfrac{\gamma}{\epsilon} + 1\right)}{1 + \dfrac{\beta}{\alpha} + \dfrac{\gamma}{\epsilon}} \qquad (2.16)$$

Assumptions about the underlying process impose constraints in applying the model to any experimental situation. These assumptions can be viewed either as simplifying assumptions that can be relaxed at some future time, or in terms of their substantive implications. In either case, we should point out these assumptions and indicate some of their substantive implications. Just as we cannot justify the constraint imposed, neither do we have enough knowledge to reject them. In the first place, describing the underlying process as a Markov chain involves the assumption that the conflict state at any point in time is affected only by the conflict state at the immediately prior point in time. Whether more complicated models which incorporate more of the past history into the underlying process would be more suitable is a question to be determined by future applications. Certainly there are many strategies to deal with the restrictions imposed in addition to relaxing the

Markovian assumption. Thus, for example, we can change our conception of time points in the underlying process and identify trial in the conflict resolution process with several trials in the manifest experimental process. Second, the model assumes that all subjects experience the same underlying process. That is, that the transition probabilities apply to all individuals. The model explicitly does not incorporate individual differences prior to the beginning of the conflict process in an effort to describe individual differences and behavior in the experiment. Rather, individual differences in behavior arise probabilistically. It is perhaps this assumption which has generated the most comment on *Conflict and Conformity*. Indeed, as was noted in that volume, Asch regarded his experimental situation as a diagnostic tool for reflecting individual differences in conformity dispositions. As *Conflict and Conformity* noted, Asch in 1956 made the following comment:

> [Individual differences] may be the product of momentary, episodic circumstances; if so, they are of minor import. Or they may be a function of consistent personal qualities which individuals bring into the experimental situation and which have as decisive a bearing on their actions as any of the other conditions we have studied.

Although Asch's position runs directly counter to what we are assuming in this model, and although much of the research involving the Asch experiment followed in the tradition of individual differences in personality factors, the analysis in *Conflict and Conformity* indicated that one does not have to assume prior individual differences in order to account for behavior in the experiment. One could then conclude that the experiment is of minor import. From a sociological perspective, such a conclusion would be far too hasty, since the experimental situation may be valuable for studying the effects of various social-psychological variables on the conformity process. As *Conflict and Conformity* argued, people conform or do not conform for a variety of reasons, but some of these reasons are present in everyone. In other words, similar personalities may behave differently in this situation or different personalities may behave similarly because of elements of the situation that activate different motivational constellations in different people. That is, enduring personality factors do affect conformity behavior but the personality factors which are operating in the situation are not necessarily the same for people with similar personality types.

40

One of the difficulties in dealing with the issue of enduring personality factors is that our conceptualization of personality factors is quite limited. The evidence regarding personality influences on behavior in the Asch situation is quite inconclusive, but it must be remembered that most of these studies deal with single personality traits. At the very least, a conception of personality that is more multifaceted would be necessary before more fruitful results are obtained.

2.4 The Model as a tool

As we have already indicated, the motivation for developing the Conflict Model was a dissatisfaction with the typical behavioral measures employed in studies utilizing the Asch situation. The use of a simple measure of frequency of conforming responses is inadequate for testing anything but the crudest hypotheses about conformity. Furthermore, such a gross measure is often too insensitive to changes in the independent variables of concern for it to be very useful in research on conformity. These points are not new and researchers concede that much more is happening in the Asch situation than is captured by their measures. It is not that the measure of frequency of conformity abstracts from the concrete reality of behavior in the Asch situation that is at issue — such abstraction is always necessary. Rather, the issue is in the nature of the abstraction, and our argument here is that the particular abstraction chosen does not capture much that is relevant and much that is interesting about behavior in this situation.

Our central thesis is that the development of the model for the situation enables us to capture in our abstractions much more of the relevant and interesting aspects of the situation than formerly was possible. The assumptions we have made enable us to describe some important features of the behavioral process in the Asch situation. This not only means that we can look at behavior through time but also that we can treat the relationship among various indices that one might wish to compute as functions of individual responses. Put very simply, the model provides a precise description that ties together various operational measures of conformity behavior.

This point is sufficiently important that, at the risk of belaboring it, we should provide an illustration. In empirical research, the issue often arises whether or not two measures provide indepen-

41

dent tests of a hypothesis. Consider, for example, testing a hypothesis using the frequency of conformity in the first half of the experiment as one measure and the frequency of conformity in the second half as the second measure. Do these two measures provide independent tests of a hypothesis? Such a question is usually resolved by rule of thumb, as, for example, "since the measures are taken on the same subjects, they are not independent". As with all rules of thumb, there are circumstances in which this rule is a good guide and circumstances in which it is not. The virtue of developing a model is that it allows us to show when two such measures are functionally independent. Thus, in the context of the assumptions of the model, we are provided with better decision criteria than such rules of thumb.

The model as a precise description provides a means for systematically studying the relation of various aspects of the conformity process to each other. We can show, for example, the relationship between the probability that a subject ends the process giving correct responses and the expected number of alternations:

$$E(A) = \frac{2p(\infty)}{\pi_0} - p(\infty) - 1$$

which may be derived from the equations in the preceding section of this chapter. Furthermore, the discussion in connection with Tables 2.1 and 2.2 should have already alerted the reader to the interdependence of these quantities.

The fact that the model provides a precise description of the conformity process is all the more significant in view of the fact that the entire process can be specified in terms of a small number of underived quantities. With the assumptions of model, we need estimate only four parameters from the data. Estimates of these four quantities allow us to derive the measures that one usually looks at in studying the Asch situation as well as values for new measures not ordinarily examined. Hence it is clear why the problem of obtaining estimates for these parameters becomes so critical, for once we have solved the problem of estimating parameters, we can obtain precise quantitative statements describing many aspects of conformity behavior in this situation.

Finally, these underived quantities themselves become the dependent variables for systematically studying experimental variations in the conformity situation. In other words, if we change the

42

subject's relationship to the confederates from that of a peer to that of a subordinate, for example, we would expect such a change to be reflected in increasing or decreasing of the values of particular transition probabilities.

We might expect, for example, β to be smaller for the experiments where the subject is a superior to the confederates than it would be where he is a peer. The experiments to be reported in the ensuing chapters were experiments designed to study the relations between the model parameters and variations in the experimental situation. Not only did these experiments provide such information, they also indicated problems with the Conflict Model which the Cohen-Lee model to be presented later attempts to solve. We turn in the next chapter to the first series of experiments.

CHAPTER 3

Relative Status and Conformity: Experiment 11

3.1 Introduction

In *Conflict and Conformity*, Cohen (1963) argued for the strategic importance of the Asch situation in developing a cumulative, theoretically grounded understanding of conformity. The simplicity of the experimental situation, the ease with which it can be repeated, and the wide-spread interest in the phenomenon make the Asch situation central in considering formulations of social conformity. Cohen noted four properties that contributed to the strategic importance of Asch's experiment in past and future conformity research. In our view, these properties are as significant today as they were in 1963. Let us expand on the significance of these four properties.

Property 1. Numerous replications indicate that the phenomenon is not transitory.

Asch experiments, or Asch-type experiments, have been done with a variety of subject populations, a variety of different stimuli, and a variety of different types of confederates. What is striking is that the experimental effect appears under all of these variations. It is possible to produce responses where individuals contradict the judgment of their senses under numerous different experimental conditions. While the magnitude of the effect may vary with variations in experimental conditions, it is possible to generate conformity to confederates in children (Berenda, 1950; Tuddenham, 1961; Query, 1968), when the judgmental mode is auditory rather

44

than visual (Gorfein *et al.*, 1960; Hicks *et al.*, 1966); when the confederates are similar to the subject (Darley, 1966) and when the confederates are markedly different from the subjects (Reitan and Shaw, 1964).

There is both a striking consistency as well as considerable variability in the results of these experiments. The reliability of this phenomenon, as well as its systematic variation as a function of experimental conditions, provides a compelling basis for the construction of explanations. We do not have a "one-shot" result, rather, we have considerable evidence of a stable phenomenon that is experimentally modifiable. These two features suggest that there are a number of regularities to be explained and also that further regularities remain to be discovered. The construction of a theory should then provide an explanation for some of these regularities as well as the apparatus by which to uncover additional regularities.

Property 2. There is considerable appreciation of the importance of the Asch phenomenon as well as some understanding of its nature.

In the first place, the conformity effect in a perceptual task, where there is a clear-cut and obviously correct answer, is striking and dramatic. The fact that it is possible in such a "simple" situation to get people to contradict their own senses has provoked a good deal of discussion, particularly of the implications of this fact for our understanding of society and human personality (see Asch 1956). Both this concern with very broad implications of the phenomenon and the repeated use of the Asch situation by a range of investigators, testify to the importance of the phenomenon.

Although our understanding of this phenomenon is now fragmentary, and certainly too fragmentary to draw broad social implications, it is sufficient to form the foundation on which various theories can be constructed. Asch's own results indicate that the conformity effect varies with variations in the properties of the stimuli, variation in the behavior of the confederates, variations in the modality of judgment (visual or auditory), variations in the properties of stimulus sequence. Other investigators have shown that the effect varies with the character of the confederates, with the modality of response (oral or written), and with many personality or cultural traits of the subjects. Furthermore, Asch has shown that the effect remains relatively constant with variations in the number of confederates when there are three or more confederates, as well as the disappearance of the effect when the naive

45

subject has as a partner a confederate who responds the same way as the subject responds. While these fragments do not force the formulation of any particular theories, they do provide elements to be incorporated into various theoretical formulations.

Property 3. There is a desire to make further use of the experimental setting as a standardized situation in which to study the effects of related variables.

A standardized test situation is one in which there is comparability of results over a series of experiments because the same basic design is used in each experiment in the series. It is possible to conduct a program of research using experiments which contain different tasks, different verbal content, and a variety of dependent measures, as well as different independent variables. Such studies, however, are not directly comparable, but are comparable only by inference. The virtue of the Asch situation is that its simplicity and the ease with which it can be repeated allow us to use the same task and same dependent variables for a number of different independent variables. If we observe differences between two studies, one of which runs college students through the Asch situation and the other which runs industrial chemists, the results are more comparable than they would be if we studied conformity using a case discussion for the students and a chemistry problem for the chemists.

A large number of investigators followed exactly this strategy in dealing with personality traits as they affect behavior in the Asch situation. There is a body of literature which deals with a number of different personality traits and does provide comparable results to assess the relative contributions of a number of different personality traits to conformity. From our point of view, given our major interest is the social relationships that obtain between confederates and subject, it is unfortunate that there is not a similarly extensive body of literature on which to build.

Property 4. A number of questions about the situation and the behavior it elicits remain unanswered.

In *Conflict and Conformity*, the issue of temporal trends in conformity behavior represents an essential theme. The evidence presented in that work clearly points to the presence of temporal trends in conformity behavior and underscores the need to be concerned with variations through time in this experimental situation.

Once we are concerned with time changes in conformity behavior, the question of when the process is in equilibrium becomes

46

important for any interpretations of experimental results. For example, if the data from two different experimental treatments are compared, the results of the comparison may differ markedly if one makes the comparison at equilibrium vs. making the comparison before equilibrium is achieved. If behavior prior to equilibrium is highly variable and under equilibrium is relatively stable, then differences between treatments may be difficult to locate if we examine the data from experiments which do not allow equilibrium to be reached.

Conflict and Conformity deals with the development of a set of tools to adequately represent temporal processes occurring in this experimental situation. The Conflict Model provides a reasonably good representation. As a representation, the model deserves investigation in its own right. For example, we can simulate the process on a computer by choosing different collections of parameter values and generating the "observations" that would result from each set. One result of these simulation studies is that two radically different processes, i.e. processes with strikingly different parameter values, can produce observations with the same mean number of conforming responses. This result suggests that the mean number of conforming responses may not be an appropriate statistic to distinguish between experimental treatments. Furthermore, combining this interpretation with our concerns for process and equilibrium requires that attention be paid to a number of other properties of the data.

Apart from questions concerning the fit of the model and its adequacy as a representation of process, fundamental substantive questions arise concerning what factors affect the form that the process or processes in this experiment take. One issue, for example, is the number of trials to equilibrium. It is certainly reasonable to postulate that one factor affecting time to equilibrium is the conflict between subject's perception and the confederates' responses. For example, assuming that equilibrium occurs when subjects have resolved the conflict, how is intensity of conflict related to conflict resolution? At the moment, we can speculate that time to resolution may be a U-shaped function of intensity. That is, both very intense conflict situations and very weak conflict situations are resolved early. What is needed is some evidence bearing on this speculation and, furthermore, some attention to the kinds of variables that would produce variation in the intensity of conflict.

The concern with process raises another issue. Can the Asch

47

situation be described by a single process, or is it necessary to employ a complex resultant of important and analytically separable processes? The Conflict Model posits a process of conflict resolution as sufficient to describe what is occurring in the Asch experiment. This by no means is a settled issue, however. Some of the analyses reported in *Conflict and Conformity* suggest that there may be more than one process occurring in the experiment and that on theoretical grounds it would be important to separate these processes either theoretically or in the design and construction of future experiments. For example, Deutsch and Gerard (1955) distinguish between informational and normative social influence. It may well be that quite different conflict processes and resolution processes result from informational influences on the one hand and normative influences on the other. If that is the case, then it might be useful to formulate one kind of model for pure informational influence and a different kind for pure normative influence. Even if it were not possible to design an experiment sufficiently purified so that only one of these processes occurred, formulating two separate models and a rule for combining them could then lead to derivations that adequately represented what takes place in the experiment.

A final example of the type of unanswered question is the problem of the role of the experimenter. In *Conflict and Conformity*, Cohen suggests that "From one viewpoint correct responses can also be regarded as conformity; the individual, when he responds correctly, conforms not only to an internalized standard, but also to an external norm. It can be argued that the experimenter acts as an external enforcing agent for the correct response" (1963, p. 57). In view of the interest in the role of the experimenter in social-psychological experiments (Rosenthal, 1966) it seems that we are required to investigate the conditions under which the experimenter is neutral in this situation and the conditions under which the experimenter acts to enforce the correct response or to reinforce the confederates. One can conceive of a major series of experiments dealing with these issues. Throughout *Conflict and Conformity*, Cohen emphasized that unanswered questions like those above required a coordinated program of research, involving experimentation, formalization, and theory construction. The present monograph should be regarded as one phase of such a coordinated program, a phase that depended upon the analyses reported in *Conflict and Conformity* and had as its objective further refinements of the model, as well as increased

48

substantive understanding of the phenomenon. The research program began with Experiment 11.

3.2 Objectives of Experiment 11

The research program begun with Experiment 11 illustrates the interplay among model, experiment and substantive concerns. There were three principal objectives for our research program. First, we intended to demonstrate the utility of the Conflict Model by showing that the model could distinguish between experimental treatments run under different initial conditions; secondly, we hoped to solve problems with the model itself, particularly problems of parameter estimation; and thirdly, we were interested in using the model, together with several experiments, to develop and evaluate substantive propositions concerning conformity and influence.

Throughout the analysis in *Conflict and Conformity*, there were suggestions for varying the initial conditions of the Asch situation in such a way that the basic structure of the model would apply, but the numerical values of the parameters would differ. For example, Cohen ran two experiménts: Experiment 1, called the "Moderate Condition" and Experiment 2, the "Extreme Condition". The difference between these two conditions concerned the response of the confederates. The stimuli that the group was asked to judge in the Asch situation consisted of a single line called the standard and three comparison lines, one of which was correct, one of which was 1¼″ shorter than the standard, and one of which was 1¾″ shorter than the standard. Hence, one line represented a "moderate error" and one line represented an "extreme error". In the "Moderate Condition" then the confederates always chose the "moderate error", while in the "Extreme Condition", they always chose the "extreme error". In all other respects the two experiments were identical. As *Conflict and Conformity* demonstrated, the parameters of the model reflected this variation since the parameter estimates obtained from the two conditions were markedly different. Furthermore, additional statistics derived from the model reflected the difference between the two experimental treatments. In short, the model and its parameters offered the possibility of sensitive discrimination that represented a summary of the many statistics one could compute from the response data.

The question now was, did the model have similar utility for the investigation of sociologically more interesting questions? Chief among these was the question of whether varying the relationship of the naive subject to the group of confederates would produce distinct differences in the model's parameters.

Experiment 11 focused on one aspect of this general question. Does the status of the subject relative to the status of the other members of the group affect not only the amount of conformity to the group, but also the process by which this conformity occurs? If we establish a status hierarchy as an initial condition of the experiment, does that status hierarchy affect the nature of the equilibrium, the length of time to equilibrium, and the events that occur prior to equilibrium? To answer these questions, the model is essential since it allows us to look at these features of the process and provides us with a sensitive means for distinguishing the effects of the various status hierarchies.

The second objective of Experiment 11 was to resolve some technical issues both in the design of this type of experiment and in the application of the model to observations. In *Conflict and Conformity* there were discrepancies between the model and the data. These discrepancies could be attributed to extraneous features of the experimental situation or to our inability to find optimum parameter estimates, or to both.

The version of the Asch situation employed in *Conflict and Conformity* represented a great deal of simplification over Asch's original work. Principally, the stimulus series and the confederates' response were held constant throughout the sequence of experimental trials, whereas Asch had varied both the stimuli and the type of confederate response from trial to trial. While these simplifications seem to serve the research objectives, it was possible that what was eliminated was not only extraneous variations, but substantively interesting features of the process. In addition, it was possible that the simplification added features that were not present in Asch's original experiment. Thus it could be argued that the overwhelming constancy introduced a strain toward self-consistency on the subject's part that would interfere with the relationship between the process of conforming and the initial status hierarchy. In Experiment 11 we intended to investigate this problem.

Of course the principal problem in applying the model was the fact that estimation procedures required a computer searching technique which did not guarantee an optimum set of estimates. Hence, it was a major objective in our research program to find an analytic solution to the estimation problem.

50

While increased understanding of the experimental situation, an analytic solution to the estimation problem, and demonstration of the model's utility in discriminating among variations in the initial status conditions of individuals exposed to the Asch situation, would all represent a successful outcome of our research program, it would still be necessary to show the substantive significance of our efforts. For that reason our first two objectives were preliminary to a third objective namely to formulate and evaluate propositions concerning the relationship of an individual's status in the group to his conformity to the group.

Now it is not at all obvious that persons of high status should behave differently in the Asch situation from persons of low status. If there are no differences, then, of course, the model should not discriminate among experimental treatments and the experimental situation would not be a particularly useful one for the study of this substantive problem. As we indicated in Chapter 1, the literature on conformity offers contradictory guides for our expectations in this type of experiment. The propositions of Homans and of Hollander suggest that it is not a simple matter to formulate hypotheses for studying status differences and conformity. The interesting possibility is that both propositions apply under certain specifiable conditions; as we already noted, Homans' proposition might apply to emerging or unstable status structures, whereas Hollander's assertion may hold for stable systems in equilibrium. If this speculation is correct, determining when the process is in equilibrium becomes crucial, but detecting such a stable state of affairs requires much more subtle analyses of the data from the Asch situation than are usually carried out. Hence, our model is necessary to evaluate this substantive speculation. One consequence of closer examination should be an understanding of some of the conditions under which such propositions are applicable.

Formulating conditions is an important step in theoretical development, but for us to pursue this strategy requires us first to demonstrate that the Conflict Model is applicable to experiments in which initial status conditions are varied and secondly, that the parameters of the model distinguish among such variations. To these ends, Experiment 11 was designed and conducted.

3.3 The design of Experiment 11

Experiment 11 consisted of three phases: first, a manipulation phase, the purpose of which was to produce variations in the status of the naive subject relative to the status of the confederates. This phase established the initial conditions for phase 2 of the experiment, which was the conformity phase. In the conformity phase, Cohen's previously simplified version of the Asch situation was employed with a few relatively minor modifications. Finally, the third phase of the experiment consisted of a post-experimental interview and debriefing, in which a full explanation of the purposes of the experiment and the techniques employed was given to the subjects.

Since the manipulation phase involved the most interesting substantive issues and was also the most novel feature of our studies, we will discuss this phase at some length before describing our specific procedures.

The first issue in developing this manipulation concerned whether to produce variations in initial status conditions by allowing subjects to bring their statuses with them into the laboratory, or by experimental manipulation. We chose to create our status variable experimentally. This decision was motivated by the desire to come as close as possible to creating identical status relations for all subjects in a given experimental treatment. If we had employed status attributes that subjects carried around with them, there would have been considerable variation in subjective definitions of the status differential between themselves and the confederates. For example, some subjects who were foremen might believe there was a large status difference between themselves and, say, lawyers, whereas other foremen would believe there was only a small status difference. Furthermore, as a corollary to our concern with subjective definitions of the situation, we could hypothesize that there would be variation in the belief that any external status dimension we might use was relevant to our experimental task. To the extent that a substantial portion of our subjects did not regard the dimension chosen as relevant, it would vitiate differences between experimental treatments. On the other hand, we believed we could produce experimentally the status relations necessary and a uniform belief that the dimension chosen was relevant to the task.

Although in the planning of Experiment 11, we rejected using external statuses that subjects brought with them, some of the studies to be reported later in this book make use of external status as well as manipulated status. At the time of these later studies, the experience of Experiment 11 and also work done in connection with "The Theory of Status Characteristics and Expectation States" (Berger, Cohen and Zelditch, 1966) increased our understanding to the point where we could use statuses that subjects brought with them.

Once the decision was made to create experimentally status differentials, the next question was what status dimension to use. There are many dimensions along which groups may be differentiated in status; a very likeable group member may be accorded high status, while a disagreeable member may be given low status; a group member who is very competent at the group task may receive high status, while an incompetent performer may be given low status. The choice of dimension could also bear on the conditions under which the Homans or Hollander propositions might apply. For example, a group member whose high status is due to being likeable may be freer to deviate from group norms than a group member whose status is due to specific task competence.

Furthermore, interesting theoretical problems arise in cases such as, for example, where it is the disagreeable member who is most competent (Hollander, 1960; Fisek and Ofshe, 1970). In groups where there are several dimensions of status that vary independently we have the problem of status inconsistency when an individual is high on one dimension and low on another, and some of the experiments we discuss later in this book concern that problem. For Experiment 11, however, our objective was somewhat simpler: to create status differentials between a subject and the group of confederates along a single dimension.

We chose competence at the task as the dimension along which to create status differentials. This choice was influenced by the work on expectation theory begun by Berger and Snell (1961; see also Berger, Conner and Fisek, 1974). The reasoning in this theory is as follows: Given that group members value a task, that is, they want to succeed at the task, they will highly evaluate performances that contribute to success. If a group member is seen as competent at the task, this will give rise to an expectation for high performance. The expectation for high performance would generate a high evaluation of the group member for whom the expectation is held; hence that member will be accorded high status. When we speak of status based on competence, then we are using a shorthand term for the chain of assumptions we have just explicated.

Another reason for choosing competence as the dimension along which to manipulate status was related to the fact that in the Asch situation there is a clearly correct answer, while the group norm represents an incorrect answer. The fact that the task was perceptual and the response alternatives were clear-cut, suggested that it would both be straightforward to manipulate competence and to make it relevant to the judgments in the Asch situation. In choosing competence, we also examined the Homans and Hollander propositions once again. While the discussion above suggested that competence as a basis of status might be more germane than likeability to Homans' assertion that the high status member reflects group norms, one could just as well argue the other way, that is, that status based on competence could be a condition under which Hollander's proposition applied. Consider, for example, an "expert" in a group of "laymen". The expert has high status because of his expertise, but the expert is also freer to give his own opinion than the laymen. But the example is deceptively simple and its analysis gives rise to a number of issues. Consider the case of the layman in a group of experts. He may be so far "out of it" that the group norms are meaningless to him and the group's sanctions do not impinge upon him. In that case he may well feel free to deviate and "call them as he sees them", since he does not define himself as a part of the group. If we chose to compare subjects who were high status relative to the confederates with subjects who were low status relative to the confederates, we might not find differences for our model to distinguish. Of course it may be that the overall proportion of conforming responses would be similar for our "expert" and "layman", but that the process of conflict resolution would differ, in which case the model should distinguish them.

Focusing on competence as the basis of status raised another problem which is also illustrated by the example of expert and laymen. We would expect an expert to behave differently in a group of experts from the way he would behave in a group of laymen. Similarly a layman should behave differently in a group of laymen than in a group of experts. The status of a group member in the group is relative and, where competence is the sole basis of status, a group of experts would be a group of status equals. From the work of Bales (1955), there is the suggestion that groups of status equals are unstable, that through interaction a differentiated status structure emerges. When an expert is confronted with other experts who are initially as competent as he is, does a differentiated status structure emerge? When a naive subject is confronted with a group of confederates who are initially as competent as he

54

is, does he come to believe that confederates are more competent than he is or less competent than he is?

The question just discussed motivated the design of the experiment. In intuitive terms, we chose to study four treatments: The "expert" in a group of "laymen", the "expert" in a group of "experts", the "layman" in a group of "experts", and a "layman" in a group of "laymen". The Berger-Snell "Theory of Self-Other Expectations" (1961) enables us to explicate these analogies more rigorously.

The central concept in Berger and Snell is the concept of performance expectation which may be interpreted as an individual's belief about how well he, relative to some other actor, will perform at the group task. Berger and Snell consider four expectation states where a state consists of pairing an expectation for self with an expectation for "other". As a simplification they only consider dichotomous expectations, high and low. They adopt the following notation for these self-other expectation states:

(++) High self, high other
(+−) High self, low other
(−+) Low self, high other
(−−) Low self, low other

employing the convention of listing expectation for self first. We should note that although Berger and Snell consider only dyadic expectation states, the theory and the notation could be generalized to more than expectation pairs. Thus (+−−) would refer to an actor who held a high performance expectation for himself and low expectations for the two other actors with whom he was interacting.

Two important features of the Berger-Snell theory and our use of it should be emphasized. First, expectation states are unobservable; they are hypothetical entities tied to observables — they are functions of prior events in interaction and have consequences for future events in interaction. For example, Berger and Snell construct a theory to describe the effects of the expectation pattern on the manner in which an individual will resolve a disagreement between self and other and the effect of that resolution on his expectation. Secondly, an expectation state is from the point of view of a given actor, so that it is possible in a dyad to have two actors each of whom is (+−).

The purpose of our manipulation phase was to create initial conditions for the study of conflict resolution and conformity. In creating performance expectations as a basis of status, we didn't want to introduce any new process into phase 2 of the experiment, but the work of Berger and his associates posed a problem for us. These studies (Berger and Conner, 1969; Berger, Conner, McKeown, 1969; Berger and Fisek, 1970; Webster, 1969) concerned the process by which stable expectation states emerge. In the present research we were not concerned with what might be termed the "process of expectation change". It was our intention to use the Berger-Snell expectation states as fixed initial conditions under which to study conformity; insofar as there is a process by which expectations change, it adds complications to our description of the Asch situation under varying status conditions. But the utility of status manipulation based on expectation states was clear from Berger's initial research. Hence, it was necessary for our purposes to assume that initially established expectation states remained constant through the conformity phase. We believed that this assumption, although questionable, was a reasonable first approximation. Our belief will be examined in the analysis of Experiment 11.

Experiment 11, then, varied initial status conditions under which conformity occurred by varying the self-other performance expectations held by our naive subjects with respect to the "perceptual" task of the Asch situation. There were four experimental treatments corresponding to the four expectation states of Berger and Snell. These treatments were labeled [HH], [HL], [LH] and [LL]; following the Berger-Snell convention of listing expectation for self first, so our [HL] treatment is where the subject has a high performance expectation for self and a low performance expectation for other. In the Asch situation, however, the naive subject is confronted with a unanimous majority of confederates who give the same incorrect answer and the confederates number anywhere from three to ten. Since the confederates do behave the same way, it is reasonable to assume that the subject does not differentiate among them so that it is possible to deal with expectation states that have only two referents — in our case, self and others or group. Thus the experimental manipulation was designed to create in our naive subjects a performance expectation for self, either high or low, and a performance expectation for the group, either high or low.

3.4 Experimental procedures

There were several constraints on the procedures for the manipulation phase. Principally these were:

(1) The manipulation should not in and of itself produce conformity. If the manipulation involved social pressure or conformity, then it might well be that "learning to conform" in the manipulation phase so enhanced conformity in the Asch phase that differences between treatments would be vitiated. More likely, conformity in the initial phase might take the conflict resolution process to the point where there was little resolution to describe in the Asch phase of the experiment.

(2) The manipulation task should be related to the "perceptual" task of the Asch phase so that the performance expectations created would be relevant to the performance required in the Asch phase.

(3) The manipulation phase should be believable to the subjects and should not affect the credibility of the Asch phase.

(4) The manipulation task should be one in which the subject cannot evaluate his own or the group's performance but must depend on the experimenter for feedback. Otherwise we could not be sure that we had created the intended expectation.

(5) For the feedback to be credible and meaningful to the subject, the manipulation task should be such that the subject's and the group's performances are comparable. In order to be credible, he should see the group performing the manipulation task and in order for his feedback to be comparable to the others, he should know that he and the group of confederates performed exactly the same task.

Some of these properties could be achieved easily if it were not for the other requirements. Hence the manipulation phase that resulted represented compromises with respect to some of the desired properties in order to achieve other desiderata. The task for the manipulation was a perceptual judgment task in which each group member had to determine whether or not a simple standard figure was contained in a more complicated "test figure". Figure 3.1 shows one of the standard and one of the test figures used. The manipulation phase employed four standard and five test figures; for each standard, the five test figures were shown and the group member judged whether or not the test figure contained the standard. Each group member thus made twenty judgments, and his performance could be scored from 0 to 20. The task was so constructed that there was a correct answer for each of the judgments, but the way in which the stimuli were presented and time allowed for each judgment made it impossible for a subject to

Figure 3.1. One standard and one test figure for the manipulation phase.

achieve a high score, or indeed a low score, except by chance. Although the subjects regarded the manipulation task as an extremely difficult one, subjects reported in the post-experimental interview that they believed that there were right answers and that the "test" was a measure of perceptual ability.

In order to allow oral responses and at the same time not produce conformity pressure, the task was divided into four parts. For the first part, one of the standard figures was distributed to each group member for thirty seconds of study. The standards were then collected and a sequence of five slides containing the test figures were projected on a screen so that all group members saw them. As each slide was removed from the screen, each group member responded in turn with his judgment; although all were responding to the same test figure on a given trial, the fact that each had a different standard for that part of the task meant that each was performing a different task on any given trial. For the entire manipulation task, each group member made the same twenty judgments, but the order in which they were made differed from member to member. This was accomplished by repeating the same five test figures for each part of the manipulation task, but insuring that each group member judged a different standard in each of the four parts of the task. After each part was completed, the standards were redistributed so that each group member had a standard figure he had not previously seen and the same test figures were again presented. Since there were four group members, the standard figures may be rotated among the participants. This rotation is shown in Table 3.1. In this way, it was possible to have oral responses without conformity pressure on any given trial. Furthermore, the task was sufficiently complicated and time pressure sufficiently strong (test figures were exposed for five seconds each) so that it is extremely unlikely that conformity pressure operated across trials. If the subject knew that one confederate has his standard in a previous part and remembered that confederate's responses, conformity pressure might have operated across trials.

TABLE 3.1
Rotation of standard figures for each group member in expectation manipulation of Experiment 11.

	Group member			
	1	2	3	4
Part I	A	B	C	D
Part II	D	A	B	C
Part III	C	D	A	B
Part IV	B	C	D	A

Note: The four standard figures are labeled "A", "B", "C", "D".

But since the way in which standards were distributed was not known to the subject and group members were asked not to show their standards to each other, it would have been difficult to figure out who had which standard during which part of the task, let alone remember how each of the three confederates responded.

The procedure for the manipulation phase was as follows: Four group members were brought into the laboratory, three confederates and the subject. They were told they were to participate in a study of perceptual ability in which there were "two different but related tests of your perceptual ability ... (that) have been used throughout the country with considerable success". The experimenter then proceeded with the instructions for the first test (the manipulation phase). These instructions are reproduced in Appendix A. Following these instructions the group was shown a sample slide containing a standard and two test figures, and the experimenter pointed out that the sample standard was contained in one of the test figures but not in the other. After insuring that the subject understood the task, the experimenter distributed the standards for Part I, announcing that the group members had thirty seconds to study their standards. At the end of thirty seconds, he collected their standards and each test figure was then projected on the screen for five seconds. The group was instructed not to give their answers until the design had been taken off the screen. After five test figures were shown, the standards were redistributed for Part II. Parts III and IV followed in the same way. At the end of Part IV, the experimenter announced a short break to allow scores to be computed, cautioning the group members not to talk to one another. He then left the room, ostensibly to obtain the scores. When he returned, the experimenter began the actual manipulation of expectation states. He first emphasized the importance of the test as "an excellent indicator of perceptual ability" and then suggested that the test had been widely used, implying that it was highly reliable. The scores were always reported from high to low, where high was a score of 18 (out of 20) and low was a score of 6. The three confederate scores varied by one or two points from the high or the low. Whether the subject received his score first or last depended of course on the treatment condition to which he had been randomly assigned. For a given treatment the same pattern of scores were used and the pattern is shown in Table 3.2.

Instructions then followed for the conformity phase of Experiment 11. Essentially, this phase used the Asch situation as modi-

TABLE 3.2
Scores assigned to group members in expectation manipulation of Experiment 11.

Treatment	Subject's score	Confederates' score
[HH]	18	16, 18, 19
[HL]	18	6, 8, 9
[LH]	8	16, 18, 19
[LL]	8	6, 8, 9

fied by Cohen (1963), although some additional changes were made. The stimulus is shown in Figure 3.2. This stimulus was used on every trial, although the letters labeling the comparison lines were changed from trial to trial. Asch had originally varied the stimulus across trials. In Experiment 11 the confederates always chose the right-most of the three comparison lines, representing a "moderate" error. In his original work, Asch sometimes had the confederates respond with a "moderate" error, Line C in Figure 3.2, and sometimes with an "extreme" error, Line A in Figure 3.2. The sequence of trials in Experiment 11 began with two "neutral" trials, in which the confederates gave correct answers and then followed with a sequence of 60 "critical" trials, where the confederates responded with "moderate" errors. In Asch's work, he interspersed "neutral" and "critical" trials.

There were two changes between Cohen (1963) and Experiment 11. In Experiments 1 and 2, Cohen (1963) varied the position of the standard with respect to the comparison lines; on half the

Standard   Comparison lines
                  A   B   C

Figure 3.2. The Asch stimulus.

61

trials the standard was presented to the left and on half the standard was presented to the right of the comparison lines, whereas the side of presentation of the standard was not significantly associated with the number of conforming responses, *change* from one side to the other was associated with *change* of response, that is, given an alternation of response when the standard changed position, that alternation was more likely to be from correct to conforming if the standard moved from right to left and more likely to be from conforming to correct when the standard moved from left to right (Cohen, 1963, p. 143). In view of this systematic effect on the direction of alternation, the design of Experiment 11 included holding constant the position of the standard relative to the comparison lines; the standard was always to the subject's left of the comparison lines as he faced the stimulus.

The second difference in the procedure of Experiment 11 from Cohen's prior studies concerned the number of confederates employed. Asch's research showed little systematic variation in the conformity effect with the size of the group of confederates once there were three or more confederates in the group. Hence, in contrast to seven confederates used in Cohen's earlier work, Experiment 11 employed only three confederates.

Two final differences should be noted. In Experiment 11 the stimuli were presented on slides from an automatically controlled projector located in the observation booth outside the experimental room. In addition, the naive subject was seated in the last seat so that the responses of the three confederates preceded his response in contrast to previous work, where the naive subject was next to last, allowing one confederate's response to always follow his own.

The slide presentation contrasted with the hand cards turned by the experimenter for each trial in Cohen (1963). As a result, the stimuli differed from previous studies in that the comparison lines were much closer to the standard and the absolute sizes of the lines were reduced, although their relative sizes remained the same as in Cohen's earlier studies. Furthermore, automatic slide presentation made it possible to reduce the possible effects of the experimenter during the conformity phase by moving him to the back of the room, since he didn't have to flip cards for the stimulus series.

Since Experiment 11 employed only three confederates, placing the naive subject last maximized the amount of influence for that number of confederates. This required sacrificing one of the possible advantages of the customary order, i.e. it is possible that placing the subject next to last prevented him from believing that it was his angle of observation or distance from the stimulus which accounted for his differing view. Although we sacrificed this advantage, we are happy to report that the subject's position did not increase the ambiguity of the stimulus; the correct answer was clearly discriminable.

Guaranteeing that all naive subjects would be in seat 4 was a simple matter. Prior to the session, seats were assigned to the confederates. When the group appeared at the laboratory, the experimenter asked each member to draw a slip of paper for his seat assignment. The number "4" was written on all slips, so the naive subject took seat 4 while the confederates went to their previously assigned seats.

Let us briefly summarize the procedure for this experiment. A group of four members, three confederates and one naive subject, arrive at the laboratory. They draw numbers for seats and the drawing gives seat 4 to the naive subject. The experimenter tells the group that they are participating in a study of visual perception which involves two different but related tests of perceptual ability. The first test, the manipulation, requires the group members to judge whether or not a standard is contained in each of a series of test figures. After twenty such judgments, the experimenter reports on the performance of each group member, assigning scores to create one of four expectation states in the subject's mind. The task is one where the subject cannot evaluate his own performance and must rely on the experimenter for evaluations of his own and the other performances. While giving instructions for the second test, the conformity phase, the experimenter tells the group that people who do well in the first test also do well in the second, which requires judgments of lengths of lines. The group member's task in the second test is to match a standard line with the one of three comparison lines to which the standard is identical in length. The stimuli are presented on slides and each presentation constitutes a trial. For each presentation, the group members give their judgment orally with the confederates' responses all preceding the naive subject's. On the first two trials, the confederates give correct answers, but on all subsequent trials they are unanimous and incorrect. All slides are identical except for the labels on the comparison lines and the confederates always choose the moderate error, the comparison line at the right of the set of three comparison lines. Following the conformity phase, the experimenter interviews the naive subject for a qualitative evaluation

63

of his reaction to the study and to determine whether or not he was suspicious of the experimental manipulations. During the interview, the experimenter explains fully to the subject the purpose of the experiment and the various manipulations employed to produce the desired conditions of the study.

3.5 Results of Experiment 11

Prior to conducting Experiment 11, we ran a pilot study to pre-test the manipulation. In this pilot study only two status conditions were investigated, [HL] and [LH]. In the pilot study we found approximately twice as many conforming responses on the average in the [LH] as in the [HL] treatment condition. These results, together with the qualitative information from the post experimental interview which indicated that the manipulation was highly successful, encouraged us to go ahead with Experiment 11.

Experiment 11 consisted of two neutral trials and 60 critical trials. The subjects were male, undergraduate, summer session students, recruited from freshman and sophomore courses. Subjects were randomly assigned to treatment conditions with the restriction that when 30 usable subjects were achieved in a given condition, assignment to that condition would terminate. Subjects were interviewed after the experiment to determine whether or not the expectation manipulation was successful. Those for whom suspicion was pronounced or for whom the expectation manipulation failed were excluded from the analysis.

The confederates were also male, undergraduate, summer session students, recruited from the Student Employment Service. It was not possible to use the same three confederates for all subjects, nor was it possible, because of scheduling difficulties, to assign confederates to treatment conditions at random. The three confederates for a particular group were drawn from a pool of eight, and the same three participated in an entire afternoon's experiments, in which usually a total of three to five groups was run. Although the confederates were carefully instructed and rehearsed for several hours prior to actual participation in the experiment, it is clear that the same confederate varied his behavior from one subject to the next and also that there were variations among confederates. Confederate behavior remains a serious source of uncontrolled variability, the magnitude of which cannot be assessed in the present data because the number of cases where the same three confederates participated in the same treatment condition is too small for analysis. While we strongly desire to maintain the face-to-face feature of this situation rather than move to a light-panel simulation of the group (Crutchfield, 1951) or a tape recorder simulation (Blake and Brehm, 1954), we recognize that maintaining the direct confrontation between subjects and confederates entails serious costs. With further development of closed-circuit television and videotape, it may be possible to simulate the confederates' responses and yet maintain the face-to-face aspect of this experimental situation.

The two experimenters for this study were male sociology graduate students, rotated at schedules' convenience through treatment conditions. Here again it was not possible to assign experimenter to treatment randomly, but this is not as serious a problem as our inability to assign confederates randomly. Since the experimenter's role is somewhat more standardized, it is reasonable to assume that there is less variation across experimenters.

Preliminary analyses of the data from Experiment 11 are presented in Tables 3.3 and 3.4. Table 3.3 shows the means and standard deviations of the number of correct responses by treatment condition. Both statistics for the [LH] treatment condition differ markedly from those for the other three, the [HH], [LH], [LL], which appear quite similar. Parenthetically we should note that the difference between the [HL] and [LH] treatments in Experiment 11 replicate the results we obtained in our pilot study.

Table 3.4 shows the mean of the number of alternations per subject in each treatment condition. The results from all treatment conditions appear quite similar on this measure, and the greatest difference appears between the [HL] and [LL] conditions, with values of 11.00 and 9.27 respectively.

TABLE 3.3
Mean and standard deviation of the number of correct responses for each condition of Experiment 11 with proportions.

Condition	Mean	Proportion	Standard deviation
[HH]	46.3	0.77	18.5
[HL]	47.7	0.80	15.1
[LH]	35.6	0.59	23.4
[LL]	47.6	0.79	16.9

Note: There were 30 subjects in each condition and each subject participated in 60 trials.

TABLE 3.4
Mean number of alternations per subject for each treatment condition of Experiment 11.

Condition	Mean number of alternations
[HH]	10.03
[HL]	11.00
[LH]	10.20
[LL]	9.27

Note: There were 30 subjects in each condition and each subject participated in 60 trials.

In terms of the traditional ways these data are usually analysed, which we represent in the above tables, the safest conclusion is that the [LH] treatment differs from the other three treatment conditions, whereas making distinctions among the other three treatments is difficult. Certainly the most common statistics for comparing treatments is the mean number of correct responses, and on this measure, the [HH], [HL] and [LL] treatments are indistinguishable.

We have previously argued that the mean number of correct responses does not provide enough information about what is going on in the experiment to be used as an adequate basis for inferences about the effects of the experimental treatments. The data we have presented support this contention, although the treatments actually may not produce any differences in conformity. We are thus confronted with two interpretations: (1) There are no differences among these three treatments, or (2) The statistics we have used are insensitive and therefore do not show differences that do exist among the conditions. The second interpretation received some support even at the present gross level of analysis. On inspection, it does appear that the proportion of correct responses in the [HH] condition does differ through time from the other conditions. Furthermore, the [LL] condition seems to produce fewer alternations than the other conditions. Thus, it is possible that a more discriminating analysis, such as our probability model would provide, might adequately summarize differences that do exist. Hence, we must hold our conclusion in abeyance until we have analyzed the data from these four treatment conditions in terms of the Conflict Model.

CHAPTER 4

The Cohen-Lee Model

4.1 Introduction

The Conflict Model was successfully used to describe the response process of subjects in three Asch-type experiments, those designated by Cohen as his Experiments 1, 2 and 3. In *Conflict and Conformity*, Cohen initially proposed a computer search method for estimation. In such a method, the computer is programmed to generate a uniform sample of possible values for the parameters, and to generate them in all possible combinations. For each set of parameter values, the probability of a correct response for each trial is computed from Markov chain theory. These computed values are then plotted against the observed proportions of correct responses on each trial. Such a graph shows the extent of agreement between the theoretical curve predicted from a given parameter set and the actual curve obtained from the subjects' responses; it thus provides a good indication of the goodness of fit between the model and subject data.

For a model with only one parameter, a method based on computer searching is possible. However, when the number of parameters to be estimated reaches four, as in the Cohen model, the computer search procedure would require hours of computer time for each model for a single data set. The cost of such computer time would be prohibitive, and the research would be extended over a period of years. The prohibitive cost of complete computer searching was clearly recognized by Cohen (1963, p. 130).

As an alternative, two other methods, Kemeny and Snell's (1962) and Cohen's procedure based on run-lengths (1962), were advanced to estimate the parameters of the Conflict Model. When these methods were applied to new data gathered by Cohen in his

67

Asch-type Experiment 11, however, the model no longer satisfactorily represented the data. This lack of fit cast doubt on the adequacy of the two estimation procedures. Further, it could reflect some basic inadequacy in the model itself. However, as the estimation problem appeared to remain unsolved, it was not possible to evaluate the adequacy of the model independently of the evaluation of the estimation procedures.

It is important to note here that the laboratory procedure for Experiment 11 represented a considerable departure from that of the previous experiments to which Cohen had applied his model. Of course, it is quite possible that a model which is adequate for one situation is not adequate for a modification of that situation. But if that is so in this case, it represents an unfortunate limitation on the utility of the model, since Experiment 11 is an extension of the original experiments — an extension that has more intrinsic interest to social psychologists.

In view of these problems, the utility of the Conflict Model seemed questionable. Yet it was not clear whether the difficulties associated with its use were associated with the structure of the model or with the method for the estimation of its parameters. The fact that the model successfully represented three Asch-type experiments suggested that it had an appropriate basic structure and that the difficulty might still rest with the estimation procedure. At this point in the research process we felt that we had two alternatives available to us. We could try to develop an entirely new model structure or we could try to improve the estimation method. We interpreted the success of the fit of the Conflict Model to Experiments 1, 2 and 3 as supporting the basic structure of that model. For this reason we chose to try to improve the estimation procedure. Interestingly enough, however, the result of pursuing this strategy was a new model. As this new model has a structure similar to that of the Conflict Model, it was designated the Cohen-Lee model. We now turn to the specification of this new model.

4.2 The Cohen-Lee model

The Cohen-Lee model, like the Conflict Model, is a four-state Markov chain with two absorbing states. However, the Cohen-Lee model departs from the Conflict Model in three basic respects: (1) it has six parameters which have to be estimated; (2) the interpretation of the initial distribution vector is altered; and (3) although the parameters which appear in the transition matrix describing the Markov chain are similar to those given by Cohen, the values which these transition probabilities may take on are severely restricted by a number of assumptions about the ways in which they are related. These restraints, together with the reinterpretation of the initial distribution vector, specify the Cohen-Lee model.

Insofar as possible, the notation used here will follow that of *Conflict and Conformity* in order to facilitate comparison of the two models. Let $p_j(n)$ denote the probability that a subject is in State j on Trial n, where $j = 1, 2, 3$ or 4. Further, let P_n be the distribution vector of the process. Consequently, we may write

$$P_n = (p_1(n), p_2(n), p_3(n), p_4(n)) \qquad (4.1)$$

As an alternative to the Cohen hypothesis that one transition takes place prior to the first response, we assume that no transition takes place before the subject's first response. This change results in an additional equation which facilitates the estimation of the parameters. Let "1-response" denote a non-conforming response and "0-response" denote a conforming response. As not one of the 120 subjects in Experiment 11 gave a sequence composed entirely of 0-responses, we assume that $p_4(1) = 0.0$. And, as a few subjects in Experiment 11 gave a 0-response on Trial 1, it became necessary to assume that $p_3(1) \neq 0.0$. Finally, incorporating Cohen's later suggestion that some subjects may commence in State 1 in addition to those who start in State 2, it was necessary to assume that neither $p_1(1)$ nor $p_2(1)$ is equal to 0.0. Consequently when applied to Experiment 11, the initial vector for the model becomes

$$P_1 = (p_1(1), p_2(1), p_3(1), 0.0) \qquad (4.2)$$

where $p_1(1) \geqslant 0.0$, $p_2(1) \geqslant 0.0$, $p_3(1) \geqslant 0.0$, and $\sum_{j=1}^{n} p_j(1) = 1.0$.
The transition matrix of the model is given by

$$A = \begin{pmatrix} 1.0 & 0.0 & 0.0 & 0.0 \\ \alpha & \lambda & \beta & 0.0 \\ 0.0 & \gamma & \rho & \epsilon \\ 0.0 & 0.0 & 0.0 & 1.0 \end{pmatrix} \qquad (4.3)$$

The probability model known as the Markov chain is specified in such a fashion that the rows of any transition matrix must sum to one. Consequently, $\lambda = 1.0 - \alpha - \beta$, and $\rho = 1.0 - \gamma - \epsilon$. The transition matrix of the Cohen model (2.1), and that of the Cohen-Lee model (4.3), have the same mathematical structure. However, in the Cohen-Lee model, the values which the transition probabilities may assume are severely limited by restraints implicit in the estimation procedure, the next topic to be considered.

4.3 Estimation of the parameters of the Cohen-Lee model

The basic source of mathematical difficulties in the estimation of the parameters is that there are transitions between states which are not associated with any directly observable change in the subject's response. Even though we know the response on a given trial, we do not, in general, know which state the subject was in when he made that response. For example, it is not possible to compute from the data a numerical quantity associated with the transition from State 2 into State 1, nor is it possible to estimate this transition probability, α, directly. Similarly, we cannot estimate ϵ or $p_1(1)$ directly. Therefore, alternative methods for parameter estimation had to be derived.

The strategy can be described in four steps. (1) A set of statistics which describe major aspects of the response process had to be identified. (2) An appropriate set of equations using these statistics had to be derived. (3) For each of these statistics, an appropriate numerical quantity based on data from subjects had to be defined. (4) By appeal to the maximum likelihood estimation principle, the numerical estimates for the parameters of the model were then obtained by setting the equations for the selected statistics equal to the appropriate numerical quantities obtained from the subject data. Thus, there were six equations to be solved for the parameter values. Six statistics were used for the estimation process. These six statistics were: $p_3(1)$, the proportion of subjects in State 3 on Trial 1; π_0, the proportion of subjects giving exclusively 1-responses; λ, the probability of the transition from State 2 back into State 2; ρ, the probability of the transition from State 3 back into State 3; $p(\infty)$, the probability of a correct response after an infinite number of trials; and $E(A)$, the expected number of alternations. Insofar as possible, we will try to develop the estimation equations by building upon the analytical work of Cohen (1963).

70

Under the hypothesis that all subjects begin in State 2 on Trial 0, we obtained for the Conflict Model the following expressions for π_0, $p(\infty)$, and $E(A)$:

$$\pi_0 = \frac{\alpha}{\alpha + \beta} \tag{4.4}$$

$$p(\infty) = \frac{1.0 + \dfrac{\gamma}{\epsilon}}{1.0 + \dfrac{\beta}{\alpha} + \dfrac{\gamma}{\epsilon}} \tag{4.5}$$

and

$$E(A) = \frac{\dfrac{\beta}{\alpha}\left(\dfrac{2.0\gamma}{\epsilon} + 1.0\right)}{1.0 + \dfrac{\beta}{\alpha} + \dfrac{\gamma}{\epsilon}} \tag{4.6}$$

(See equations 2.7, 2.15, 2.16.)

In Experiment 11, two treatment conditions had values for $p(\infty)$ which were about the same, but their values for $E(A)$ were clearly different. This suggested that a better estimation procedure would employ both quantities. When the expressions for $p(\infty)$ and $E(A)$ were examined with this in mind, it was observed that the two ratios, β/α and γ/ϵ, appeared in each. As it was only in this ratio form that the transition probabilities appeared in either quantity it seemed that these ratios were important *as ratios*. This suggested that further restrictions should be imposed on the transition probabilities. These suggestions were combined by requiring that the estimation procedure include expressions for $p(\infty)$ and $E(A)$ in each of which the ratios of the transition probabilities be treated as ratios. Thus, let $L = \gamma/\epsilon$ and $R = \beta/\alpha$. By making these substitutions into (4.5) and (4.6), we have

$$p(\infty) = \frac{1.0 + L}{1.0 + R + L} \tag{4.7}$$

and

$$E(A) = \frac{R(2.0L + 1.0)}{1.0 + R + L} \tag{4.8}$$

71

Now let n_{ij} denote the observed number of response transitions from response i to response j on consecutive trials occurring before the last alternation. Then, by applying an argument similar to that made by Kemeny and Snell (1962) for the Conflict Model[1], two of the parameters of our new model may be estimated by

$$\hat{\lambda} = \frac{n_{11}}{n_{11} + n_{10}} \tag{4.9}$$

and

$$\hat{\rho} = \frac{n_{00}}{n_{00} + n_{01}} \tag{4.10}$$

By definition, $L = \gamma/\epsilon$, $R = \beta/\alpha$, $\gamma = 1.0 - \alpha - \beta$, and $\rho = 1.0 - \gamma - \epsilon$. We may perform simple algebraic manipulations upon these definitions to obtain expressions for α and ϵ as follows: Rewrite

$$R = \beta/\alpha$$

as

$$\alpha R = \beta$$

Then use this expression for β in $\lambda = 1.0 - \alpha - \beta$ to obtain

$$\lambda = 1.0 - \alpha - \alpha R$$

Solving for α, we obtain

$$\alpha + \alpha R = 1.0 - \lambda$$

$$\alpha(1.0 + R) = 1.0 - \lambda$$

$$\alpha = \frac{1.0 - \lambda}{1.0 + R} \tag{4.11}$$

Similarly, rewrite

$$L = \gamma/\epsilon$$

---

[1] See Appendix B.

72

as

$$\epsilon L = \gamma$$

Then substitute ϵL for γ in

$$\rho = 1.0 - \gamma - \epsilon$$

to obtain

$$\rho = 1.0 - \epsilon L - \epsilon$$

Solving for ϵ, we obtain

$$\epsilon L + \epsilon = 1.0 - \rho$$

$$\epsilon(L + 1.0) = 1.0 - \rho$$

$$\epsilon = \frac{1.0 - \rho}{1.0 + L} \tag{4.12}$$

These expressions for α and ϵ will be useful later.

It should be recalled that the expressions for $p(\infty)$ and $E(A)$ given above as (4.7) and (4.8) were derived for the Conflict Model; that is, they were derived under the assumption that all of the subjects began in State 2 on Trial 0. In the Cohen-Lee model, however, subjects may start in States 1, 2, or 3; and subjects start on Trial 1. It follows for this model that

$$p(\infty) = p_1(1) + p_2(1) \text{ Pr(absorbed into State 1 given that}$$
the subject started in State 2) + $p_3(1)$ Pr(absorbed
into State 1 given that the subject started in
State 3) $\tag{4.13}$

The expression for the expected number of alternations must also be modified. Consequently,

$$E(A) = p_2(1) \text{ E(alternations given that the subject started}$$
in State 2) + $p_3(1)$ E(alternations given that the
subject started in State 3) $\tag{4.14}$

Following the procedure developed in *Conflict and Conformity*

73

and given that the process begins in State 3, it is possible to construct the sequences leading to exactly K alternations in order to derive expressions for (4.13) and (4.14) (see Table 2.1). The derivation is facilitated by the preparation of Table 4.1, which gives the number of occurrences of each transition event in sequences leading to K alternations for a few values of K, under the hypothesis that the process starts in State 3.

The derivation is presented in terms of sequences of states rather than in terms of responses. Hence, a sequence 2——2 is a sequence in which the subject was in State 2 for some consecutive number of trials. We defined sequences of the type 2——2 as a transition event because we wished to include not only single transitions, but also sub-sequences consisting of identical states, for which we could assign probabilities. In Chapter 2, we demonstrated that the probability of any sequence of the form 2——2, containing $(i + 1)$ 2's, is given by $\Sigma_{i=0}^{\infty} (1.0 - \alpha - \beta)^i$, which we have shown to be equal to $1.0/(\alpha + \beta)$. Analogously, we found the probability for any sequence of the form 3——3 to be given by $1.0/(\gamma + \epsilon)$. The product of each and every type of transition event occurring in a sequence gives the probability of that sequence.

Table 4.1 is an analog of Table 2.1. The entries in the column labelled α of Table 4.1 are identical with the entries in the column labelled ϵ of Table 2.1. The same relationship obtains between β in one table and γ in the other as well as between $1/(\alpha + \beta)$ and $1/(\gamma + \epsilon)$. This "mirror-image" relationship between the two tables simplifies the derivation of an expression for the expected number of alternations, given that the process starts in State 3, because it allows us to employ the expression for E(A), given above in (4.6). If ϵ is replaced by α, γ replaced by β, β replaced by γ, and α replaced by ϵ, we obtain

$$E(A \mid \text{subject started in State 3}) = \frac{\frac{\gamma}{\epsilon}\left(2.0\frac{\beta}{\alpha} + 1.0\right)}{1.0 + \frac{\gamma}{\epsilon} + \frac{\beta}{\alpha}} \qquad (4.15)$$

Rewriting (4.15) employing the equivalences $L = \gamma/\epsilon$ and $R = \beta/\alpha$, we then obtain

$$E(A \mid \text{subject started in State 3}) = \frac{L(2.0R + 1.0)}{1.0 + R + L} \qquad (4.16)$$

74

TABLE 4.1
Number of occurrences of each transition event in sequences leading to k
alternations for a few values of k, given that the process starts in State 3.

umber f alter- ations k	Sequence			Transition event					
			(Probability)	2—2 $\frac{1}{\alpha+\beta}$	2—3 β	3—2 γ	2—1 α	3—3 $\frac{1}{\gamma+\epsilon}$	3—4 ϵ
	3—34			0	0	0	0	1	1
	3——32——21			1	0	1	1	1	0
	3——32——23——34			1	1	1	0	2	1
	3——32——23——32——21			2	1	2	1	2	0
	3——32——23——32——23——34			2	2	2	0	3	1

Combining (4.8) and (4.16) according to (4.14), the expected
number of alternations for the Cohen-Lee model becomes

$$E(A) = p_2(1)\,\frac{R(2.0L + 1.0)}{1.0 + R + L} + p_3(1)\,\frac{L(2.0R + 1.0)}{1.0 + R + L} \qquad (4.17)$$

Next, an expression for $p(\infty)$ must be obtained. First, it is necessary to see that, when the asymptote is reached, the proportion of
subjects absorbed into State 1 is the proportion of subjects making
a 1-response; that is, the total probability of absorption into State
1 is identical to the asymptotic probability of a 1-response. As
specified in (4.13), the expression for $p(\infty)$ must consist of three
parts. The portion to be obtained here is the expression for
Pr(absorbed into State 1 given that the subject started in State 3).
If k denotes the number of alternations, absorption into State 1,
given that the process starts in State 3, may occur only if k is odd.
The results necessary for the derivation have already been presented in Chapter 2. (It is useful to construct a table from Table 4.1
analogous to Table 2.2.) For ease in presentation, we will introduce the definition

$$Z = \frac{\beta\gamma}{(\alpha + \beta)(\gamma + \epsilon)} \qquad (4.18)$$

Then

$$p(\infty \,|\, \text{subject started in State 3}) = \sum_{k \text{ odd}}^{\infty} \text{Pr(exactly k alternations)}$$

75

$$= \frac{\alpha\gamma}{(\alpha + \beta)(\gamma + \epsilon)} \sum_{k\,odd}^{\infty} Z^{(k-1)/2} = \frac{\alpha\gamma}{(\alpha + \beta)(\gamma + \epsilon)} (1.0 + Z + Z^2 + ...)$$

$$(4.19)$$

For the series $(1.0 + Z + Z^2 + ...)$, we may employ (see Cohen, 1963 [5.12]) the equality

$$\sum_{k=0}^{\infty} Z^i = \frac{1.0}{1.0 - Z}$$

$$(4.20)$$

Consequently,

p(∞ | subject started in State 3) =

$$= \left(\frac{\alpha\gamma}{(\alpha + \beta)(\gamma + \epsilon)}\right)\left(\frac{1.0}{1.0 - \dfrac{\beta\gamma}{(\alpha + \beta)(\gamma + \epsilon)}}\right)$$

$$(4.21)$$

This expression may be simplified as follows:

p(∞ | subject started in State 3)

$$= \left(\frac{\alpha\gamma}{(\alpha + \beta)(\gamma + \epsilon)}\right)\left(\frac{1.0}{\dfrac{(\alpha + \beta)(\gamma + \epsilon) - \beta\gamma}{(\alpha + \beta)(\gamma + \epsilon)}}\right)$$

$$= \left(\frac{\alpha\gamma}{(\alpha + \beta)(\gamma + \epsilon)}\right)\left(\frac{(\alpha + \beta)(\gamma + \epsilon)}{(\alpha + \beta)(\gamma + \epsilon) - \beta\gamma}\right)$$

$$= \frac{\alpha\gamma}{(\alpha + \beta)(\gamma + \epsilon) - \beta\gamma}$$

$$= \frac{\alpha\gamma}{\epsilon(\alpha + \beta) + \alpha\gamma}$$

$$(4.22)$$

Employing the equivalences for R and L as well as the obtained expressions for α and ϵ, (4.11) and (4.12), this may be written as

p(∞ | subject started in State 3) $= \dfrac{L}{1.0 + R + L}$

$$(4.23)$$

76

Combining this expression with the previously derived expressions in (4.13), the desired result — the probability of a correct response after an infinite number of trials for the Cohen-Lee model — is given by

$$p(\infty) = p_1(1) + p_2(1) \frac{1.0 + L}{1.0 + R + L} + p_3(1) \frac{L}{1.0 + R + L} \qquad (4.24)$$

It may be shown that the expression for the probability of a sequence of all 1-responses, denoted by π_0 here, may be given by

$$\pi_0 = p_1(1) + p_2(1) \frac{\alpha}{\alpha + \beta} \qquad (4.25)$$

By making the substitutions $\alpha + \beta = 1.0 - \lambda$ and $\alpha = (1.0 - \lambda)/(1.0 + R)$ the expression may be rewritten as

$$\pi_0 = p_1(1) + p_2(1) \frac{1.0}{1.0 + R} \qquad (4.26)$$

Before we can obtain numerical estimates for the parameters of the model by setting these equations equal to appropriate numerical quantities obtained from the data, we must make some arbitrary decisions as to what quantities are appropriately associated with the six statistics we have employed. A special problem arises with the selection of the numerical quantity for representing $p(\infty)$ for an arbitrary decision has to be made as to what trials would be selected as representing the asymptotic values of the correct response. In order to keep the other quantities as statistically independent of one another as possible, we decided to use Trials 1 through 55 as the basis for the estimates of π_0 and $E(A)$.

Let the observed proportion of subjects with all 1-responses in Trials 1 through 55 be represented by a. Let b denote the observed proportions of 1-responses counted for all subjects in a given treatment condition, but only over the last five trials of the response sequence. Set c equal to the observed number of alternations counted from Trial 1 through Trial 55, divided by the number of subjects. Finally, set d equal to the proportion of subjects who give a 0-response on Trial 1.

The estimate of $p_3(1)$, denoted by $\hat{p}_3(1)$, is d. The theory of Markov chains specifies that the sum of the probabilities in the distribution vector is one. Hence, for the Cohen-Lee model, $p_1(1)$

+ $p_2(1)$ + $p_3(1)$ = 1.0, as previously mentioned when the initial distribution vector (4.1) was introduced. This permits the substitution of $(1.0 - p_2(1) - d)$ for $p_1(1)$. First, we rewrite (4.26) employing this substitution as

$$\pi_0 = 1.0 - p_2(1) - d + p_2(1)\left(\frac{1.0}{1.0 + R}\right)$$

Next, we employ the maximum likelihood principle to set this equation for π_0, equal to a, the observed proportion of subjects with all 1-responses in Trials 1 through 55. This results in

$$a = 1.0 - p_2(1) - d + p_2(1)\left(\frac{1.0}{1.0 + R}\right)$$

which we solve for $p_2(1)$ as follows:

$$p_2(1) - p_2(1)\left(\frac{1.0}{1.0 + R}\right) = 1.0 - a - d$$

$$p_2(1)\left(1.0 - \left(\frac{1.0}{1.0 + R}\right)\right) = 1.0 - a - d$$

$$p_2(1)\left(\frac{R}{1.0 + R}\right) = 1.0 - a - d$$

$$p_2(1) = \frac{(1.0 + R)(1.0 - a - d)}{R} \tag{4.27}$$

The most tedious derivation is one that produces an estimate for R and uses the expressions for both $p(\infty)$ and $E(A)$. The derivation is divided into three steps. First, we use $p(\infty)$ to obtain an expression for L; then we use $E(A)$ to obtain another expression for L; finally, these two expressions for L, each in terms of R and the observed quantities (a, b, c, d) are set equal to each other and solved for R. We begin by copying the previously obtained equation for the asymptotic probability of a correct response as follows:

$$p(\infty) = p_1(1) + p_2(1)\left(\frac{1.0 + L}{1.0 + R + L}\right) + p_3(1)\left(\frac{L}{1.0 + R + L}\right)$$

Substitute $(1.0 - p_2(1) - d)$ for $p_1(1)$. Replace $p(\infty)$, the asymptotic probability of a 1-response by b, the observed proportion of 1-responses counted over the last five trials of all the response sequences. Replace, p_3, the proportion of subjects in State 3 on Trial 1, by d, the proportion of subjects who made a 0-response on Trial 1. Then subtract the left-hand side from both sides of the equation, put the entire equation over the lowest common denominator, and simplify. The result is

$$0 = 1.0 - b - d - bR + R - p_2(1)R - dR - Lb + L \qquad (4.28)$$

Substitute the expression (4.27) for $p_2(1)$ in (4.28) and solve for L to obtain

$$L = \frac{(1.0 + R)(b - a)}{1.0 - b} \qquad (4.29)$$

The second step is to obtain another expression for L but this time based upon

$$E(A) = p_2(1)\left(\frac{R(2.0L + 1.0)}{1.0 + R + L}\right) + p_3(1)\left(\frac{L(2.0R + 1.0)}{1.0 + R + L}\right)$$

into which we substitute the expression for $p_2(1)$; replace $p_3(1)$ by d; replace $E(A)$ by c, the observed number of alternations counted from Trial 1 through Trial 55 (divided by the number of subjects); and solve for L. This result is

$$L = \frac{(1.0 + R)(a + c + d - 1.0)}{2.0(1.0 - a)(1.0 + R) - (c + d)} \qquad (4.30)$$

Finally, set these two expressions for L, (4.29) and (4.30), equal to each other, and solve for R. The result, denoted by $\hat{R}$, may be taken as an estimate for R.

$$\hat{R} = \frac{2.0a - b + c + d - 1.0}{2.0(b - a)} \qquad (4.31)$$

Replace R by $\hat{R}$ in (4.29), solve for L, and denote the result by $\hat{L}$. Replace R by $\hat{R}$ in (4.27), solve for $p_2(1)$ and denote the result by $\hat{p}_2(1)$. As $\hat{p}_3(1)$ is directly estimated by d, the estimate for $p_1(1)$ is obtained by subtraction, as indicated by $\hat{p}_1(1) = (1.0 - \hat{p}_2(1) -$

79

d). The expressions presented before for α, (4.11); λ, (4.9); ρ, (4.10); and ϵ, (4.12) immediately yield the estimates

$$\hat{\alpha} = \frac{1.0 - \hat{\lambda}}{1.0 + \hat{R}} \tag{4.32}$$

and

$$\hat{\epsilon} = \frac{1.0 - \hat{\rho}}{1.0 + \hat{L}} \tag{4.33}$$

Recalling that $R = \beta/\alpha$ and $L = \gamma/\epsilon$, we see that

$$\hat{\beta} = \hat{R}\hat{\alpha} \tag{4.34}$$

and that

$$\hat{\gamma} = \hat{L}\hat{\epsilon} \tag{4.35}$$

This completes the estimation procedure.

At this point in the research we have achieved a method for the estimation of the parameters of the Cohen-Lee model. It was necessary to interpret the initial distribution vector as directly specifying which state the subject was in on the basis of his response on the first trial. This interpretation introduced an additional equation which could be used in the estimation process. Further, an analysis of previously available Asch data suggested that most subjects eventually adopted the strategy of making either all 0-responses or all 1-responses. However examination of some of the response sequences of particular subjects suggested that the way the subject moved into this "absorbed" condition was relatively independent of which absorbed state he reached. These two factors were interpreted as arguing for the position that two statistics were of particular importance. Thus, $E(A)$, the expected number of alternations, and $p(\infty)$, the asymptotic probability of a 1-response, were used for a basis of the estimation strategy. $E(A)$ was selected because it would reflect the larger aspects of the way the subject finally reached an absorbing state. That is, we argued that the number of alternations reflected the larger aspects of the path to absorption. We also argued that $p(\infty)$ reflected the larger aspects of the equilibrium condition for that particular treatment condi-

80

tion. To incorporate these statistics in the estimation procedure, we had to derive analytical expressions for each of them in terms of the initial distribution vector and the transition probabilities. These expressions were then used in the set of equations employed in the derivation of the estimates of the model. But by doing this we have created further restrictions upon the relationships among these parameters of the model. Because of these additional restrictions on the parameters of the model and because of the reinterpretation of the initial distribution vector from that originally posited by Cohen for his Conflict Model, we have come to regard the Cohen-Lee model as distinctive.

Unfortunately, we have not as yet "solved" the estimation problem for we are unable to claim on the basis of any statistical theory that these are the "best" estimates. Because of this, any interpretations of the model must be qualified, as we are still left with the problem of the uniqueness of the estimates. That is, because we cannot claim that these estimates are optimal, we are unable to assert that there are not other sets of estimates which do as good a job of estimation as those we have obtained. Because there is this possibility of other estimates which are adequate we are forced to admit that it is not only possible but quite likely that other "acceptable" estimates would lead to different interpretations of this substantive underlying response process which we are attempting to represent. We can, however, investigate how well the model fits the response data of the subjects in Experiment 11. This then is our task for the following chapter.

CHAPTER 5

Fit of the Cohen-Lee Model to Experiment 11

5.1 Introduction

Although the Conflict Model had been developed for and successfully applied to three Asch experiments, a later Asch-type experiment, designated Experiment 11, produced data to which the Conflict Model could not be applied successfully. Experiment 11 differed from the three previous experiments in that the subjects were first exposed to a task designed to specify their anticipated level of performance in the later Asch task. Our hope has been to employ the Asch situation as a basis for studying the relationship between expectations for ability and conformity behavior.

We could assume that the failure of the Conflict Model to represent the data from Experiment 11 was an indication that the model is itself inadequate or, more seriously, that the goal of employing the Asch situation as a vehicle for understanding the relationship between conformity behavior and ability expectations is not obtainable. However, we would be willing to make either of these assumptions only as a last resort. The work on Experiments 1, 2, and 3 seemed to support the assumption that the Markovian state structure was fundamentally sound. Consequently, we decided to attempt to improve the estimation procedure. Interestingly enough, however, the research toward this goal resulted in the new model, designated the Cohen-Lee model, to describe the conceptualized process underlying the response behavior of subjects in Asch-type experiments. The structure of this new model, together with a method for the estimation of its parameters, was presented in the previous chapter. We can now turn to an assessment of how well this model represents the response data from subjects in Ex-

82

periment 11. We will first present the detailed analysis for the [HL] and [LH] conditions; then we will present a more global analysis of all four conditions.

5.2. Observed quantities from response data

Table 5.1 presents the quantities used to estimate the parameters of the Cohen-Lee model for the [HL] and [LH] conditions of Experiment 11. The proportion of subjects with all 1-responses in Trials 1 through 55, designated a, was used in the estimation of π_0. The proportion of 1-responses observed in Trials 56 through 60, designated b, was used in the estimation of $p(\infty)$. In the estimation of $E(A)$, the observed number of alternations from Trial 1 through Trial 55, divided by the number of subjects and designated c, was employed. The letter d represented the observed proportion of subjects who gave a 0-response on Trial 1 and was used to estimate $p_3(1)$.

We used computer simulation to assess the fit of the model. We generated data from pseudo-subjects (homostats) by applying transition probabilities trial-by-trial and deciding for each homostat on each trial which state he entered. We produced 10 samples of 30 homostats; each homostat was run for 60 trials. We of course used

TABLE 5.1
Observed quantities used to obtain the estimates for the Cohen-Lee model.

Observed quantity	Condition	
	[HL]	[LH]
(a) The proportion of subjects with all 1-responses Trials 1 through 55	0.333	0.167
(b) The proportion of 1-responses in Trials 56 through 60	0.773	0.600
(c) The number of alternations from Trial 1 through Trial 55, divided by the number of subjects	10.500	9.600
(d) The proportion of subjects who give a 0-response on Trial 1	0.067	0.200
n_{11}	265	213
n_{10}	160	147
n_{01}	155	141
n_{00}	115	216

83

the values for the initial distribution vector and for the transition matrix which were obtained by the estimation procedure suggested for the Cohen-Lee model.

5.3 Detailed analysis of the [HL] condition

The application of the estimation procedure described in the previous chapter (Eqns. 4.29—4.35) to the data of the 30 subjects in the [HL] condition of Experiment 11 resulted in an initial distribution vector:

$$P_1 = (0.28, 0.66, 0.06, 0.0)$$

and in the transition matrix

State on Trial n + 1

$$A = \text{State on Trial n} \quad \begin{array}{c} 1 \\ 2 \\ 3 \\ 4 \end{array} \begin{array}{cccc} 1 & 2 & 3 & 4 \\ \left(\begin{array}{cccc} 1.0 & 0.0 & 0.0 & 0.0 \\ 0.03 & 0.62 & 0.35 & 0.0 \\ 0.0 & 0.55 & 0.43 & 0.02 \\ 0.0 & 0.0 & 0.0 & 1.0 \end{array} \right) \end{array}$$

For the [HL] condition of Experiment 11, Table 5.2 presents the contrast between, first, the theoretical value of the equilibrium probability of a 1-response, $p(\infty)$, as given by (4.24), and, second, the comparison quantity, the mean number of 1-responses observed over the last five trials of the experiment. The value of the comparison quantity for the [HL] condition was 0.77. (This comparison quantity was employed in the estimation of the parameters of the model.) When the parameters were used to compute the theoretical or predicted value of the statistic $p(\infty)$, 0.77 was the result. The mean number of 1-responses over the last five trials was then obtained for the 300 homostats and produced a value of 0.74. The sample values of the mean number of 1-responses in the last five trials ranged from 0.67 to 0.81.

There were 3 samples in which the value of the comparison quantity, the mean number of 1-responses over the last 5 trials, was above the 0.77 predicted for $p(\infty)$ and 7 samples in which it was below this predicted value. Similarly, there were 3 simulated samples whose values for the comparison quantity were above and 7 below the observed mean of 0.77.

TABLE 5.2

Contrasts for the statistic $p(\infty)$, the equilibrium probability of a 1-response, for the [HL] condition of Experiment 11.

Value of the	
statistic $p(\infty)$, as predicted by the model	0.77
comparison quantity observed in subjects (N = 30)	0.77
comparison quantity observed in aggregate of homostats (N = 300)	0.74
comparison quantity observed in simulation	
1	0.81
2	0.70
3	0.67
4	0.81
5	0.69
6	0.81
7	0.75
8	0.75
9	0.71
10	0.71
Number of simulated samples for the comparison quantity which are	
above	3
at	0
below	7
the value predicted from the model	
Number of simulated samples for the comparison quantity which are	
above	3
at	0
below	7
the value observed in subjects	

Note: The value of $p(\infty)$ as predicted by the model was obtained by solving Equation (4.24). The comparison quantity is the mean number of 1-responses over the last 5 trials. There were 30 subjects in the [HL] condition. There were 10 simulations with 30 homostats in each simulation.

Table 5.3 reports the contrasts for the statistic $E(A)$, the expected number of alternations, for the [HL] condition of Experiment 11. The analytical expression for $E(A)$ for the model is given by (4.17). The number of alternations observed up to the last 5 trials, divided by the number of subjects, is the comparison quantity. For the 30 subjects in the [HL] condition of Experiment 11, its value was 10.50. (This comparison quantity was used in obtaining the estimates for the parameters of the model.) The model predicts a value of 10.50. A value of 8.65 was obtained for the comparison quantity from the 300 homostats. The comparison quantity ranged from 6.30 to 10.43. The distribution of the com-

85

TABLE 5.3

Contrasts for the statistic E(A), the expected number of alternations, for the [HL] condition of Experiment 11.

Value of the	
statistic E(A), as predicted by the model	10.50
comparison quantity observed in subjects (N = 30)	10.50
comparison quantity observed in aggregate of homostats	
(N = 300)	8.65
comparison quantity observed in simulation	
1	6.30
2	9.30
3	9.13
4	8.87
5	8.67
6	8.77
7	10.43
8	7.20
9	9.53
10	8.23
Number of simulated samples for the comparison quantity which are	
above	0
at	0
below	10
the value predicted from the model	
Number of simulated samples for the comparison quantity which are	
above	0
at	0
below	10
the value observed in subjects	

Note: The value of E(A) as predicted by the model was obtained by solving Equation (4.17). The number of alternations observed up to the last 5 trials, divided by the number of subjects, is the comparison quantity. There were 30 subjects in the [HL] condition. There were 10 simulations with 30 homostats in each simulation.

parison quantity for the simulated samples as above, at, or below the value predicted from the model was the same as its distribution with respect to the value observed in subjects. All 10 samples had values which were below both the values to which they were being compared.

Table 5.4 reports the contrasts for the statistic π_0, the probability of a response sequence consisting entirely of 1's for the [HL] condition. This statistic is given by (4.26). The comparison quantity is the proportion of subjects who had response sequences consisting entirely of 1's on Trials 1 through 55. For the 30 sub-

TABLE 5.4
Contrasts for the statistic π_0, the probability of a response sequence consisting entirely of 1-responses, for the [HL] condition of Experiment 11.

Value of the	
statistic π_0, as predicted from the model	0.33
comparison quantity observed in subjects (N = 30)	0.33
comparison quantity observed in aggregate of homostats	
(N = 300)	0.33
comparison quantity observed in simulation	
1	0.33
2	0.30
3	0.27
4	0.40
5	0.27
6	0.33
7	0.27
8	0.40
9	0.37
10	0.33
Number of simulated samples for the comparison quantity which are	
above	3
at	3
below	4
the value predicted from the model	
Number of simulated samples for the comparison quantity which are	
above	3
at	3
below	4
the value observed in subjects	

Note: The value of π_0 as predicted by the model was obtained by solving Equation (4.26). The proportion of subjects who had response sequences consisting entirely of 1-responses (not counting the last 5 trials) is the comparison quantity. There were 30 subjects in the [HL] condition. There were 10 simulations with 30 homostats in each simulation.

jects in the [HL] condition, the comparison quantity was found to be 0.33. The model accurately predicts a value of 0.33, but the observed value was used to estimate the parameters of the model. The comparison quantity for the 300 homostats was 0.33. The range of values obtained for the comparison quantity over the simulated samples was from 0.27 to 0.40. There were 3 samples whose comparison quantities were above, 3 at, and 4 below the value predicted from the model. The model generated 3 samples with values of the comparison quantity above, 3 at, and 4 below the value observed in the subjects.

5.4 Detailed analysis of the [LH] condition of Experiment 11

Table 5.5 presents the contrast between $p(\infty)$ (the equilibrium probability of a 1-response) and the observed comparison quantity (the mean number of 1-responses over the last 5 trials) for the [LH] condition of Experiment 11. This mean was 0.60. (The comparison quantity was used to estimate the parameters of the model.) When the parameters were used to predict the value of $p(\infty)$, the result was 0.60. The comparison quantity for the 300 homostats for the model was 0.60. An examination of the distribution of the mean of 1-responses over the last 5 trials for the 10

TABLE 5.5

Contrasts for the statistic $p(\infty)$, the equilibrium probability of a 1-response, for the [LH] condition of Experiment 11.

Value of the	
statistic $p(\infty)$ as predicted by the model	0.60
comparison quantity observed in subjects (N = 30)	0.60
comparison quantity observed in aggregate of homostats (N = 300)	0.60
comparison quantity observed in simulation	
1	0.85
2	0.55
3	0.65
4	0.54
5	0.54
6	0.55
7	0.65
8	0.63
9	0.60
10	0.48
Number of simulated samples for the comparison quantity which are	
above	4
at	1
below	5
the value predicted from the model	
Number of simulated samples for the comparison quantity which are	
above	4
at	1
below	5
the value observed in subjects	

Note: The value of $p(\infty)$ as predicted by the model was obtained by solving Equation (4.24). The comparison quantity is the mean number of 1-responses over the last 5 trials. There were 30 subjects in the [LH] condition. There were 10 simulations with 30 homostats in each simulation.

88

TABLE 5.6

Contrasts for the statistic E(A), the expected number of alternations, for the [LH] condition of Experiment 11.

Value of the	
statistic E(A), as predicted from the model	9.60
comparison quantity observed in subjects (N = 30)	9.60
comparison quantity observed in aggregate of homostats	
(N = 300)	8.26
comparison quantity observed in simulation	
1	7.27
2	8.83
3	9.10
4	8.33
5	6.33
6	7.53
7	8.90
8	7.53
9	7.27
10	11.53
Number of simulated samples for the comparison quantity which are	
above	1
at	0
below	9
the value predicted from the model	
Number of simulated samples for the comparison quantity which are	
above	1
at	0
below	9
the value observed in subjects	

Note: The value of E(A) as predicted by the model was obtained by solving Equation (4.17). The number of alternations observed up to the last 5 trials, divided by the number of subjects, is the comparison quantity. There were 30 subjects in the [LH] condition. There were 10 simulations with 30 homostats in each simulation.

simulated samples shows that the range of the values for the model was from 0.48 to 0.85. The simulation of the model produced 4 values above, 1 at, and 5 below the value of 0.60 predicted by the model.

Contrasts for the statistic E(A) for the [LH] condition are presented in Table 5.6. The comparison quantity and E(A) were defined in the same way as those for the [HL] condition. The observed value of the comparison quantity for the [LH] condition for the 30 subjects was 9.60. The comparison quantity for the homostats was 8.26. The range of values for the comparison quantity computed for the homostats was from 6.33 to 11.53. Nine simulated samples yielded comparison quantities which were below the predicted value, while one sample had a value above the predicted value. Also, 9 simulated samples yielded comparison quantities which were below the value observed in the responses of the subjects, and 1 above.

The contrasts for the statistic π_0 for the [LH] condition are presented in Table 5.7. (That statistic, as previously noted, is defined by (4.26).) The observed comparison quantity — the propor-

TABLE 5.7
Contrasts for the statistic π_0, the probability of a response sequence consisting entirely of 1-responses, for the [LH] condition of Experiment 11.

Value of the	
statistic π_0, as predicted from the model	0.17
comparison quantity observed in subjects (N = 30)	0.17
comparison quantity observed in aggregate of homostats (N = 300)	0.15
comparison quantity observed in simulation	
1	0.17
2	0.10
3	0.13
4	0.07
5	0.13
6	0.20
7	0.20
8	0.23
9	0.17
10	0.07
Number of simulated samples for the comparison quantity which are	
above	3
at	2
below	5
the value predicted from the model	
Number of simulated samples for the comparison quantity which are	
above	3
at	2
below	5
the value observed in subjects	

Note: The value of π_0 as predicted by the model was obtained by solving Equation (4.26). The proportion of subjects who had response sequences consisting entirely of 1-responses (not counting the last 5 trials) is the comparison quantity. There were 30 subjects in the [LH] condition. There were 10 simulations with 30 homostats in each simulation.

tion of the 30 human subjects in the [LH] condition who had response sequences consisting entirely of 1-responses on Trials 1 through 55 — was used to estimate the parameters of the model. This comparison quantity was 0.17, the predicted value. The value of the comparison quantity for the 300 homostats was 0.15. The range of the comparison quantity over the simulated samples was from 0.07 to 0.23. For the model there were 3 samples whose comparison quantities had values above that predicted from the model, 2 with values equal to it, and 5 that fell below it. The same distribution was obtained when the contrast was to the value observed in data from the 30 subjects.

Up to this point, the evaluation has been based on the model's ability to reproduce the quantities used to estimate the parameters. This is a necessary, but not a sufficient, condition for a good-fitting model. For the most part, the above results are very encouraging, demonstrating consistency in the model and an isomorphism between the structure of the model and the structure of the data. The simulation results for alternations show a surprising departure from both the computed and observed values of $E(A)$, but then there is considerable sampling variability for the homostats. We do not yet understand why the variability with respect to this quantity is so large and this remains a problem for future investigation.

5.5 Plots of the proportion of correct responses given trial by trial

A better basis for assessing the goodness of fit between model and data is an examination of the plots of the trialwise probability of a 1-response. The theory of Markov chains states that the mean proportion of 1-responses on succeeding trials can be computed from the initial distribution vector, P_1, and the transition matrix, A. The mathematical details of the computations involved are available elsewhere (Kemeny, 1959). In a computer program designed to carry out these computations, the initial distribution vector and the transition matrix are read and the predicted mean proportion of 1-responses for each of the 60 trials of the experiment is computed. These theoretical mean proportions are prepared for plotting as a continuous curve. In addition, the observed response data from the subjects are read and the mean number of 1-responses on each trial is computed. These observed mean proportions are also prepared for plotting as a continuous curve. For each of the 4 treatment conditions of Experiment 11, such a plot has been prepared with the theoretical curve plotted on the same graph used to present the observed curve.

5.5.1 Analysis of the [HH] condition

Figure 5.1 presents the trialwise proportion of 1-responses for the [HH] condition, wherein the predictions of the model seem to be approximately constant from Trials 5 through 60 at the value of 0.74. Although the model appears to be fairly satisfactory for Trials 35 through 60, the agreement between the predicted and the observed responses on the initial segment of trials is not very satisfactory. Yet the model seems to be adequate for representing the equilibrium condition of subjects in the experiment. The theoretical curve employed the estimates given below.

The initial distribution was

$$P_1 = (0.32, 0.54, 0.13, 0.0)$$

and the transition matrix was

$$
\begin{array}{c}
\text{State on Trial } n + 1 \\
\begin{array}{cccc}
1 & 2 & 3 & 4
\end{array}
\end{array}
$$

$$
A = \text{State on Trial } n \quad
\begin{array}{c}
1 \\ 2 \\ 3 \\ 4
\end{array}
\left(
\begin{array}{cccc}
1.0 & 0.0 & 0.0 & 0.0 \\
0.03 & 0.66 & 0.31 & 0.0 \\
0.0 & 0.50 & 0.47 & 0.03 \\
0.0 & 0.0 & 0.0 & 1.0
\end{array}
\right)
$$

5.5.2 Analysis of the [HL] condition

Figure 5.2 displays the trialwise probability of a 1-response for the [HL] condition. Here the model predicts correctly the first 2 trials but is below the observed values for Trials 3 through 35. Again the model correctly represents the final stages of the response process. For convenience, we repeat the initial distribution and the transition matrix for this condition below.

The initial distribution vector is given by

$$P_1 = (0.28, 0.66, 0.06, 0.0)$$

92

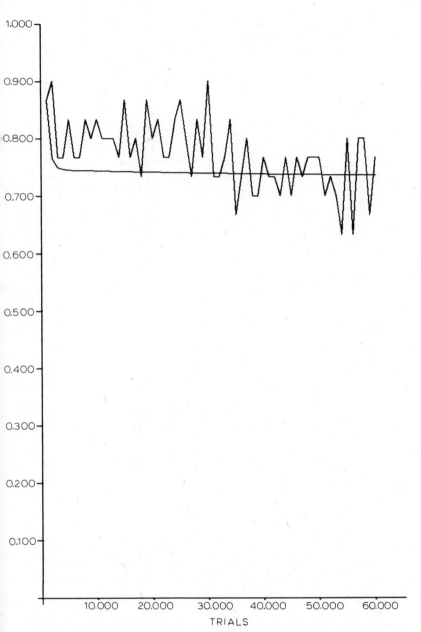

Figure 5.1. The irregular curve connects the proportion of 1-responses observed on each trial for the [HH] condition of Cohen's Experiment 11. The smooth curve is the theoretical proportion of 1-responses predicted by the Cohen-Lee model for the same data. N = 30.

and the transition matrix is given by

$$
\text{A = State on Trial n}
\begin{array}{c}
\\ 1 \\ 2 \\ 3 \\ 4
\end{array}
\overset{\textstyle \text{State on Trial n + 1}}{
\begin{array}{cccc}
1 & 2 & 3 & 4 \\
\left(1.0 \right. & 0.0 & 0.0 & 0.0 \\
0.03 & 0.62 & 0.35 & 0.0 \\
0.0 & 0.55 & 0.43 & 0.02 \\
\left. 0.0 \right. & 0.0 & 0.0 & 1.0
\end{array}}
$$

5.5.3 Analysis of the [LH] condition

The model produces a better fit to the observed proportion of 1-responses for the [LH] condition of Experiment 11, as may be seen in Figure 5.3. The examination of the curves giving trialwise probability of a 1-response indicates that the model appropriately represents the entire process from the first trial through the last trial. The initial distribution vector is

$P_1 = (0.10, 0.70, 0.20, 0.0)$

and the transition matrix is

$$
\text{A = State on Trial n}
\begin{array}{c}
\\ 1 \\ 2 \\ 3 \\ 4
\end{array}
\overset{\textstyle \text{State on Trial n + 1}}{
\begin{array}{cccc}
1 & 2 & 3 & 4 \\
\left(1.0 \right. & 0.0 & 0.0 & 0.0 \\
0.04 & 0.59 & 0.37 & 0.0 \\
0.0 & 0.36 & 0.61 & 0.03 \\
\left. 0.0 \right. & 0.0 & 0.0 & 1.0
\end{array}}
$$

5.5.4 Analysis of the [LL] condition

From the trialwise proportion of 1-responses we see that the model successfully represents the data obtained from subjects in the [LL] condition (Figure 5.4). The initial distribution vector for this condition was estimated to be

$P_1 = (0.21, 0.76, 0.03, 0.0)$

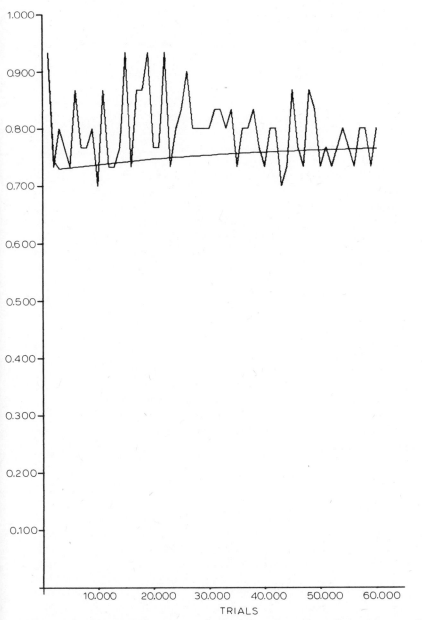

Figure 5.2. The irregular curve connects the proportion of 1-responses ob-served on each trial for the [HL] condition of Cohen's Experiment 11. The smooth curve is the theoretical proportion of 1-responses predicted by the Cohen-Lee model for the same data. N = 30.

95

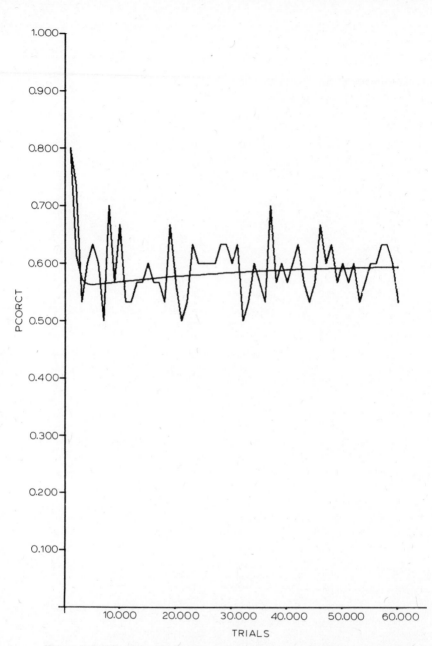

Figure 5.3. The irregular curve connects the proportion of 1-responses observed on each trial for the [LH] condition of Cohen's Experiment 11. The smooth curve is the theoretical proportion of 1-responses predicted by the Cohen-Lee model for the same data. N = 30.

96

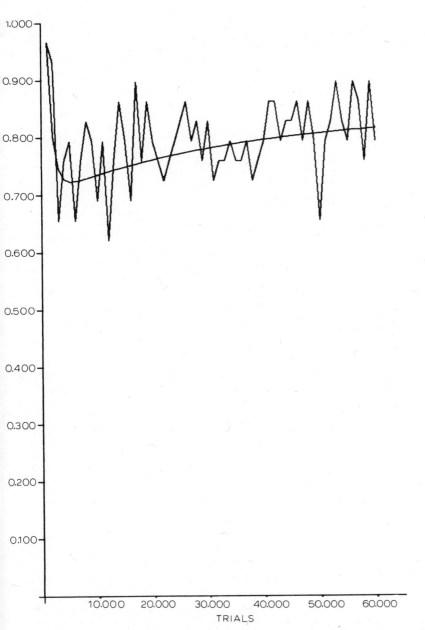

Figure 5.4. The irregular curve connects the proportion of 1-responses observed on each trial for the [LL] condition of Cohen's Experiment 11. The smooth curve is the theoretical proportion of 1-responses predicted by the Cohen-Lee model for the same data. N = 30.

97

and the transition matrix was estimated to be

$$
\begin{array}{c}
\text{State on Trial } n + 1 \\[4pt]
\begin{array}{cccc}
\quad 1 & \quad 2 & \quad 3 & \quad 4
\end{array}
\end{array}
$$

$$
A = \text{State on Trial } n \;
\begin{array}{c}
1 \\ 2 \\ 3 \\ 4
\end{array}
\left(
\begin{array}{cccc}
1.0 & 0.0 & 0.0 & 0.0 \\
0.04 & 0.73 & 0.23 & 0.0 \\
0.0 & 0.40 & 0.58 & 0.02 \\
0.0 & 0.0 & 0.0 & 1.0
\end{array}
\right)
$$

5.6 Initial evaluation of the Cohen-Lee model

Although Figures 5.1 and 5.2 indicate that the model does not represent the first 35 trials of either the [HH] or the [HL] condition as well as we might like, the model satisfactorily represents the response process in the last set of trials. But, in the [LH] and [LL] conditions, the model satisfactorily represents the response process on all trials. The results of the simulation studies also suggest that the model is a reasonable one to accept. But additional data from Asch-type experiments are available. These include Experiments 1, 2, and 3, which were used to develop the Conflict Model, and Experiments 20 and 21, which were not used to develop either model. Consequently, we next turn to reporting the fit of the Cohen-Lee model to these additional sets of data.

CHAPTER 6

Fit of the Cohen-Lee Model
to Experiments 1,2,3,20, and 21

6.1 Introduction

The data from the subjects in Experiments 1, 2, and 3 were used to verify the structure of the Conflict Model. Thereafter, an additional study, Experiment 11, was designed and differed from the three earlier experiments in that the Asch portion was preceded by a manipulation designed to create specific expectations for task performance. The failure of the Conflict Model to represent the response process of subjects in Experiment 11 led to the development of the Cohen-Lee model.

After the completion of Experiment 11, two additional studies were designed and conducted. Each of these two studies, designated Experiments 20 and 21, consisted of two treatment conditions. As in Experiment 11, the expectations for a task-relevant ability were manipulated preceding the Asch situation. None of the data from Experiments 20 and 21 was used in the development of either model. As Experiments 20 and 21 were quite similar, they will be described together. First, however, we shall describe Experiments 1, 2, and 3.

6.2 Experiments 1, 2, and 3

The stimulus, one originally used by Asch, was the same in all three experiments. Subjects were shown a pair of cards, one of which contained the standard — an 8-inch line. The other card, referred to as the set of "comparison lines", contained three lines, one 6¼ inches, one 8 inches, and one 6¾ inches in length, arranged in that order from left to right. This same stimulus was used on every trial. However, to reduce the possibility that subjects would realize that the stimulus did not change, two other adjustments were made. First, on half the trials the standard was presented to the left of the comparison lines, while on the other half of the trials the standard was presented to the right of the comparison lines. Second, the comparison lines were identified by letters of the alphabet which were changed from trial to trial. All three experiments began with two neutral trials on which the assistants indicated that the 8-inch line matched the standard. These neutral trials were immediately followed by a sequence of critical trials, and only two neutral trials were administered in each experiment.

The subjects in Experiments 1 and 2 were undergraduate students at a New England college. Some were voluntary participants, and some were recruited through the college employment office. The assistants used for different subjects varied, but all were upperclassmen. Seven assistants were used for each subject.

On all critical trials in Experiment 1 the assistants indicated that the 6¾-inch line was the "correct" match to the standard. (Thus, Experiment 1 is also referred to as the "moderate condition" in *Conflict and Conformity.*) In Experiment 2 the assistants indicated that the 6¼-inch line matched the standard on all critical trials. (Thus, Experiment 2 is also referred to as the "extreme condition" in *Conflict and Conformity.*) Experiments 1 and 2 included 36 critical trials. Data on 33 subjects are available from Experiment 1, and data on 27 subjects are available from Experiment 2.

Experiment 3 was conducted for 80 trials to facilitate a more careful process analysis of the data. All the subjects in Experiment 3 were undergraduate males. These subjects did not come from the same college as those subjects obtained for Experiments 1 and 2. Data from 50 subjects are available from Experiment 3. Experiment 3 was conducted, as was Experiment 1, with the assistants choosing the 6¾-inch line as "correct" on all critical trials.

The subjects in all three conditions were given the following instructions:

This is an experiment in visual perception. It is a task involving the discrimination of lengths of lines. I shall show a pair of cards. On one of these will be a single line; on the other will be three lines differing in length. Each of the three lines will have a letter beneath it to identify it. One of the three lines will be exactly equal to the single line on the other card — you will decide in each case which is the equal line. You will state your judgment in terms of the letter identifying the line. Sometimes the card with the single line will be on your right, and sometimes it will be on your left.

As the number of comparisons is few and the group small, I shall call upon each of you in turn to announce your judgments, which I shall record here on a prepared form. Please be as accurate as possible. Suppose you give me your estimates in order starting at the left. Are there any questions? (Cohen, 1963, p. 175)

6.2.1 Analysis of Experiment 1

Figure 6.1 displays the trialwise proportion of the subjects' 1-responses together with the predictions from the model. As we can see, the response process that occurred in the experiment had two phases. The first phase was from Trial 1 to Trial 6, in which the proportion of correct responses averaged 0.78. The second phase begins with a sharp drop in the proportion of correct responses between Trial 6 and Trial 8, and from this point through the 36th trial (the last trial of the experiment) the proportion of correct responses hovers around an average value of 0.68. The theoretical curve predicted from the model shows excellent agreement with the data throughout phase 2 of the process, but it does not successfully represent the first six trials of this experiment.

The estimates for the model are:

$$P_1 = (0.19, 0.81, 0.0, 0.0)$$

and

$$
A = \text{State on Trial } n \quad
\begin{array}{c}
\\
1 \\
2 \\
3 \\
4
\end{array}
\overset{\displaystyle \text{State on Trial } n+1}{
\begin{array}{cccc}
1 & 2 & 3 & 4 \\
\left(\begin{array}{cccc}
1.0 & 0.0 & 0.0 & 0.0 \\
0.05 & 0.64 & 0.31 & 0.0 \\
0.0 & 0.45 & 0.49 & 0.06 \\
0.0 & 0.0 & 0.0 & 1.0
\end{array}\right)
\end{array}}
$$

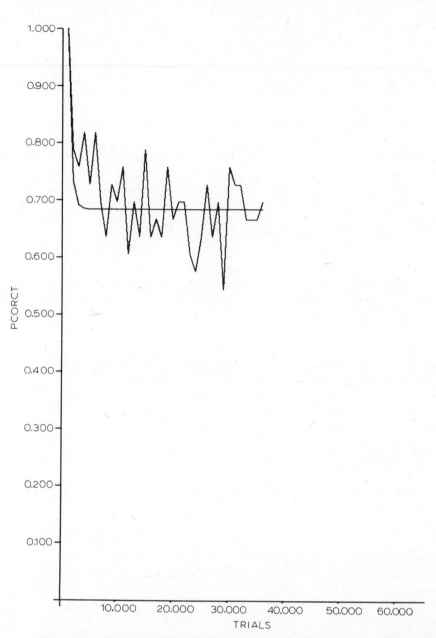

Figure 6.1. The irregular curve connects the proportion of 1-responses observed on each trial for Experiment 1 ("moderate condition"). The smooth curve is the theoretical proportion of 1-responses predicted by the Cohen-Lee model for the same data. N = 33.

102

6.2.2 Analysis of Experiment 2

Figure 6.2 contains the information for the analysis of Experiment 2. There it may be seen that the responses of the subjects seem to be best described by a curve which increases from about 0.70 through a value of 0.85. There seems to be an overall gradual increase in the proportion of 1-responses from Trial 2 through Trial 36, the last trial of the experiment. Again we notice a marked initial drop in the proportion of 1-responses from Trial 1 to Trial 2. Trial 1 begins with the proportion of about 0.89 and drops to a proportion of 0.60 on Trial 2. From here the proportion continues to oscillate but the amount of oscillation gradually decreases over the remaining trials. From Trial 14 the curve slowly increases from a value of 0.71 to a value of 0.89 on Trials 34 and 35, but drops to 0.86 on the last trial. The theoretical curve does remarkably well in describing this general trend.

The estimates for the initial distribution vector and the transition matrix are as follows:

$P_1 = (0.01, 0.88, 0.11, 0.0)$

and

State on Trial n + 1

		1	2	3	4
	1	1.0	0.0	0.0	0.0
A = State on Trial n	2	0.09	0.68	0.23	0.0
	3	0.0	0.42	0.55	0.03
	4	0.0	0.0	0.0	1.0

6.2.3 Analysis of Experiment 3

Experiment 3 was conducted for 80 trials. As may be seen in Figure 6.3, the observed responses oscillate greatly over the first few trials but the magnitude of the oscillation decreases until the process becomes stable at about Trial 41. The over-all response process again is marked by a very sharp drop in the proportion of 1-responses from Trial 1 to Trial 3. From Trials 3 to about 40, the mean value is about 0.68, and the response curve tends to rise slightly through this sequence of trials. The last segment of the process seems to be from about Trial 40 to Trial 80 and is best

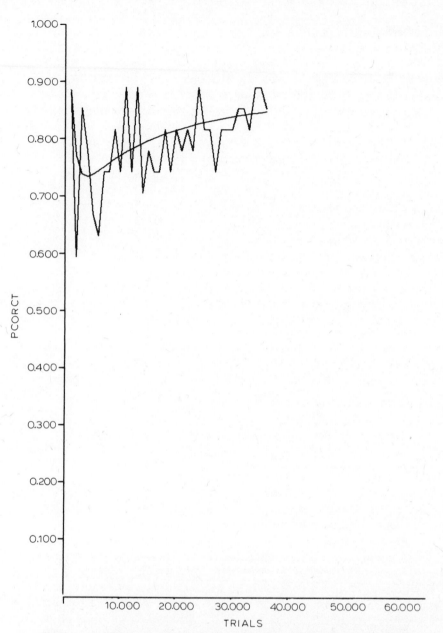

Figure 6.2. The irregular curve connects the proportion of 1-responses observed on each trial for Experiment 2 ("extreme condition"). The smooth curve is the theoretical proportion of 1-responses predicted by the Cohen-Lee model for the same data. N = 27.

104

characterized by a value of 0.73 for the proportion of 1-responses. The theoretical curve predicted for the model cuts across the observed curve for several trials equally scattered throughout the 80 trials of the experiment. However, it seems to be deficient in two respects. First, it does not drop sufficiently low on the first two trials; and second, it does not seem to represent the gradual climb in the response process, for it appears to be almost a straight line from Trial 5 onward.

The estimates for the initial distribution vector and the transition matrix are as follows:

$$P_1 = (0.12, 0.80, 0.03, 0.0)$$

and

$$\begin{array}{c} & \text{State on Trial } n+1 \\ & \begin{array}{cccc} 1 & 2 & 3 & 4 \end{array} \\ A = \text{State on Trial } n \quad \begin{array}{c} 1 \\ 2 \\ 3 \\ 4 \end{array} \left(\begin{array}{cccc} 1.0 & 0.0 & 0.0 & 0.0 \\ 0.03 & 0.75 & 0.22 & 0.0 \\ 0.0 & 0.46 & 0.52 & 0.02 \\ 0.0 & 0.0 & 0.0 & 1.0 \end{array}\right) \end{array}$$

6.3 Experiments 20 and 21

After the completion of Experiment 11, two additional experiments, 20 and 21, were designed to continue the study of the effect of expectations upon the response process of subjects. In addition, the sex of the participants was a factor in the design of these additional experiments. The subjects in both Experiments 20 and 21 were female; in Experiment 20 female assistants were used, and in Experiment 21 male assistants were used. The subjects in Experiment 20 were 16 to 22 years old and were recruited either from a state college or from a junior college. The subjects in Experiment 21 were from 17 to 22 years old, and all were recruited from a junior college. For most subjects the host experimenter was male, although for a few subjects a female host was employed. In both Experiments 20 and 21, the subjects were assigned at random to either the [HL] or [LH] conditions; [HL] and [LH] were produced using the same manipulation as Experiment 11.

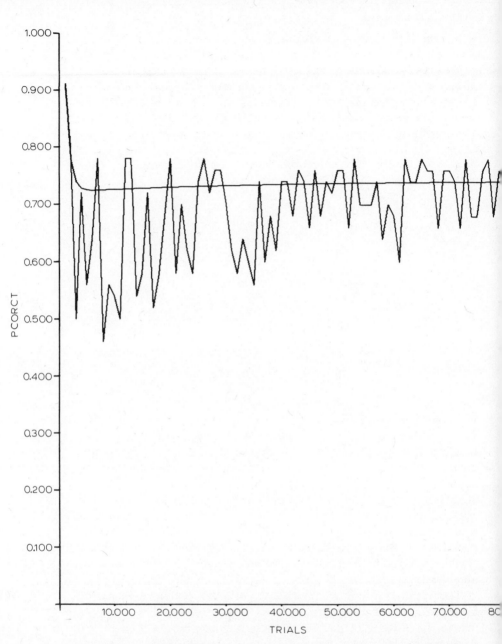

Figure 6.3. The irregular curve connects the proportion of 1-responses observed on each trial for Experiment 3. The smooth curve is the theoretical proportion of 1-responses predicted by the Cohen-Lee model for the same data. N = 50.

106

6.3.1 Analysis of Experiment 20

The results for the [HL] condition of Experiment 20 are presented in Figure 6.4, where we can see that the proportion of 1-responses obtained from the data of the 33 subjects available for analysis fluctuates around a value of 0.75 over the last 20 trials. The theoretical proportion of 1-responses predicted by the model for the same data adequately coincides with the obtained proportions.

The estimates for the initial distribution vector and the transition matrix are as follows:

$$P_1 = (0.25, 0.57, 0.18, 0.0)$$

and

$$
A = \text{State on Trial } n \quad
\begin{array}{c}
\\
1 \\
2 \\
3 \\
4
\end{array}
\overset{\displaystyle \text{State on Trial } n+1}{
\begin{array}{cccc}
1 & 2 & 3 & 4 \\
\left(\begin{array}{cccc}
1.0 & 0.0 & 0.0 & 0.0 \\
0.04 & 0.62 & 0.34 & 0.0 \\
0.0 & 0.33 & 0.65 & 0.02 \\
0.0 & 0.0 & 0.0 & 1.0
\end{array}\right)
\end{array}}
$$

The results for the [LH] condition of Experiment 20, reported in Figure 6.5, contrast markedly with those obtained for the [HL] condition. The proportion of 1-responses on Trial 1 is about 0.67, drops precipitously from the first three trials to a value of 0.30, and then oscillates for the remainder of the experiment between the values of 0.23 and 0.40. The general impression is of a curve slowly dropping to an average value of about 0.31. The theoretical proportion of 1-responses predicted by the model is an adequate representation of these data obtained from the 32 subjects available for analysis.

The estimates for the initial distribution vector and the transition matrix are as follows:

$$P_1 = (0.03, 0.66, 0.31, 0.0)$$

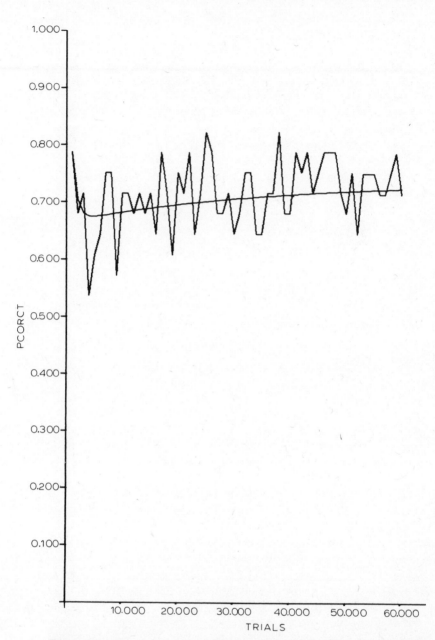

Figure 6.4. The irregular curve connects the proportion of 1-responses observed on each trial for the [HL] condition of Experiment 20. The smooth curve is the theoretical proportion of 1-responses predicted by the Cohen-Lee model for the same data. N = 33.

108

and

$$\text{State on Trial } n + 1$$

$$\text{A = State on Trial } n \quad \begin{array}{c} 1 \\ 2 \\ 3 \\ 4 \end{array} \begin{pmatrix} \begin{array}{cccc} 1 & 2 & 3 & 4 \\ 1.0 & 0.0 & 0.0 & 0.0 \\ 0.03 & 0.43 & 0.54 & 0.0 \\ 0.0 & 0.33 & 0.63 & 0.04 \\ 0.0 & 0.0 & 0.0 & 1.0 \end{array} \end{pmatrix}$$

6.3.2 Analysis of Experiment 21

The proportion of 1-responses observed on each trial for the [HL] condition of Experiment 21 begins at 0.86 on Trial 1, drops rapidly to a value of 0.67 on Trial 3, and then steadily climbs to a value of 1.0 on Trials 22 and 24 (see Figure 6.6). The proportion then drops again and stabilizes around a value of 0.80 for the remainder of the experiment. Although the model predicts a theoretical value that intersects the observed proportions from Trials 1 through 14 and Trials 37 through 60, there is no agreement between the observed proportion and the theoretical proportion for Trials 15 through 36.

The estimates for the initial distribution vector and the transition matrix are as follows:

$$P_1 = (0.45, 0.44, 0.11, 0.0)$$

and

$$\text{State on Trial } n + 1$$

$$\text{A = State on Trial } n \quad \begin{array}{c} 1 \\ 2 \\ 3 \\ 4 \end{array} \begin{pmatrix} \begin{array}{cccc} 1 & 2 & 3 & 4 \\ 1.0 & 0.0 & 0.0 & 0.0 \\ 0.03 & 0.74 & 0.23 & 0.0 \\ 0.0 & 0.51 & 0.46 & 0.03 \\ 0.0 & 0.0 & 0.0 & 1.0 \end{array} \end{pmatrix}$$

The proportion of 1-responses observed on each trial for the [LH] condition of Experiment 21 again contrasts markedly to that observed for the [HL] condition. As may be seen in Figure 6.7, the observed proportion for the [LH] condition begins on Trial 1 with a value of 0.84 and drops to a value of 0.42 on Trial 3. From Trial 3 on, the proportion seems to oscillate around a value of 0.48. The theoretical curve predicted by the model ade-

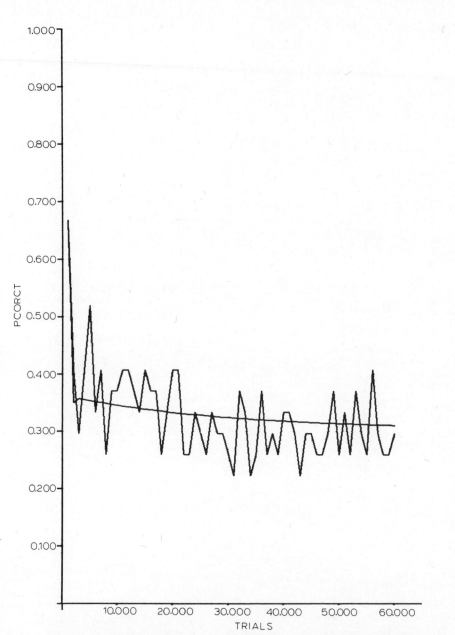

Figure 6.5. The irregular curve connects the proportion of 1-responses observed on each trial for the [LH] condition of Experiment 20. The smooth curve is the theoretical proportion of 1-responses predicted by the Cohen-Lee model for the same data. N = 32.

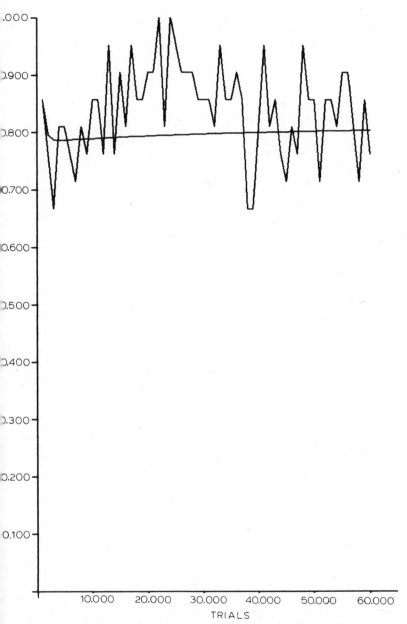

Figure 6.6. The irregular curve connects the proportion of 1-responses observed on each trial for the [HL] condition of Experiment 21. The smooth curve is the theoretical proportion of 1-responses predicted by the Cohen-Lee model for the same data. N = 28.

111

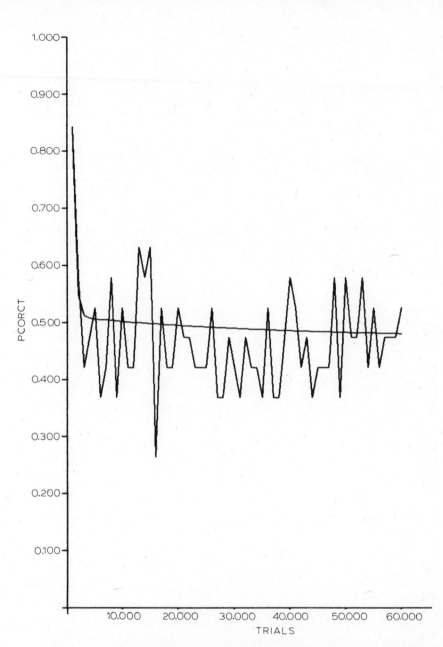

Figure 6.7. The irregular curve connects the proportion of 1-responses observed on each trial for the [LH] condition of Experiment 21. The smooth curve is the theoretical proportion of 1-responses predicted by the Cohen-Lee model for the same data. N = 28.

112

quately represents the observed proportion of 1-responses from the 28 subjects in this condition.

The estimates for the initial distribution vector and the transition matrix are as follows:

$P_1 = (0.14, 0.72, 0.14, 0.0)$

and

$$
\begin{array}{c}
\qquad\qquad\qquad \text{State on Trial n + 1} \\[4pt]
\qquad\qquad\quad 1 \qquad 2 \qquad 3 \qquad 4 \\[4pt]
A = \text{State on Trial n} \;
\begin{array}{c} 1 \\ 2 \\ 3 \\ 4 \end{array}
\left(
\begin{array}{cccc}
1.0 & 0.0 & 0.0 & 0.0 \\
0.03 & 0.50 & 0.47 & 0.0 \\
0.0 & 0.41 & 0.56 & 0.03 \\
0.0 & 0.0 & 0.0 & 1.0
\end{array}
\right)
\end{array}
$$

A comparison of the proportion of 1-responses obtained from subjects in these two experiments shows that for each of the two conditions the proportion of 1-responses is higher for subjects in Experiment 21 than in Experiment 20. This result suggests that female subjects are less susceptible to influence attempts from male assistants than from female assistants. The difference between the two experiments is especially marked for the [LH] condition. Thus, there is apparently an interaction effect between ability expectations and the sex of the participants.

6.4 Evaluation of the Cohen-Lee model

At this point we have completed the presentation of 6 Asch-type experiments representing 11 distinct sets of data. For each of the 11 data sets, the curves reporting the proportion of 1-responses observed on each trial together with the theoretical proportion predicted by the model for the same data have been presented. These curves provide evidence supporting our claim that we have succeeded in representing the underlying process of conflict resolution engaged in by subjects in the Asch situation. Furthermore, comparison of the figures in Chapters 5 and 6 indicate that factors such as expectations for performance and the sex composition of the group produce marked variations in the conflict resolution process. The picture is clear, but finer details remain to be examined — both with respect to goodness of fit and to the role of variations in fixed initial conditions. In the next chapter, we turn to a finer analysis of these issues.

CHAPTER 7

The Use of the Cohen-LeeModel as a Tool in the Construction of Theory

7.1 Introduction

Despite our abiding concern for developing an empirically-supported theory about conflict, conformity, and influence, we were also aware that data are useless without the analytical tool that would describe the process that produced the observed conformity behavior. The development of this tool, the Cohen-Lee model, is described in previous chapters.

Even given this tool, however, we have yet to use it. In this chapter we will use the model to make inferences about the process of conformity. But in our use of the model to make inferences, it is incumbent upon us to show that our procedures meet the methodological requirements which we have set forth in our critique of the traditional approaches to the analysis of conformity and influence studies (see Chapter 1).

Insofar as our description meets our methodological requirements by being dynamic, conditional, and systemic, it will enhance our ability to discover stable relations and to formulate precise theories. We hope that the statement of these precise theories will promote a critical development of new studies which may now be expected to produce cumulative knowledge.

7.2 Demonstrations of the substantive utility of the model

One way to justify a model is to demonstrate its substantive utility. In using this method, we have three objectives: to show

114

that the model is an adequate description of the observations we have collected in our experiments, to show that the numerical values of the parameters distinguish between different experimental treatments and do so in a substantively reasonable way, and to generate new questions and to indicate new directions for both empirical and theoretical investigations. While our performance on this last criterion can be evaluated only with more hindsight than we have available at present, we will present some of these questions.

7.3 Fit of the model

In Chapters 5 and 6 we examined the fit of the model to eleven different data sets collected using the Asch situation. Eight of these data sets — Experiments 11, 20, and 21 — were collected in the present project, while three of them — Experiments 1, 2, and 3 — were previously reported in *Conflict and Conformity*. An inspection of the tables and figures in the previous two chapters does provide evidence that we have achieved our first objective, for the model provides a good description of the experimental observations.

For the [HL] and [LH] conditions of Experiment 11, Tables 5.2 to 5.7 show that the model reproduces values for those statistics used in estimation that are identical with the empirical values for these treatments. We presented data for the probability of being absorbed into State 1, the expected number of alternations, and the probability of a sequence of entirely correct responses. The ability of the model to reproduce the statistics is evidence both for the consistency of the model and for the presence (in the empirical data) of the relationships among these quantities which is postulated by the model.

Examination of Figures 5.1 to 5.4 and 6.1 to 6.7 indicates that the model provides a good description of eight of the eleven data sets presented.[1] (We include data from Experiments 1, 2, and 3 because we believe that the Cohen-Lee model should not only represent Asch experiments when there are manipulated initial conditions, but also it should accomplish what the Conflict Model was able to do; namely, represent observations in the Asch situation when there are no manipulated extrinsic variables.) In view of

---

[1] We regard the fit of figure 6.6 Experiment 21 [HL] as marginally good.

the small sample size for each of these data sets and the considerable variability in the observed proportion of correct responses on each trial, the degree of fit shown in these figures is very encouraging.

We should comment on the three cases in which the theoretical curve for the trialwise probability of the correct response departs systematically from the observed data. We refer to Figures 5.1, 5.2, and 6.3, for the [HH] and [HL] conditions of Experiment 11 and for Experiment 3. The failure of our model to describe Experiment 3 is not at all surprising, since we had previously discovered a discrepancy between the Conflict Model and the data from Experiment 3 which was attributed to physical aspects of the manner in which the experiment was conducted. The spatial location of the stimuli introduced systematic effects in the observations which are outside the scope of both models. While Experiment 3 was useful to us in that it suggested ways to modify the experimental procedure and required us to control more carefully the presentation of the lines to be judged, we should not regard the failure of the model to describe the data from this experiment as serious.

The discrepancies with respect to the [HH] and [HL] conditions of Experiment 11 do require our consideration. If we examine the irregular curve of Figure 5.1, the observed proportion of 1-responses on each trial for the [HH] condition, we note a surprising jump between the first and second halves of the experiment. There is a sharp and unexpected discontinuity in these data which did not occur in the other data sets that we present. This discontinuity suggests that other factors beyond those we had considered operated in this experimental treatment. Now we believe that this is the one data set where our assumption that the performance expectations we created at the beginning of the experiment remained constant throughout the conformity phase is most seriously in question.

Examining Figure 5.2, which refers to the [HL] condition of Experiment 11, we see another type of discontinuity which is not as marked as that observed in the [HH] condition. Trials 10 through 27 depart from the picture presented by the plot for the remaining trials. The observations for this segment are both more variable and somewhat displaced from the proportion of correct responses observed on either earlier or later trials. A similar perturbation is seen in Figure 6.6, where there is a displacement in Trials 15 through 30. If the observations for the [HL] condition of Experiment 11 are reliable, Figure 5.2 suggests that the process

116

that is occurring here is more complex than the process we capture in the Cohen-Lee model. But we hesitate to attribute what is occurring in these observations to changing performance expectations, because the discontinuity is not as sharp as that observed in the [HH] condition and the same discontinuity is not found in the [HL] condition of Experiment 20. The figures for the [HL] conditions of Experiments 11 and 21 suggest that additional features of the phenomenon need further consideration.

Despite these discrepancies, we regard the model as a reasonable first approximation to the description of the [HH] and [HL] conditions of Experiment 11 and the [HL] condition of Experiment 21. It certainly provides a better representation that any alternative models available. As the fit of the model to the data sets from the other experimental treatments is remarkably good, we believe we can proceed to the next step, that of examining how the model distinguishes between different experimental treatments.

7.4 Employing the model to distinguish between experimental treatments

One of the major tests of the utility of the model is its ability to distinguish between different experimental treatments in a substantively reasonable way. The hypotheses we presented in Chapter 1 were a first approximation to what we regard as substantively reasonable expectations for the obtained values of the parameters of the model. In this discussion, we will concentrate on Experiments 11, 20, and 21. In Experiment 11 we wanted to see if the model's parameters could distinguish among experimental treatments in which the manipulation of status was based on performance expectations. (The design and procedures for Experiment 11 were given in Chapter 3.) In Experiments 20 and 21 we had the additional concern with the manipulation of similarity to the subject of his potential reference group. Before investigating the model's ability to distinguish between experimental treatments, we must describe Experiments 20 and 21, which were designed to study the effects of differing reference groups upon conformity.

In planning Experiments 20 and 21, we wished to separate beliefs about ability from other effects of status similarity or status differentiation. Although the standard research question is "Do females conform more then males?", we felt that this question was insufficiently specified. In pilot studies, Terry (1961) and Sable (1962) argued that females would conform to males more than males would conform to females only if the subjects believed that the task was a male task. In other words, if one removed ability expectations conveyed by beliefs about sex, one would find no differences in the degree to which males and females conformed to a reference group of the opposite sex. Terry attempted to remove the ability information conveyed by sex by defining his task as sex-linked. He used a color-matching task for all his experimental treatments, but in half of these treatments defined the task as a male task and in half defined it as a female task. Sable, on the other hand, attempted to rule out sex as an indicator of ability by directly manipulating the abilities of his subjects as we did in Experiment 11. In both studies the prediction was that, when one controlled the task performance expectations, sex differences in conformity would disappear. Both studies were based on small samples and produced anomalous results. It was clear, however, that there were residual effects of sex of subject even when ability expectations were controlled. Although their samples were small and the interaction effects between sex and ability expectation were unclear, these two studies provided the incentive to examine the effects of group composition in addition to the effects of those status factors which operate to create beliefs about task ability.

Experiments 20 and 21 therefore represented an effort to control the subject's beliefs about his own ability as compared with the ability of the other participants, and the two experiments taken together were designed to provide a comparison of how a subject would behave when those in his reference group were of the opposite sex. Initially, we anticipated that the values of the parameters of the model would reflect both the effects of ability and the effects of similarity of reference group and that these two effects could be distinguished. We formulated simplified linear hypotheses similar to those employed to justify the application of the model to Experiment 11. These hypotheses, however, were conditional on the basis of the self-other performance expectations; thus, for example, we hypothesized that, given a high-low expectation, the probability of the subject's rejecting the group (represented by the value of α) would be greater when the reference group was composed of members who were of the opposite sex than when it was composed of members who were the same sex. We also anticipated a similar result for low-high treatments.

118

Note that we restricted our comparisons to treatments representing the same self-other expectation states.

Our hypotheses for these two experiments were similar in form to those presented in Chapter 1. For Experiments 20 and 21, then, we had a series of linear hypotheses that produced the ordering of a single parameter of the model according to two principal treatment variables, the ability of the subject as compared with that of the confederates and the similarity of the subject to his reference group.

Although we were aware at the time that these hypotheses were oversimplified, we thought that they would reasonably approximate the link between our treatment variables and the process occurring in the experiment. We now believe that these hypotheses were not only oversimplified, but were in fact misleading. They were, and still remain, useful for a non-dynamic analysis; but the simplifying assumptions they involve cannot possibly lead to a successful representation of the process that concerns us. In other words, although our hypotheses distinguish among the different initial states of our eight treatments, they are inadequate for making inferences about dynamic phenomena.

These hypotheses were formulated in terms of the original Conflict Model, which assumed that all subjects began the response process in State 2 regardless of experimental treatment. The hypotheses then related elements of the transition matrix to the subject's relative status. But the Cohen-Lee model no longer assumes a common starting point for all subjects; hence, insofar as the differential status of the subject (created by experimental manipulation) produces different starting points for different experimental treatments, the processes by which these treatments move from the starting point to equilibrium are no longer directly comparable. In other words, while the structure of the process may be similar in form across experimental treatments, the numerical quantities that describe the process will not necessarily be comparable across treatments. In any case, given an initial distribution, a transition matrix will allow us to map an initial vector into an equilibrium vector for the system. We cannot, however, directly compare the mappings for different initial vectors. We argue that the transition parameters are comparable only if the initial conditions of the treatments being compared are identical or if the effects of differences in initial conditions can be partialed out. Clearly the way we initially formulated our hypotheses concerning the effects of relative status did not take these issues into account.

One of the outstanding virtues of the Cohen-Lee model is that it enables us to estimate values for the initial distribution and to separate the description of the process from the description of the starting state. But to pursue our original hypotheses without modification would be to abandon this virtue, for we now believe that the relative status of the individual in the group affects both the subject's starting state and the way he will resolve the conflict. Our original hypotheses looked only at the process and ignored the possibility that some, if not all, of the effect of relative status may be represented by the initial distribution vector. Thus, while it may be appropriate to compare initial vectors of our experimental treatments in terms of hypotheses like those we originally formulated, a comparison of transition matrices depends upon having removed differences in initial vectors.

To illustrate this problem, consider the following. Suppose that our reasoning is correct that the probability of rejecting the group increased with the relative status of the individual. Recall that we define rejection of the group with being absorbed into State 1. We hypothesized, therefore, that α, the probability of moving into State 1, would increase as the relative status of the individual increased. But comparing α's across experimental treatments could lead us to incorrectly reject our basic hypothesis, since α does not reflect the proportion of subjects in State 1 on Trial 1. It is conceivable that the smallest α could be encountered for a treatment condition with the highest proportion initially in State 1; hence, to be correct we must examine more than quantities from the transition matrix, one at a time. Our hypotheses, by treating elements of the matrix singly, ignored the fact that the quantities were part of a system and as such were interdependent. One cannot reason about α without also reasoning at the same time about β, and λ, and $p_1(1)$. Hence, our strategy for testing these hypotheses must be systemic; that is, minimally, we must deal with a row of the transition matrix, rather than with the elements of a row as independent quantities. Obviously, these considerations suggest that we reformulate some of our hypotheses.

If we restrict the hypotheses in Chapter 1 to refer to the initial trial only, we obviate some of the difficulties that we have discussed in this section. The hypotheses then would be:

1. On the initial trial, if the individual has greater ability than the group, he is more likely to reject the group than if his ability is less than or equal to the group's.

2. On the initial trial, if the individual has less ability than the group, he is less likely to reject the group than if his ability is greater than or equal to the group's.
3. On the initial trial, if the individual has greater ability than the group, he is less likely to accept an influence attempt by the group than if his ability is less than or equal to the group's.
4. On the initial trial, if the individual has less ability than the group, he is more likely to be influenced by the group than if his ability is greater than or equal to the group's.

The modified hypotheses dealing with Experiments 20 and 21 would now read:

5. On the initial trial, if the subject holds a high-low expectation, then the probability of rejecting the group would be greater when the reference group was dissimilar in sex than when it was similar.
6. On the initial trial, if the subject holds a low-high expectation, then the probability of rejecting the group would be greater when the reference group was dissimilar in sex than when it was similar.
7. On the initial trial, if the subject holds a high-low expectation, then the probability of accepting an influence attempt from the group is greater when the group is similar in sex than when it is dissimilar.
8. On the initial trial, if the subject holds a low-high expectation, then the probability of accepting an influence attempt from the group is greater when the group is similar in sex than when it is dissimilar.

By restricting the scope of these hypotheses to the initial trial, we believe that we have stated them in an appropriate conditional form. Since these hypotheses refer to the start of the process, our concerns about dynamic properties do not affect them.

Let us identify State 1 on Trial with the concept, "the initial rejection of the group", and State 3 on Trial 1 with, "initial acceptance of an influence attempt from the group". Then $p_1(1)$ and $p_3(1)$ are the appropriate quantities to examine for these hypotheses. Then we make the following predictions:

From Hypotheses 1 and 2:
  $p_1(1)$: HL > HH, HL > LL, HL > LH, HH > LH, LL > LH;
From Hypotheses 3 and 4:
  $p_3(1)$: LH > HL, LH > LL, LH > HH, HH > HL, LL > HL;
From Hypotheses 5 and 6:
  $p_1(1)$: 21HL > 20HL, 21HL > 11HL, 21LH > 20LH, 21LH > 11LH;

121

From Hypotheses 7 and 8:

$p_3(1)$: 20HL > 21HL, 11HL > 21HL, 20LH > 21LH, 11LH > 21LH.

Table 7.1 presents the parameter values for all eight data sets, and these values clearly distinguish between experimental treatments. The probability of being in State 1 on Trial 1 ranges from a low of 0.03 in Experiment 20 [LH] to a high value of 0.45 in Experiment 21 [HL]. The probability of being in State 3 on Trial 1 ranges from 0.03 in Experiment 11 [LL] to 0.31 in Experiment 20 [LH]. Furthermore, if we regard our test of substantive reasonableness of the parameter differences as the correspondence of these differences to the predictions generated by our hypotheses, we find that forty-two of the fifty possible comparisons are as we predicted. (There are fifty comparisons if one ignores the differences between Experiments 11 and 21 and, for example, compares Experiment 11 [HL] with 11 [LH] and then with Experiment 20 [LH] and then with Experiment 21 [LH]. A more conservative procedure would avoid comparing Experiment 11 with either Experiment 20 or 21 on the grounds that the other two experiments differ in important respects from Experiment 11, although not from each other; thus, one would compare Experiment 11 [HL] only with Experiment 11 [LH], 11 [HH], or 11 [LL]. (The subjects in Experiment 11 were Stanford males who tend to hold very high expectations for their performance abilities. The subjects in Experiments 20 and 21 were junior college females who do not hold as high expectations for their own performance abilities. Furthermore, the experiments were conducted on the campus of

TABLE 7.1
Initial state parameters for all treatments of experiments 11, 20, and 21.

Experiment-condition	$p_1(1)$	$p_3(1)$
E11 [HH]	0.32	0.13
E11 [HL]	0.28	0.07
E11 [LH]	0.10	0.20
E11 [LL]	0.20	0.03
E20 [HL]	0.24	0.18
E20 [LH]	0.03	0.31
E21 [HL]	0.45	0.11
E21 [LH]	0.14	0.14

Note: Male subjects were used in Experiment 11 and female subjects were used in Experiments 20 and 21.

Stanford University. Thus, a variety of status factors in addition to those which were explicitly introduced as treatment factors in the design of the experiment may have been present.) Using this more conservative procedure, there are eighteen possible comparisons. Of these, sixteen are as we predicted. We then conclude that the initial state parameters differentiate between experimental treatments and do so in a substantively reasonable way.

One additional feature of the data in Table 7.1 should be noted. When we look at the probability of being in State 1 on Trial 1, we find the treatments involving female subjects are both at the top and the bottom of the rank order of the initial state parameters. Because of this we argue against a simple linear interpretation of the effects of sex of subject. (For Experiment 21 [HL] we find that the initial probability of rejecting the group is 0.45, while for Experiment 20 [LH] that probability is 0.03.) This result is clearly inconsistent with the unconditional assertion that females conform more than males. Of course, we would need data on male subjects with female confederates to examine the assertion that, other things being equal, females conform more than males; but, even in the absence of such data, it is clear that what other things are equal is more important than the sex of the subject in determining the degree of *initial* non-conformity. Even with our cautions in mind, comparing Experiments 11 and 20 suggests that, when the referent is similar and ability expectations are held constant, initially females conform more than males, or males are initially more likely to reject the group than females. The comparison of Experiments 20 and 21, however, indicates that females are more willing to be non-conformists when the referents are males. This result clearly does not support the belief that females are generally submissive.

We cannot leave this analysis without noting two qualifications. While we are confident in our conclusion that our experimental treatments differ with respect to where the subjects start the process, the analysis does not meet all the methodological requirements we have set for ourselves. In the first place, we do not examine these initial vectors as vectors; rather, we look at the first and third elements of each treatment vector and compare them independently. Thus, our approach does not meet the systemic requirement that hypotheses deal with these initial vectors as vectors.

The second qualification concerns our analysis of the probability of being in State 3 on Trial 1. These quantities are estimated

123

from the data and are based on the responses for a single trial of the experiment. As such, they are subject to considerable sampling variability and we must be cautious in our interpretations of them. It would be desirable to make use of more of the data to increase the stability of our estimates of $p_3(1)$, but to do so would "contaminate" our estimates of the initial starting point of the system with future observations. To some extent, our estimates of the probability of being in State 1 on Trial 1 are already contaminated. Hence it would be most desirable to obtain estimates of this initial vector from sources other than the experimental data themselves, i.e., from some extrinsic measures. For the present, however, we must recognize that our estimates of the initial vector depend upon future responses of our subjects.

Our analysis does indicate that our concern about the comparability of treatments after the initial starting point is justified. Since each of these experimental treatments has a different starting point, a direct comparison of quantities other than the initial vector clearly is not justified. To examine these other quantities requires that the effects of the differences in the initial starting distributions be removed.

7.5 The generation of new questions

Now that we have established that our experimental treatments differ on the initial starting point of the process, we have complicated the problem of comparing treatments. Those familiar with Markov chain theory will wonder why we concern ourselves with this issue, for the basic assumption in a Markov chain, the independence of path assumption, is that the effect of initial starting states soon disappears, so that the individual's state on Trial n+1 depends only on his state on Trial n and the parameters. In general that is true, but we have a special type of Markov chain. Because we have an absorbing chain, States 1 and 4 are very different from States 2 and 3. Hence, subjects who start the process absorbed in State 1 and those who are subject to the transition probabilities are clearly different. Both because there are such marked differences among our experimental treatments on the initial probability of being in State 1, and because an individual who starts in State 1 is subject to only one transition probability (the probability is 1.0 that he will stay there on all trials), we cannot directly compare experimental treatments without taking into account the marked differences in proportion of subjects in State 1 on Trial 1. But to make statements about the process of conflict resolution, we must make conditional statements so that they refer only to those individuals who are either in State 2 or in State 3 on Trial 1.

We initially thought that the obvious way to make process statements would be to reason about the elements of the transition matrix. At the same time, we thought that the hypotheses presented in the previous section would be appropriate starting points for our analysis. But our hypotheses do not take into account the possibility that the treatment variables in these experiments may have their total effect on the initial distribution and may have no effect whatsoever on the process of conflict resolution. In our original formulation, there was no thought of partitioning the effects of our treatment variables into "initial" effects and "process" effects; now that we know that some of the effect of our treatment variables is "used up" in differentiating the experimental treatments in their starting points, we no longer believe that the same kinds of statements would apply to those subjects who are in conflict on Trial 1. In other words, while adding the phrase, "on the initial trial", was an appropriate condition, we do not believe that simply adding the condition, "given that an individual is in conflict on Trial 1", would solve the problem. The elements of the transition matrix of a Markov chain are constants through time and, although our originial hypotheses applied to any point in time, the sharp discrimination between treatments on Trial 1 and the less marked differences among the eight transition matrices argue against any straightforward extrapolation to all points in time. Indeed, the elements of the transition matrix may not be the most appropriate properties by which to distinguish the effects of our experimental treatments.

We first began to doubt the utility of using single parameters to test our hypotheses when we noted the small magnitudes of α and ϵ in all our treatments. As we have no way to estimate the variance of these quantities, we were concerned about interpreting small differences and we then realized that the systemic requirements we had imposed on the analysis ruled out looking at single elements of the matrix. The same problems would not exist if we looked at quantities where these small magnitudes were constrained by other information from the data, in other words, quantities where α and ϵ entered into functional relationships with other empirical statistics. In part, this is the import of the systemic requirement.

125

For these reasons, we abandoned the original hypotheses and asked instead "What features of the process varied with our experimental treatments?" Our first question was: "Do any effects of performance expectations or similarity of reference group remain after the initial trial differences are partialed out?" The following analyses represent an effort to use the model to answer this question.

We see three possible approaches. First, we could examine statistics such as the mean number of correct responses or the probability of a correct response at the end of the process, computed only for those subjects who are initially in States 2 or 3. (The model enables us to compute values for these statistics conditional on beginning in States 2 or 3.) A second approach would be to standardize the initial vectors for all eight treatments and then recompute any of the quantities by using one standardized vector for all eight conditions. In effect, the standardization would permit us to reason hypothetically as follows: "If all eight experimental treatments had the same initial distribution, what could we say about conflict resolution?" A third approach would be to seek those parameters of the model, or functions of the model's parameters, that are already conditional in that they refer only to those subjects who start in either State 2 or State 3.

As an example of the first approach, consider the asymptotic probability of a correct response. The first column of Table 7.2, which presents the *unconditional* value of this statistic for the eight experimental treatments, shows that there are indeed differences among treatments in the equilibrium vector of the system. Let us examine the value obtained for the probability of a correct response in equilibrium. In general, the value obtained in [HL] treatments is higher than that obtained in [LH] treatments. For Experiments 20 and 21, in the [HL] treatments the value is higher for the case in which the reference group is dissimilar; likewise, in the [LH] treatments. Finally, the undifferentiated treatments, [HH] and [LL], are more similar to [HL] than to [LH] treatments. Can these differences be explained by the differences in the initial distribution vector of the various treatments? Put another way, are these differences preserved when we examine the appropriate conditional quantities?

The model enables us to compute separate values of the asymptotic probability of a correct response for subjects who began in State 1, State 2, or State 3. For subjects in State 1 on Trial 1, this probability is, of course, 1.0. Equation 4.24 enables us to compute

126

TABLE 7.2

The asymptotic probability of a correct response, $p(\infty)$, unconditionalized and conditionalized on the initial distribution for eight experimental treatments.

Experiment-condition	Unconditional	Conditional		
	$p(\infty)$	$p(\infty \mid S_2 \text{ or } S_3)$	$p(\infty \mid S_2)$	$p(\infty \mid S_3)$
	Column 1	Column 2	Column 3	Column 4
E11 [HH]	0.75	0.63	0.61	0.58
E11 [HL]	0.77	0.68	0.69	0.66
E11 [LH]	0.60	0.55	0.56	0.52
E11 [LL]	0.82	0.77	0.79	0.76
E20 [HL]	0.72	0.63	0.64	0.60
E20 [LH]	0.35	0.33	0.32	0.29
E21 [HL]	0.84	0.71	0.71	0.67
E21 [LH]	0.56	0.49	0.48	0.45

Note: Male subjects were used in Experiment 11 and female subjects were used in Experiments 20 and 21.

the asymptotic probability of a correct response conditional upon the individual's state on Trial 1. Column 2 of Table 7.2 presents the statistic for the individual in conflict (i.e., not in State 1) on Trial 1. These probabilities have been normalized from those obtained by using Equation 4.24, so that the equilibrium vector for those in conflict sums to one. (Normalizing treats those in conflict as the total sample and asks what proportion of them are absorbed in State 1 at infinity.)

In column 2 of Table 7.2, we see that the probability of being absorbed in State 1, given that the individual was initially in a conflict, is reduced from the unconditional probability roughly in proportion to the magnitude of the probability of being in State 1 on Trial 1; the largest difference between Column 1 and Column 2 of the table is for 21 [HL], and the smallest is for 20 [LH]. These two treatments had the largest and smallest values for $p_1(1)$. The effects of our treatment variables, however, still appear in the conditional quantities, although the magnitude of these differences is reduced slightly for every comparison of [HL] versus [LH] and for the comparison between Experiments 20 and 21. This analysis shows that some of the effect of our treatment variables can be attributed to differences in starting distributions, but most of the effect remains even when we control for differences in starting states. In short, our treatment variables do differentiate among subjects beyond merely determining what proportion of subjects in a given treatment are "exposed" to the conflict.

Columns 3 and 4 of the table reinforce this conclusion. If we assume that subjects who begin in the same state are comparable across experimental treatments, we see differentiation by experimental treatment for subjects who begin in the same state. When we compare Columns 3 and 4 of Table 7.2, we note small but consistent differences between $p(\infty)$ given S_2 and $p(\infty)$ given S_3. At first sight these differences appear to be inconsistent with the independence of path assumption in Markov chain theory. But, on closer examination, these differences can be explained by what happens at the end of Trial 1. Recall that in all treatments, $p_2(1)$ is considerably larger than $p_3(1)$. Consequently, a proportion of the subjects in State 2, α, is absorbed in State 1 at the same time that a proportion, β, move to State 3. But on Trial 2, the proportion of subjects in State 2 is about equal to the proportion in State 3, and the process proceeds symmetrically from that point on. (Simple computation shows that differences between Columns 2 and 3 are almost identical to $\alpha p_2(1)$ for each treatment.) This result supports our conclusion that our treatment variables influence the process over and beyond determining the distribution of subjects on Trial 1.

The second approach to the problem of partialling out the differences due to variations in the initial state probabilities across treatments is to standardize the initial vector. What we want, then, is one initial vector that will describe the starting state of all subjects regardless of the treatment condition to which they are assigned. The estimate we chose for this vector was the average of the distribution vectors of the eleven Asch experiments available for analysis. Consequently, the "Asch initial distribution vector" was taken to be (0.19, 0.69, 0.12, 0.0). The initial vectors for each of the eleven data sets are given in Table 7.3.

In the analysis below, the arguments are hypothetical and assume that all subjects start the process at the same point, which is described by the distribution vector (0.19, 0.69, 0.12, 0.0). In this hypothetical analysis, the Asch average distribution vector will be used for every treatment condition, but the transition matrix will be the one originally estimated for the Cohen-Lee model for each specific treatment condition. By applying Markov chain theory, we can obtain the distribution vector for any trial as the process unfolds. For example, if we wanted to describe the process for the [HL] condition of Experiment 11, we would employ as the

TABLE 7.3
Initial distribution vectors as estimated by the Cohen-Lee Model.

Experiment-condition	Proportion of subjects		
	in State 1 $p_1(1)$	in State 2 $p_2(1)$	in State 3 $p_3(1)$
E1	0.19	0.81	0.00
E2	0.01	0.88	0.11
E3	0.12	0.80	0.03
E11 [HH]	0.32	0.54	0.13
E11 [HL]	0.28	0.66	0.07
E11 [LH]	0.10	0.70	0.20
E11 [LL]	0.20	0.76	0.03
E20 [HL]	0.24	0.57	0.18
E20 [LH]	0.03	0.66	0.31
E21 [HL]	0.45	0.44	0.11
E21 [LH]	0.14	0.72	0.14
Average	0.19	0.69	0.12

Note: All computations were conducted with five significant digits.

initial distribution vector

$$P_1 = (0.19, 0.69, 0.12, 0.0)$$

and the transition matrix given by

State on Trial n + 1

$$A = \text{State on Trial n} \quad \begin{array}{c} 1 \\ 2 \\ 3 \\ 4 \end{array} \begin{pmatrix} 1.0 & 0.0 & 0.0 & 0.0 \\ 0.03 & 0.62 & 0.35 & 0.0 \\ 0.0 & 0.55 & 0.43 & 0.02 \\ 0.0 & 0.0 & 0.0 & 1.0 \end{pmatrix}$$

On the other hand, if we were concerned with the [LH] condition of Experiment 11, we would employ as the initial distribution vector

$$P_1 = (0.19, 0.69, 0.12, 0.0)$$

and would use as the transition matrix

State on Trial n + 1

$$
A = \text{State on Trial n} \quad
\begin{array}{c}
1 \\
2 \\
3 \\
4
\end{array}
\begin{array}{cccc}
1 & 2 & 3 & 4 \\
\begin{pmatrix}
1.0 & 0.0 & 0.0 & 0.0 \\
0.04 & 0.59 & 0.37 & 0.0 \\
0.0 & 0.36 & 0.61 & 0.03 \\
0.0 & 0.0 & 0.0 & 1.0
\end{pmatrix}
\end{array}
$$

The distribution vectors for Trials 1, 20, 40, and 60 for Experiments 11, 20, and 21, as computed from the standardized Asch initial vector, are presented in Table 7.4. If the subjects in each of the treatment conditions began the process as described by the same Asch initial vector, then we see that in each of the eight conditions over half of the subjects have been absorbed into either State 1 or State 4 by the twentieth trial; over seventy per cent of the subjects have been absorbed by the fortieth trial; and at least eighty-four per cent of the subjects have been absorbed by the sixtieth trial.

Two important conclusions can be drawn from the results presented in Table 7.4. First, let us consider the sum of $p_2(n) + p_3(n)$ for n = 20, 40, and 60. This sum is the proportion of subjects not yet absorbed on Trial n and can be viewed as a measure of the speed of conflict resolution; the higher this sum, the slower the rate of resolution. Table 7.5 presents these data. Because the speed of conflict resolution is similar for all eight experimental treatments, we conclude that the performance expectation and reference group variables do not affect the rate of conflict resolution when differences in initial distributions are controlled.

When we contrast the three [HL] conditions with the three [LH] conditions for the distribution vector for Trial 60, we clearly see that the manipulations in task-relevant ability have consistent effects in the unfolding of the process. As we can see in Table 7.6, those subjects who are high in task-relevant ability have a higher probability of absorption into State 1 than those subjects who are low in the task-relevant ability.

The [HH] and the [LL] conditions of Experiment 11 were omitted from this analysis because these two treatment conditions have undifferentiated expectation states. Recall that in the development of the theory we assumed that the expectation states do

130

TABLE 7.4

Distribution vectors for trials 1, 20, 40 and 60 for Experiments 11, 20, and 21 as computed from the standarized Asch initial vector.

Experiment-condition	Trial	Distribution vector			
		p_1 (trial)	p_2 (trial)	p_3 (trial)	p_4 (trial)
E11 [HH]	1	0.19	0.69	0.12	0.00
	20	0.40	0.29	0.18	0.13
	40	0.52	0.17	0.10	0.21
	60	0.59	0.10	0.06	0.26
E11 [HL]	1	0.19	0.69	0.12	0.00
	20	0.43	0.28	0.18	0.11
	40	0.57	0.16	0.10	0.17
	60	0.65	0.09	0.06	0.21
E11 [LH]	1	0.19	0.69	0.12	0.00
	20	0.42	0.21	0.21	0.17
	40	0.53	0.10	0.10	0.26
	60	0.59	0.05	0.05	0.31
E11 [LL]	1	0.19	0.69	0.12	0.00
	20	0.46	0.30	0.18	0.07
	40	0.61	0.17	0.10	0.11
	60	0.71	0.10	0.06	0.14
E20 [HL]	1	0.19	0.69	0.12	0.00
	20	0.43	0.22	0.23	0.13
	40	0.56	0.12	0.12	0.20
	60	0.62	0.06	0.07	0.25
E20 [LH]	1	0.19	0.69	0.12	0.00
	20	0.32	0.16	0.27	0.25
	40	0.38	0.08	0.14	0.40
	60	0.42	0.04	0.07	0.47
E21 [HL]	1	0.19	0.69	0.12	0.00
	20	0.43	0.33	0.15	0.10
	40	0.57	0.19	0.08	0.16
	60	0.65	0.11	0.05	0.19
E21 [LH]	1	0.19	0.69	0.12	0.00
	20	0.36	0.21	0.25	0.18
	40	0.46	0.12	0.14	0.29
	60	0.51	0.07	0.08	0.35

not change throughout the response process. Unfortunately, this assumption may not be tenable for the [HH] performance expectation. Imagine yourself to be in the [HH] condition. You are told that you and all of the other participants are very high on a

131

TABLE 7.5

Proportion unabsorbed on trial n, as given by $p_2(n) + p_3(n)$ as computed from the standarized Asch initial vector.

Experiment-condition	Trial 20	Trial 40	Trial 60
E11 [HH]	0.47	0.27	0.16
E11 [HL]	0.46	0.26	0.15
E11 [LH]	0.42	0.20	0.10
E11 [LL]	0.48	0.27	0.16
E20 [HL]	0.45	0.25	0.13
E20 [LH]	0.43	0.22	0.11
E21 [HL]	0.48	0.27	0.16
E21 [LH]	0.46	0.26	0.15

task-relevant ability. You see a decision-making task where the answer appears obvious to you. Yet, you hear trial after trial on which the other participants unanimously respond with an alternative that obviously appears to be incorrect. How can you reconcile this continuous disagreement with the fact that all of the participants have the same high task-relevant ability?

A subject who realizes this has a number of alternative interpretations available. He might, for example, assume that the task-relevant ability is not in fact relevant. He might assume that the other participants have somehow lost their ability while he has retained his. Or he might assume that he has lost the ability while the others have retained theirs.

In analyzing these data, we can reasonably assume that the result of the continuous disagreements, combined with the undif-

TABLE 7.6

Distribution vectors for trial 60 for the differentiated conditions of Experiments 11, 20, and 21 as computed from the standarized Asch initial vector.

Experiment-condition	Distribution vector			
	$p_1(60)$	$p_2(60)$	$p_3(60)$	$p_4(60)$
E11 [HL]	0.65	0.09	0.06	0.21
E20 [HL]	0.62	0.06	0.06	0.25
E21 [HL]	0.65	0.11	0.05	0.19
E11 [LH]	0.59	0.05	0.05	0.31
E20 [LH]	0.42	0.04	0.07	0.47
E21 [LH]	0.51	0.07	0.08	0.35

ferentiated expectation states in which both the subject and the other participants are manipulated to be high on task-relevant ability, produces a distribution of subjects some of whom act as if they have moved into a [HL] state and others who have moved into a [LH] state.

If [HH] indeed does produce by differentiation a mixture of [HL] and [LH] subjects, we would expect that the values for the final distribution vector would fall between those obtained for the [HL] and [LH] conditions of Experiment 11. This comparison is presented in Table 7.7, which lists $p(\infty)$ and E(A) vector for the [HH], [HL], and [LH] conditions of Experiment 11.

The subjects who are undifferentiated and low in task-relevant ability also present difficulties for the analysis. Again, the combination of continuous disagreement, coupled with the knowledge that all participants were low on task-relevant ability, probably is interpreted by the subject to mean that at the beginning of the experiment none of them have any ability directly relevant to the task. The subject probably then reasons that he therefore need pay no attention to the responses of the other participants; since they are unanimously giving the same incorrect answer, he will ignore their responses. Thus, the [LL] subject is probably most likely to violate the scope conditions of expectation theory, for he probably is more inclined than a subject in any other treatment condition to exhibit complete loss of collective orientation.

Thus, a [LL] subject will probably behave like a [HL] subject. Consequently, we should not be surprised to find that the proportion of subjects absorbed into State 1 for the [LL] condition of Experiment 11 is higher than the proportion absorbed into State 1 for any other treatment condition!

TABLE 7.7
Comparison of the [HH] condition with the [HL] and the [LH] conditions of Experiment 11.

Condition	$p(\infty)$	E(A)
[HL]	0.74	11
[HH]	0.67	10
[LH]	0.63	8

Note: The values under $p(\infty)$ give the asymptotic probability of a 1-response, as predicted by the Cohen-Lee model, using the standardized Asch initial vector.

133

We are not satisfied that we understand the [HH] and [LL] treatments. The problem arises when we recall the data for $p_1(1)$ (Table 7.1). Given the arguments just presented, $p_1(1)$ for the [HH] treatment should fall between the values of $p_1(1)$ for the [HL] and [LH] treatments, while it should be greatest for the [LL] treatment. The data in Table 7.1 show that exactly the reverse is true. $p_1(1)$ is greater for the [HH] treatment than for the comparable [HL] treatment of Experiment 11, while the [LL] value falls between [HL] and [LH]. The invariant relations for [HL]-[LH] comparisons and for similar-dissimilar reference groups do not hold for [HH] and [LL].

The third approach we suggested earlier would be to seek those quantities that refer only to subjects all of whom start in either State 2 or State 3. In addition to being conditional, the quantities must have other properties. We seek statistics that are dynamic, in that they reflect the underlying resolution process; sufficient, in that they summarize varied aspects of the phenomenon we are attempting to describe; and stable, in that they are based on sufficiently large numbers of observations so that sampling variability is minimal. We are also concerned that the quantities we choose do not deal with single elements of the process in isolation but, instead, reflect systemic properties. Our concern with the systemic property is related to the statistical criterion of sufficiency. Roughly speaking, to the degree that a statistic summarizes the information contained in a set of data, it is sufficient; the model postulates a series of relationships among various features of the phenomenon; and, to the degree that the statistics we choose reflect these relations, those statistics will have the property of sufficiency. In short, we desire quantities which contain the maximum amount of information about each set of data examined.

If we can find such quantities, then they can be used to compare different experimental treatments such that inferences about the process of conflict resolution could be made. Ideally these quantities should also lend themselves to substantive interpretation in a straightforward manner. But the desire to summarize diverse features of the experimental process runs counter to ease of substantive interpretation. Dealing with single elements, we were able to offer a substantive interpretation for α, β, γ, and ϵ; but we have seen the pitfalls of our simplistic interpretation of these variables. On the other hand, dealing simultaneously with the operation of these quantities causes serious substantive difficulties, for it is hard to think in multi-dimensional terms. Never-

134

theless, if these difficulties can be overcome, the results will be much more fruitful than more simplistic interpretations of single quantities.

We began our effort to formulate a statistic that describes the process and has the properties desired by re-examining the equations for L (4.30), and for R (4.31), which, for convenience, we reproduce here:

$$L = \frac{(1.0 + R)(a + c + d - 1.0)}{2.0(1.0 - a)(1.0 + R) - (c + d)}$$

$$R = \frac{2.0a - b + c + d - 1.0}{2.0(b - a)}$$

Note, first, that the quantities L and R use a great deal of information from a data set. R depends upon (a) the proportion of subjects who make a correct response on Trials 1 through 55; (b) the observed proportion of 1-responses counted over the last five trials of all the response sequences; (c) the observed number of alternations counted from Trial 1 through Trial 55 (divided by the number of subjects); and (d) the observed proportion of subjects who made a 0-response on Trial 1. Similarly, L depends upon a, c, d, and R. These equations suggest that the likely candidates for the statistics we desired would be functionally related to R and L.

By rewriting Equations (4.34) and (4.35), we see that $R = \beta/\alpha$ and $L = \gamma/\epsilon$, which appear as ratios in the expressions for $p(\infty)$ and $E(A)$. In terms of our model, then, R and L not only refer to elements of the transition matrix, but are also appropriately conditional and therefore independent of the initial starting distribution. (Although in the derivations in Chapter 4 we used expressions for R and L to estimate the initial distribution, it is possible to rewrite the equations eliminating the estimate for $p_2(1)$ and obtain identical results for R and L.) Hence, not only do R and L summarize a great deal of information about the process, but they are also directly comparable across experimental treatments, since they do partial out any differences in initial distributions.

The values of the ratio R/L were computed for each of the experimental treatments and are presented in Table 7.8. These values range from 0.273 in the [LL] condition of Experiment 11 to 2.297 in the [LH] condition of Experiment 20, but more importantly, the higher values are associated with [LH] treatments and the smaller values with [HL] treatments. The smallest value, as we have already noted, occurs in Experiment 11 [LL]. The value of the ratio for Experiment 11 [HH] falls in between that obtained in the [HL] and the [LH] treatments.

Two factors aided us in interpreting this ratio. First, the ratio is higher when there is a high performance expectation for the group of confederates than when there was a low performance expectation for the group. Second, the simple manipulation of Equations (4.34) and (4.35) shows that the ratio R/L is equal to $\beta\epsilon/\alpha\gamma$. The numerator of this ratio represents the product of the probabilities of moving in the direction of the group as a referent, while the denominator represents the product of the probabilities of moving toward the self as a referent. Hence, we interpret R/L as a measure of the "pulling power" of the group relative to the "pulling power" of the self.

Table 7.8 shows one additional feature of the process. For all experimental treatments except those in Experiment 20 [LH] and Experiment 21 [LH], the ratio R/L is less than 1. Hence, we can infer that, for nearly all of our treatments, the pulling power of the self as a referent is stronger than the pulling power of the group as a referent. We attribute the greater pulling power of the self to the asymmetric nature of the judgment task; after all, the judgments involved what was clearly a perceptually correct answer. To overcome long-ingrained habits of self-reliance in perceptual responses, the individual not only must have high performance expectations for the group and low expectations for self, but also should be female.

One virtue of the ratio we are using, and our interpretation of it, is that it suggests an alternative conceptualization of the influence process occurring in this situation. In viewing Asch-type ex-

TABLE 7.8
Values of the quantity R/L for eight experimental treatments.

Experiment-condition	R/L
E11 [HH]	0.669
E11 [HL]	0.471
E11 [LH]	0.838
E11 [LL]	0.273
E20 [HL]	0.599
E20 [LH]	2.297
E21 [HL]	0.436
E21 [LH]	1.144

136

periments, one usually thinks of influence as working from the group on the individual; our ratio suggests that two kinds of influence processes operate in opposite directions. One of these processes originates with the group and operates on the actor, and the other begins with the self and operates on the actor. In this general context of reference group analysis, pressures emanating from the self as a referent are comparable to pressures emanating from other social referents (see Cohen, 1962).

We cannot leave this discussion without commenting on two major problems with our measure and its interpretation, problems that remain for future research and conceptualization. There are difficulties in interpreting R/L because it is a ratio of products. Our interpretations of relative pulling power avoid the issue, for example, of treating two ratios as equal where one has both a larger numerator and a larger denominator than the other. Do we want to consider these situations as representing identical pulling power? Only further analysis of the properties of our ratio and further empirical investigations will answer questions like this one.

The second problem with our ratio is related to what it does not capture. An important aspect of the process concerns the probability of remaining in the same non-absorbed state, either State 2 or State 3, from one trial to the next, but our index does not include both the movement and the stationary aspects of the process; more desirable would be an index that would allow us to contrast relative pulling power with relative staying power. For example, in our [LH] treatments, a ratio greater than one combined with a high probability of remaining in State 2 would be very different from the same ratio combined with a low probability of remaining in State 2. At present, we are unable to construct a meaningful quantity that captures both movement and "stationarity" in one index.

The failure to find such an index, together with our reasons for not using single parameters as measures, makes it difficult to test hypotheses about the intensity of conflict. In Chapter 1 we hypothesized:

Where the individual is differentiated from the group, he will experience less conflict than where he is equal in ability to the group.

In fact, the problems of operationalizing this hypothesis led us to look more closely at the details of the process. In Chapter 1, we also hypothesized:

Where the individual is differentiated from the group, he will resolve the conflict earlier than when he is equal in ability to the group.

From this second hypothesis, our original conception of the phenomenon is clear; we expected that the undifferentiated experimental treatments would have lower values of both α and ϵ than the differentiated treatments. When we rejected using single parameters as indices, we were forced to rethink our ideas concerning the intensity of conflict. The first distinction we originally made was that subjects in high intensity conflict situations would show greater movement between the non-absorbed states than would subjects in low intensity conflict situations; and, further absorption in States 1 or 4 should occur relatively early in the process for subjects experiencing low intensity conflict situations. But looking more closely at the model shows the inadequacy of this first distinction; States 2 and 3 are characterized by two components, what we might call an inertia component as well as a movement component. That is, we must consider both the tendency to remain in one of the non-absorption states and the tendency to move between States 2 and 3. This argument represents one of the principal motivations for desiring an index that captures both directions of movement and the inertia of the process.

Nor were these our only difficulties. For example, we assumed that conflicts of lower intensity would be resolved more quickly than conflicts of higher intensity; but one could just as easily assume that the greater intensity of the conflict, the greater the pressure to resolve it and, therefore, the greater the speed of resolution. If our model enabled us to choose between these two assumptions, our original formulation of the hypotheses might have been incorrect, but we would still be able to say something about conflict intensity. Unfortunately, as we have already seen, when the effects of the distribution on Trial 1 are removed, the rates of conflict resolution for the eight experimental conditions are about the same. The wide differences in the probability of conflict resolution at Trial 1 suggest that the two assumptions stated above are not as incompatible as they first appear. What may be incorrect is the view that the relationship between intensity of conflict and probability of resolving that conflict is linear. Suppose that conflict intensity has a threshold above which the probability of resolving conflict varies directly with the intensity of the conflict and below which the probability of resolution varies inversely with the intensity. For highly intense conflict situations, then, the probability of resolving conflict on Trial 1 is high.

138

Resolving conflict on Trial 1 then reduces the intensity of the conflict. In fact, it may fall below the threshold so that the observed relationship between intensity and probability of resolution results.

While this speculation is interesting, an adequate conceptualization of conflict intensity and an operationalization of the variables it contains remain as problems for future research. Clearly, however, our hypotheses relating conflict intensity to ability differentiation are not adequately formulated, so that no purpose would be served by attempting to test them.

Before leaving this issue, we should consider one last problem. Our hypotheses combine undifferentiated conditions, whether they are highs or lows. These hypotheses also pool differentiated conditions and ignore the difference between the individual in the [HL] category and the individual in the [LH] category. One could reasonably ask whether the pooling of either the differentiated or undifferentiated treatments is justified. That is, are there any consistent differences between the undifferentiated and the differentiated treatments? The data relevant to this question are presented in Table 7.9 which deals only with Experiment 11, but which brings together the principal quantities we have examined in this chapter. These data indicate that there is no basis for pooling [HH] and [LL] treatments; for example, sometimes [HH] looks like [HL] and sometimes it looks like [LH], and when [HH] and [LL] look similar they are both similar to [HL]! These results suggest that hypotheses that combine undifferentiated treatments are inadequate; rather, our conceptualization of the undifferentiated ability states must take into account whether the ability is high or low.

TABLE 7.9
Comparison quantities for differentiated versus undifferentiated status treatments (Experiment 11).

Experiment-condition	$p_1(1)$	$p_3(1)$	$p(\infty)$	$p(\infty \mid S_2$ or S_3 on Trial 1)	R/L
E11 [HH]	0.32	0.13	0.75	0.63	0.669
E11 [HL]	0.28	0.07	0.77	0.68	0.471
E11 [LH]	0.10	0.20	0.60	0.55	0.838
E11 [LL]	0.20	0.03	0.82	0.77	0.273

7.6 Homans and Hollander revisited

Recall from Chapter 1 that one of the motivations for this research was to choose between or to reconcile the propositions advanced by Homans and Hollander. Homans proposed that, "the higher the social rank of the person, the more closely he will follow the group norms", while Hollander proposed that, "high status persons will have freedom to deviate from group norms". At the outset of the present research, we believed that we could reconcile these two propositions by applying them to different stages of the interaction process. We argued that the hypotheses could not be evaluated by data, but required further explication, and that a process conceptualization seemed to be a prerequisite for this task. Consequently, we assumed that high-status persons would initially reflect the norms of the group more than low-status persons, particularly in newly-formed *ad hoc* groups; but that, later on in the process, these high-status people would attain greater security and hence would experience greater freedom to deviate from the norms of the group. If these assumptions were correct, one would expect that: (a) the initial probability of being in State 3 in the [HL] treatments would be larger than in the [LH] treatments, (b) the initial probability of being in State 1 would be lower in the [HL] treatments than in the [LH] treatments, (c) the asymptotic probability of a correct response would be higher in the [HL] treatments than in the [LH] treatments, and (d) there would be a turnover point somewhere in the process where the effectiveness of influence of the group as a referent clearly decreased. The relevant quantities for testing these expectations are presented in Table 7.10, where once again we bring together previously presented information in a format convenient for examining these hypotheses. In Table 7.10 we treat Experiments 11, 20, and 21 as three replications in which to test the combined Homans-Hollander propositions. Contrary to what one would expect from applying Homans' proposition to the initial stages of the group interaction, the initial probability of conforming to the group is greater in the [LH] treatments than in the [HL] treatments (Column 2, Table 7.10). Furthermore, the initial probability of rejecting the group, $p_1(1)$, is greater for [HL] treatments than for [LH] treatments. These results are clearly consistent with Hollander's hypothesis, as are the results in the remainder of the table. Both the asymptotic probability of a correct response and the asymptotic probability of a correct response

TABLE 7.10
Comparison quantities for differential status treatments.

Experiment-condition	$p_1(1)$	$p_3(1)$	$p(\infty)$	$p(\infty \mid S_1$ or S_3 on Trial 1)	R/L
E11 [HL]	0.28	0.07	0.77	0.68	0.471
E11 [LH]	0.10	0.20	0.60	0.55	0.838
E20 [HL]	0.24	0.18	0.72	0.63	0.599
E20 [LH]	0.03	0.31	0.35	0.33	2.297
E21 [HL]	0.45	0.11	0.84	0.71	0.436
E21 [LH]	0.14	0.14	0.56	0.49	1.144

given that the individual is in a conflict state on Trial 1 show that a high-status subject is more likely to be a non-conformist than is a low-status subject.

The last column of Table 7.10 shows the value of our ratio R/L for each of the six treatments. In every case the relative pulling power of the group is greater when the individual's ability status is low and the group's is high. Since this ratio is based upon quantities which in the model are assumed to be constant through time, we can infer that the group's pulling power is greater for the [LH] treatments at every point in time. The same inference can be drawn from a comparison of the graphs displaying the trial-by-trial probability of a correct response (see Chapters 5 and 6). If we compare Figure 5.2 with Figure 5.3 (the graphs for Experiment 11), and Figure 6.4 with Figure 6.5 (Experiment 20), and Figure 6.6 with Figure 6.7 (Experiment 21), we can see that the probability of a correct response for the [HL] treatments is greater than the probability of a correct response for [LH] treatments at every point in time. In each of the three comparisons, the two trial-by-trial curves rarely overlap.

In this analysis, we find no evidence to support Homans' proposition, but our results are for the most part consistent with Hollander's hypotheses that "high status persons will have freedom to deviate from group norms". Since Hollander's proposition applies to the initial trial, the equilibrium state, and through every point in between, we believe we can reformulate his proposition to reflect process considerations. Given the nature of the experimental task in these studies, the way in which we created high and low status, and the anomalous and unexpected results obtained in the [LL] treatment, we believe that our reformulation should reflect the

141

limitations of the scope of the Hollander-type proposition. We offer the following reformulation:

Proposition 7.1. Given a task that requires both a specific ability and a status order based on that ability (where the status order is constant over time), then, at any point in time, the referential pulling power of the group relative to the referential pulling power of the self is greater when the status of the group is high than when it is low.

In the statement of Proposition 7.1, the expression, "referential pulling power of the group relative to the referential pulling power of the self", is an interpretation of the ratio, R/L, of the model. Thus, Proposition 7.1 implies that each of the following four inequalities will be observed:

(R/L for the [HH] condition) > (R/L for the [HL] condition)
(R/L for the [HH] condition) > (R/L for the [LL] condition)
(R/L for the [LH] condition) > (R/L for the [HL] condition)
(R/L for the [LH] condition) > (R/L for the [LL] condition)

We offer this proposition as an empirical generalization. It is our hope that a proposition such as this will serve to generate theory. Clearly, our assertion is not earth-shaking, but to interpret the proposition as simply asserting that high ability groups have more referential power than low ability groups is to miss its significance. In the first place, we have clearly set limits on where we want to apply the proposition. We do not assert that the proposition would apply to situations where the status order is not based on ability or where the status order is not constant. While some people may believe the relationship is more general than our restrictive conditions allow, the proposition at least makes clear what restrictions must be relaxed. Secondly, we assert the conditions as sufficient. Therefore, the inclusion of other features in the group interaction, such as providing a reward for successful task performance, should not affect the relationship between status of the group and relative referential pulling power.

The fact that this proposition is an extremely strong assertion is perhaps best understood when the fact that our conditions do not impose any constraints on the characteristics of the individual is noted. Observe that the Proposition 7.1 does not require that the individual have lower ability status than the group in those situations that are to be compared. This last example suggests that our generalization may be much too strong; it may be necessary to

142

impose conditions on the characteristics of self for the proposition to be true. In short, we are claiming that ability status will override other types of relationships between the individual and the group, or between the individual and the task situation. Finally, as examination of Table 7.8 indicates, the generalization is consistent with the results of all the comparisons in that table, that is the comparisons for which the group ability status varies, regardless of the individual's ability status.

Rather than being trivial, we have suggested that the generalization as formulated may not even be true. Perhaps the best reflection of our views here is that we are not presenting a parallel generalization relating the referential pulling power of the self to the ability status of the self. To do so would not be consistent with our own data. Such a generalization would require, for example, that the ratio R/L be smaller in [HL] than in [LL] conditions. In Table 7.8 that is not the case. Hence, we are not asserting a simple universal relationship between ability status and referential pulling power.

We offer this proposition as a tool that could be useful to researchers with a wide range of theoretical interests. It can serve both as an explanatory principle or as an object proposition to be explained by other principles. In other words, as we have formulated a dynamic proposition and indicated its scope of application, we claim that the proposition can be useful for two distinct strategies of theory construction. On the one hand, it can be used together with other propositions to explain some of the variety of experimental results that have been obtained in conformity and influence experiments. On the other hand, the proposition itself can be taken as the thing to be explained and can lead to the formulation of more general explanatory principles.

The use of our proposition as an explanatory principle is handicapped by the shortage of relevant studies dealing with ability characteristics of the group. The extensive literature on conformity and social influence by and large concerns characteristics of the individual. In those cases where a group property, or a property of the relationship between the individual and group is investigated, the properties considered are usually things like the permanence of the group or the attractiveness of the individual to the group. Hence what is needed is a program of research directed at the relationship of the individual to the group with respect to the group task. In this connection we may speculate that such a program might clear up the contradictory findings that Allen (1965)

143

reports with respect to "attractiveness of the group". If we recall that one of the ways in which attractiveness is experimentally manipulated (Back, 1951) is to vary the efficacy of the group as a mediator on individual goals by explicitly telling the subject that this is a good group and we expect high performance from him, then our principle suggests that some manipulations of attractiveness may be implicitly manipulating the ability status of the group while other manipulations may not. If such is the case, then our principle could possibly reconcile the contradictions, for we could expect the group's referential pulling power to be greater in those situations where attractiveness implicitly manipulated ability. The formulation of our principle, as this example demonstrates, does provide a starting point for a series of experiments aimed at a systematic understanding of the conditions under which groups determine individual behavior.

The use of Proposition 7.1 as an object proposition is more difficult to illustrate. It is our belief that ability status is an instance of a more general relationship between the individual and the group. It may be that this more general relationship is one of dependence where dependence on the group for solution of a task problem is similar to dependence upon the group for emotional satisfaction. If such were so, then a general formulation of the dependence phenomenon should explain our generalization. However, dependence is so little understood that we are unwilling to commit ourselves to that direction and merely present it as illustrative.

The results in Table 7.10 allow us to formulate a second general principle. It will be recalled that the purpose of Experiments 20 and 21 was to evaluate the effects of similarity with respect to sex between the individual and the group. In order to assess the effects of similarity, we restrict ourselves to comparisons between Experiment 20 and Experiment 21; Experiment 11 was conducted much earlier than Experiments 20 and 21, with a different subject population and under slightly different conditions. For this reason, as we have already noted, there are some questions whether Experiment 11 is comparable to Experiments 20 and 21. Furthermore, as we have already indicated, we want to restrict our analysis to comparisons where expectations for ability are held constant. Thus, we compare Experiment 20 [HL] with Experiment 21 [HL] and Experiment 20 [LH] with Experiment 21 [LH]. Recalling that in Experiment 20 the subject was female and the assistants were female, while in Experiment 21 the subject was female and the assistants were male, we can see several things in Table 7.10. For the [HL] comparison, Experiment 20 has a smaller initial probability of rejecting the group, a greater initial probability of being influenced by the group, a small asymptotic probability of a correct response, and a greater value of our ratio R/L. The same results obtain when we compare the [LH] treatments of Experiments 20 and 21. In sum, when the group is similar to the individual on a salient status attribute, such as sex, there is less tendency to reject the group initially, less tendency to reject the group in equilibrium, greater tendency to be initially influenced by the group; and, finally, the relative referential pulling power of the group is greater. These results suggest a principle of similarity which we believe can be fruitful in theory construction efforts. Let us introduce the idea of a diffuse status characteristic, by which we mean a status attribute that applies across many different situations and which is more general in its basis than status based upon ability at a specific task (see Berger, Cohen, and Zelditch, 1966, for a precise definition of diffuse status characteristic).

Proposition 7.2. Given a task that requires both a specific ability and a status order based on that ability (where the status order is constant over time), then, at any point in time for a given ability status, the referential pulling power of the group relative to the referential pulling power of the self is greater when the group is similar to the self on a salient diffuse status characteristic than when the group is dissimilar.

Although there has been considerable discussion of reference group theory, there is little in the way of general principles in the reference group literature. The concept of reference group is mainly a strategic injunction to look for characteristics of groups as explanations of individual behavior (Merton, 1957). While we subscribe to the injuction, we feel that there are no clear guidelines as to what properties under what circumstances determine individual behavior. Although the concept of similarity requires considerable explication, we believe that our formulation of "similarity on a salient diffuse status characteristic" should direct research attention away from compiling lists of specific properties of groups which should be studied to a more general focus. We argue that it is more strategic to look at where the group and the individual share a status characteristic, whatever that status characteristic may be, than it is to make lists of characteristics to be investigated.

145

In the way we have formulated the proposition we look at similarity as "objective"; that is, similarity as defined by an outside observer. Some of Fiedler's work on "assumed similarity" (Fiedler, 1954) may lead to a reconsideration of Proposition 7.2, defining similarity from the individual's point of view, but that is another problem for further investigation.

We offer this similarity principle as a first building block in the development of theories of reference group behavior. We hope that the way in which we have formulated this similarity principle will advance reference group theory, and also provide a link between reference group phenomena and other approaches to conformity and influence, such as expectation theory and status characteristic theory.

The analysis we have undertaken in this chapter provides a foundation for further experimental work using an Asch-type or other situation. Some of this new work would be designed to increase substantive generality, while some would be designed to increase precision. Our substantive propositions represent two lines of research where we believe dynamic consideration can be put aside, for we have explicitly postulated invariance over time in Propositions 7.1 and 7.2. We also believe that much can be gained by looking at the process in these conflict situations, but as yet we are not able to formulate similar generalizations about variations through time. We began our work with a concern that the inability of the investigator to guarantee equilibrium may lead to misleading inferences about the nature of the conformity phenomenon and the relationship of extrinsic variables to that phenomenon. Our work has met this concern by enabling us to indicate two areas in which dynamic properties reasonably can be ignored.

CHAPTER 8

An Overview of This Project

8.1 Introduction

This monograph has dealt with a great many details of the process of building and testing a mathematical model. In one sense, a concern with the details is very much a part of our philosophy, for we believe that the type of sociological knowledge that will be both cumulative and useful is rigorous and that rigor cannot be achieved without paying attention to many details. In part, our objective has been to show why the road to knowledge is a difficult and demanding one. However, there is a danger that such close attention to detail may obscure the major results of our project. The purpose of this chapter, then, is to summarize what we regard as our principal accomplishments.

We believe that both the substantive and methodological results of our investigations provide material for researchers with a wide range of theoretical interests. Although the principal concerns of the authors are in the area of reference group theory for one author and a general theory of conflict resolution for the other, our substantive generalizations as well as our model are not restricted to the service of these concerns. For that reason, in summarizing we have chosen to cover the range of our results rather than systematically develop our own theoretical interests. Both a theory of reference group phenomena and a general theory of conflict resolution await further monographs.

8.2 Major substantive findings of our studies

In using our model to analyze the experiments we have conducted, we have drawn several substantive conclusions.

147

(1) We have shown that the process begins in different ways.

Both the probability that an individual has initially resolved the conflict, and the probability that the individual is initially influenced by the group can vary widely from condition to condition. Furthermore, differences in initial vectors are associated with: (a) ability status of the individual relative to the group and (b) similarity of the individual to the group on a diffuse status characteristic.

The following propositions summarize our findings about the differences in initial vectors:

Proposition 8.1.1. Given a task that requires an ability, the higher the ability status of the individual relative to the group, the greater the probability that the individual will initially reject the group.

Proposition 8.1.2. For a given ability status, the initial probability of the individual's rejecting a reference group that is dissimilar on a salient diffuse status characteristic is higher than initial probability of the individual's rejecting a reference group that is similar on a salient diffuse characteristic.

Proposition 8.1.3. Given a task that requires specific ability, the higher the ability status of the group relative to the individual, the greater the individual's initial susceptibility to influence from the group.

Proposition 8.1.4. For a given ability status the individual's initial susceptibility to influence is greater for a reference group that is similar on a salient diffuse status characteristic than it is for the reference group that is dissimilar.

(2) The same equilibrium vector was not obtained for all treatment conditions.

The differences in the equilibrium vectors cannot be attributed to the effects of variations in the initial vectors. Variations in both conditional and unconditional equilibrium vectors are associated with the ability status of the individual relative to the group and the similarity of the individual to the group on a salient diffuse status characteristic.

Proposition 8.2.1. Given a task that requires a specific ability, the higher the ability status of the individual relative to the group, the greater the equilibrium probability of rejecting the group.

Proposition 8.2.2. For a given ability status, the equilibrium probability of rejecting a reference group that is dissimilar to the individual on a salient diffuse status characteristic is higher than the equilibrium probability of rejecting a reference group

148

that is similar on a salient diffuse status characteristic.

Proposition 8.2.3. Differences between relative high and relative low ability status and between similar and dissimilar reference groups are reduced, but still obtain, when the effects of differences in the initial vector are removed, either by employing the conditional equilibrium vector or by standardizing the initial vector.

(3) The rates of conflict resolution are similar for all ability statuses and similar-dissimilar reference groups when differences in the initial vectors are removed.

We hypothesize that the speed of resolving the conflict is related to the nature of the series of judgments. The constancy of the stimulus series in these experiments may overwhelm any relationship between ability status or type of reference group and measures of the speed of conflict resolution. Hence, any relationship that we postulate must be conditional on the nature of the judgment series.

(4) The universal proposition that females conform more than males is false.

Under certain conditions, females may conform more than males; but the nature of these conditions is more important than the sex of the individual. The highest initial probability of rejecting the group and the highest equilibrium probability of rejecting the group were obtained from a treatment involving female subjects.

(5) The pulling power of the group as a referent is less than the pulling power of the individual as a referent except for low-ability females.

We speculate that this result may be due to the asymmetric nature of the experimental task. The pressure from the group as a referent is competing with all the ingrained patterns of perceiving and reporting the perceptually correct response.

It is clear, however, that the nature of the experimental series cannot fully explain why in most cases the ratio of pulling powers is less than 1, while the ratios for female subjects in the two low-ability status treatments (Experiments 20 and 21) are greater than 1, when all subjects responded to the same judgment series. Hence, factors in the subjective definition of the situation as made by the subjects must be better understood before we will be able to explain these findings.

(6) No consistent picture emerges from the comparison of undifferentiated ability-status treatments ([HH] and [LL]) with differentiated ability-status treatments ([HL] and [LH]).

149

While much remains to be understood about undifferentiated ability status in this situation, it is clear that we cannot combine undifferentiated treatments but must analyze them separately according to the ability level they represent.

(7) There is no evidence in our experiments for Homans' proposition that "the higher the social rank of a person, the more closely he will follow the group norm". Contrary to our *a priori* notions, this hypothesis does not apply to any point in the process. An alternative interpretation of Homans' proposition must be followed if we are to determine how his assertion applies to social interaction; i.e., questions other than "when (in time) does it apply?" should be explored.

(8) Our findings are for the most part consistent with Hollander's proposition that "high status persons will have freedom to deviate from group norms". Whether Hollander intends high status to be a necessary condition or a sufficient condition for freedom to deviate from group norms is not clear from his formulation; but because the highest value of the equilibrium probability of a correct (non-conforming) response and the smallest relative pulling power were in the [LL] treatment, we conclude that high ability status is a sufficient condition for freedom to deviate but not a necessary condition.

(9) Our analysis led us to formulate two general propositions in Chapter 7. We propose that they can serve as a basis for further theoretical and empirical work. These propositions are:

Proposition 8.9.1. Given a task that requires both a specific ability and a status order based on that ability (where the status order is constant over time), then, at any point in time, the referential pulling power of the group relative to the referential pulling power of the self is greater when the status of the group is high than when it is low.

Proposition 8.9.2. Given a task that requires both a specific ability and a status order based on that ability (where the status order is constant over time), then, at any point in time for a given ability status, the referential pulling power of the group relative to the referential pulling power of the self is greater when the group is similar to the self on a salient diffuse status characteristic than when the group is dissimilar.

8.3 What can we now say about the questions posed in Chapter 1?

Although one series of studies cannot answer definitively the general questions posed in Chapter 1, we believe that the strategy we have chosen will, in the long run, provide these answers. Without claiming to be definitive, we believe we better understand the issues we raise than we did at the outset of this research. We reconsider these issues, recognizing two qualifications: (1) any assertions that we now are able to make will undoubtedly be modified by further empirical and theoretical work; and (2) some of the issues we raised in Chapter 1 were closer to the central focus of the present research than others, and therefore, we have both a broader and deeper understanding of some issues than others. Let us return to the questions posed in Chapter 1; for convenience, we will recapitulate the questions here.

Question 1. What is it about the group that affects individual conformity?

Question 2. What is it about the individual that affects his acceptance of social influence?

The present research did not deal with these questions in the general form in which they were posed, but our formulation and our analysis of eight data sets enable us to make two important negative statements and to advance tentatively some additional propositions.

Neither ability status of the group by itself nor ability status of the individual by itself is sufficient to determine all the aspects of conformity behavior that we have examined. For some aspects, for example, [HH] and [LH] behave very differently, while [LL] and [HL] behave quite similarly.

The fact that no consistent picture emerges when one looks only at ability status of the group or only at ability status of the individual has two implications. First, it argues for a differentiation of the phenomenon. With our model we have differentiated aspects of the phenomenon which can be examined separately. Secondly, neither characteristics of the individual nor characteristics of the group are by themselves a fruitful way to look at this phenomenon. (Although Propositions 8.9.1 and 8.9.2 may seem to be an exception to this assertion, we believe that future research will require us to further conditionalize these assertions according to the relative ability of the individual.) Rather, both the ability status of the individual and the ability status of the group operate to determine properties of conformity in the situation.

The model's assumption that an individual who initially resolves the conflict is unaffected by the group fits the data from all treatments. This result suggests an approach to introducing characteristics of individual personalities into the process. We can ask the following question: "Do individuals have characteristics that will allow us to determine which subject from a population exposed to a fixed manipulation will start the process in State 1?" We believe that consideration of this question may lead to a more fruitful way to introduce personality variables than correlating personality measures with conformity scores. We might also ask whether groups have characteristics (independent of the individual's relation to the group) that will enable us to predict which groups will contain a higher proportion of subjects initially in State 1. We know from Asch's work that the unanimity of group pressure will affect the asymptotic probability of a correct response. But what of non-behavioral characteristics of the group? Here might be a fruitful place to investigate homogeneity with respect to ability status or sex. Employing the obvious reasoning that an individual will have greater difficulty making a single response to a differentiated entity than to a homogeneous entity, we would speculate that the initial probability of being in State 1 would be smaller for heterogeneous than homogeneous groups.

Even if we control for similarity of referents and ability status, there seem to be residual effects of sex of subject on both the initial and equilibrium vectors. We advance this argument tentatively, for we have serious reservations about the comparability of Experiments 11 and 20 and 21. (As we have noted several times, comparing male subjects who were students at Stanford University with female subjects who were junior college students undoubtedly introduced additional status considerations.) Nevertheless, we believe that this issue merits further empirical research and further theoretical analysis. In the present research, even in the face of the confounding effects of different subject populations, the effects of sex of subject are less powerful than either ability status or similarity of referent. Since we reject the notion that females are more submissive than males and cite our results in Experiment 21 [HL] (where we observed the highest initial probability of rejecting the group) as support for our position, we believe we must look for other characteristics associated with sex differences in order to explain the effects of sex of subject on conformity behavior.

Question 3. What kinds of individual behavior can be influenced?

This question does not represent a central focus of the present research. We have dealt with a simplified experimental situation that does not invoke a repertoire of individual behaviors. We have not systematically varied types of behavior to ascertain those which can be modified. Nevertheless, our formulation and analysis are instructive. We claim that it is not necessary, nor always fruitful, to restrict consideration to overt behavioral responses. Our analysis of conflict suggests that the nature of the conflict involved in an individual's response to conformity pressures is itself modifiable. Our model formulates several properties of the conflict process, and our analysis has shown how these properties are affected by extrinsic variables.

Of course, a full-scale attack on this question would require a conceptualization of the types of individual behavior. This conceptualization could contain dimensions such as: verbal-physical, public-private, attitudinal-factual, etc. Our work suggests that, even if one undertook a dimensional analysis, some dimensions could be captured in a theoretical model rather than by direct empirical measures.

Question 4. How does the relationship between the individual and the group affect his conformity?

This issue has been the central focus of our research, and we need not recount all of our findings. Suffice it to say that our research convinces us of the utility of employing status as an explanatory concept for conformity behavior and conflict resolution. We have dealt with two types of status; and status is, after all, a *relational* variable. We have shown that both ability status and similarity on a diffuse status characteristic affect diverse aspects of the Asch phenomenon. These status variables affect how the individual begins the process of conflict resolution, his equilibrium state, and his state at any point in time. We have captured our main findings in two general propositions, which are both conditional and dynamic. These propositions, together with the Cohen-Lee model and our experimental situation, can generate a series of comparable and cumulative studies, but whether or not they are invariant under the conditions we have stated is a question for further empirical research. Our propositions are systemic in that the concept of pulling power incorporates separate but related aspects of the conflict resolution process. But the propositions need to be systemic in another sense: they must be imbedded in a system of theoretical principles. The construction of such theories is the main task before us.

Question 5. What properties of the situational context in which the group is interacting affect conformity?

As we did not systematically vary the situational properties of our experiment, we have relatively little to say on this question. We do, however, wish to raise two issues as suggestions for future research. In the first place, our experiments involve what may be called a "pure task" situation. The group is brought together solely for the purpose of this judgment task; it has no existence prior to the experiment, nor can it anticipate any future existence after the experiment ends. The only significance of the relationship between the individual and the group is that produced by the experimental task. The observed effects of ability status may well depend on this situational context, so that altering this aspect of the context should produce changes in the relationship between ability status and aspects of the conflict resolution process.

Suppose, for example, we modified our experiment slightly by indicating to our experimental subjects that after the completion of the perceptual judgment they would have an opportunity to get acquainted with the other members of the group. Would this modification alter the values of the model's parameters? Would it alter the relationship that we have observed between ability status and the quantities that describe the process? On the assumption that the anticipation of further interaction with other members of the group would intensify the conflict in the situation, we would anticipate some changes in the parameters, but not in the relationships to extrinsic variables.

The second contextual issue is that the conflict process described occurs in an experiment. A growing body of social science writers (e.g., Rosenthal, 1966) argue that the role of the experimenter must be taken into account in describing behavior in an experimental context. The present series of experiments provides some anecdotal evidence in support of this contention.

To conduct Experiments 20 and 21 efficiently, we used several different experimenters. Most of the groups were conducted by male experimenters, but a few were run by two different female experimenters. Expediency, rather than experimental design, dictated which groups were run by female experimenters; hence, the number of cases with female experimenters is too small to compute any of the model's quantities. Nevertheless, our impression is that the relative pulling power of the group was less when the experimenter was female than when the experimenter was male.

Although we cannot present quantitative evidence on the effects of the sex of the experimenter, we raise the point here because it suggests another interpretation for our ratio R/L. We have interpreted this ratio as the pulling power of the group as a referent relative to the pulling power of the self as a referent. Perhaps we should also consider the experimenter as a referent in this situation, a referent for the correct response (see Schulman, 1967). Then we would interpret our ratio of R/L as the pulling power of the group as a referent relative to the pulling power of the self as a referent plus the pulling power of the experimenter as a referent. The possibility of this interpretation reinforces our view that many pressures operate in this situation, and that these pressures emanate from different referents. Furthermore, this interpretation can be systematically investigated; we can vary the similarity of the experimenter to the subject on a salient diffuse status characteristic and test how these variations affect the ratio R/L.

Question 6. How does group influence come about?

This question is the most fundamental of all we have considered. The Cohen-Lee model is one possible answer to this question; it represents a process by which influence occurs. The model postulates an initial probability distribution determined by extrinsic variables, a conflict resolution process which occurs probabilistically through time in which the probabilities are related to extrinsic variables; and it asserts that the process terminates when all individuals have rejected either the group as a referent or the self as a referent. In short, the interpreted model is a representation of our conceptualization of the influence process.

We do not argue that either the representation or the conceptualization is unique. We believe, however, that the analyses we have pursued and the ideas we have advanced flow directly from our conceptualization and its formal representation. Furthermore, we contend that a cumulative and fruitful research program is impossible without an explicit formulation of how influence emerges and any resulting conflict is resolved. We invite alternative formulations and the cumulative series of empirical studies that they would promote so that our own formulation may be confronted with these alternatives.

Question 7. Under what conditions do individuals conform to groups?

Throughout our discussion we have emphasized that scientific research is conditional. We have distinguished two kind of conditions: on the one hand are conditional statements that indicate the scope of applicability of a model or a theoretical proposition. On the other hand, what are termed fixed initial conditions represent a set of initial values for a system of variables; for example, the

155

statement, "in Experiment 21 [HL] the initial probability of rejecting the group is 0.45", specifies fixed initial conditions. With this distinction, and as a result of using our model, we now regard Question 7 in its most general form as capable of only trivial answers — given that the individual has not rejected the group, he will conform to the group. But Question 7 apparently asks for scope conditions, and our trivial answer specifies fixed initial conditions.

Our experience in this project has clarified the issue. As Question 7 is raised, it asks for *the scope of a phenomenon*; but, as we have defined scope conditions, they clearly do not refer to phenomena — one does not apply a phenomenon. The factors that affect the existence of a phenomenon, then, are not the subject matter of scope conditions but rather of theoretical assertions. Furthermore, it is too much to expect that all the diverse phenomena that are subsumed under the term conformity can be dealt with in one set of theoretical assertions. What can be done is to indicate the scope of applicability of one particular view of a conformity process. In this respect, we have indicated that a task requiring an ability is a crucial condition for the applicability of our model and the substantive propositions we have advanced. In addition, when we posit fixed ability status as a scope condition for Proposition 7.2, we rule out those situations in which the diffuse status characteristics also provide information about the relative abilities of subject and confederate.

We recognize that we have only begun to formulate the scope of applicability of our model and our theoretical propositions. Further constraints are needed, and a further specification of the properties of a task is required. We mention this latter point because we believe that an analysis of task properties would provide clearer guidelines for the applicability of our model.

8.4 Our research strategy: A review and a forward look

In this monograph we have advanced a research strategy that we believe will assist in closing the gap between theory and empirical investigation. We have illustrated how the efforts to build, test and use a formal model altered the questions we asked about the phenomena, and, in the process, enabled us to formulate answers to these revised questions. In this section we want to look at (1) our general strategic concerns; (2) some questions concerning the future utility of the Asch experiment; (3) the use of our model as a model in the analysis of experiments; and (4) an informal recapitulation of the model as an emerging theory of conflict resolution. First, let us consider our general strategic concerns.

As we look back on our work, we see the continuity of our concerns from the beginning of the research reported in *Conflict and Conformity* to the end of the present study. The original concerns for comparability across studies, invariance over time, and abstract properties of a situation rather than a holistic view of a phenomenon have been extended, clarified, and molded into a strategy. The problems of comparing Experiments 11, 20, and 21 discussed in Chapter 7 clearly justified our efforts to provide a solid foundation for comparing different experiments. The Cohen-Lee model enables us to partition effects into initial effects, process effects, and equilibrium effects, and thereby provides a testable alternative to asserting by fiat that studies are comparable.

We can now argue that studies are comparable when they are identical in fixed initial conditions or when the quantities examined are independent of the initial conditions, or when the effects of initial conditions can be partialed out. Our model provides both a measure of the fixed initial conditions (the initial vector) and a method for computing the required independent quantities. Furthermore, we have illustrated another approach to comparability, that of standardizing data sets. While our method was somewhat crude, we hope to explore more refined standardization procedures in future studies.

Although the majority of subjects in our experiments reach equilibrium earlier in the process than we had anticipated, the analysis presented justifies our concern with equilibrium. We do not have invariance over time — for example, the ordering of our eight treatments is not the same for $p_1(1)$ as it is for $p(\infty)$. To those who would object that we would make many of the same inferences about the effects of ability status or similarity of referent from a comparison of means (mean number of correct responses), while ignoring equilibrium, we have two responses. First, we have much more specific knowledge of what is, and what is not, affected by these extrinsic variables. Surprisingly, speed of conflict resolution was similar for all treatments, but this similarity remains hidden when one compares only means. Second, because we can support the equilibrium assumption for each data set and can show that equilibrium occurs relatively early, we can confidently compare means; in other words, given that equilibrium occurs early, the model justifies comparing means by guaranteeing that means computed over the equilibrium segment will not vary. Without the model, one can only fall back on comparability by fiat — the means are comparable because we assume they are comparable!

Perhaps the most significant feature of our strategy is that it offers a viable alternative to either an atomistic or a holistic approach. The present project served to clarify the systemic nature of our work and its relationship to alternative strategies. The conceptualization we have developed is neither atomistic nor holistic. For example, we regard studies which choose a single characteristic of individuals (or of groups or of the group task) and relate this variable to conformity scores as an atomistic orientation. On the other hand, studies which attempt to deal *simultaneously* with many characteristics of individuals, many properties of the situation, many attributes of the group, and many initial, process, and equilibrium measures of performance (treating the large set of variables through some form of multi-variate analysis) constitute a holistic approach. Let us briefly indicate why we assert that our approach is neither atomistic nor holistic.

In contrast to an atomistic approach, we have dealt with a number of relationships simultaneously, rather than seriatim and independently. An atomistic approach gives equal weight to every pairwise correlation, whereas we have segregated some relationships as scope conditions, some as fixed initial conditions, and some as explanatory principles.

In contrast to an holistic approach, we have not tried in our research to capture all of the relevant features of the Asch situation. It may be that properties of the situation which we have ignored would be the best predictors of frequency of conforming. Perhaps the prediction of conforming would be best handled through a multiple correlation technique in which we seek out as many independent variables as we can in order to maximize the observed correlation. The holistic strategy would require us to go even further. That is, to obtain as many dependent variables as we could and relate these either one at a time through multiple correlation or simultaneously through factor-analytic techniques to all the relevant independent variables. Once having concluded such an analysis, its generality at least would be in doubt, for attempting to capture the whole situation virtually guarantees that some of that which is captured is idiosyncratic either to the particular experiments that we have run or to the Asch situation per se.

Since our concern is with generality, we have focused rather on drawing out those features of the phenomenon that are both general and potentially useful for testing ideas about the relationship between the individual and the group and his propensity to conform to the group. We hope that others who pursue this problem will come up with better conceptualization than our own, but we are convinced that a strategy which tries to deal with the whole situation will not be successful. (At the beginning of this monograph we argued against the notion of a theory of the Asch situation. We remain firm in that conviction and call for approaching the Asch experiment as a useful tool rather than as a phenomenon per se.)

We should make it clear that when we are critical of the atomistic or holistic approaches, we are not aiming our criticism at the investigator who does *one* bivariate or *one* multivariate study. What we regard as the atomistic strategy is a program of research which goes from correlating ability status with mean conformity to correlating eye color with mean conformity, and on and on. While one or two of these studies may contribute significantly, the series of correlations adds up to very little in the way of knowledge about the phenomenon. We know almost nothing of the invariance properties of these correlations, nor do we know which relationships are conditional on other relationships somewhere in the series.

We are neither so foolish nor so imperialistic as to argue that every investigator should adopt a systemic strategy at the outset of his research. The attempt to explain a bivariate correlation or the effort to extract a set of more abstract factors from a factor analysis might provide both the foundation and the motivation for a systemic strategy. What we believe is clear from our own studies — that a systemic strategy offers a clear basis for the cumulation of research findings and holds the promise of closing the gap between theorizing and empirical investigation.

8.5 The utility of the Asch situation

As a result of our work we have raised serious questions about the utility of the Asch situation for the study of the *process* of conflict resolution. Before a definitive judgment can be made on this question a number of additional experiments would be required. Independent of this question, there are issues concerning one's approach to this experimental situation even when it is used to test non-dynamic hypotheses. We want to comment briefly on both of these issues.

The fact that our studies show a relatively high proportion of subjects who have resolved the conflict on Trial 1 and the fact that all treatments reached equilibrium at roughly the same rate raises serious questions concerning this situation for the study of processes, but our surprise that equilibrium occurs early itself generates interesting questions. We have already conjectured that the constant stimuli of this experimental situation may explain the rapid absorption and the similarity across treatments of the speed of conflict resolution. Hence, we would propose modifying the situation to eliminate stimulus constancy. Returning to Asch's original procedure of varying the stimuli to be judged may allow us to put the process under a microscope; perhaps stimulus constancy produces a pressure for self-consistency that overwhelms factors like ability status that otherwise might produce variation in the time required to reach equilibrium.

But stimulus constancy is not the whole story. The fact that our estimates indicate that a substantial proportion of conflict resolution occurs on the first trial suggests that we look to our procedures for manipulating ability status. Because the scores used to create high and low ability were markedly different, perhaps a more subtle manipulation would reduce initial conflict resolution. Therefore, it seems necessary to explore alternative manipulations of ability status. What is required is an ability manipulation that produces stable expectations (our model is predicated on the assumption that beliefs about ability remain constant throughout the process), yet does not resolve the conflict at Trial 1 for a large proportion of the subjects. Further exploration should enable us to decide whether or not this is practically feasible.

One factor that may obscure any process that does occur is the variability of the behavior of the experimental assistants from trial to trial and from subject to subject. Thus, another modification of the situation that we would recommend concerns the behavior of the confederates. An experimental procedure employing video simulation of the confederates and computer administration of the experiment could eliminate the error variance of confederate behavior.

Further experiments incorporating these modifications should help to decide the issue of the utility of Asch-type situations for process studies, but the issue cannot be resolved on the basis of experimental results alone. Our strategy requires utilizing our model to analyze and to interpret the experimental data. It may well be that further modifications in the model together with new experimental procedures are necessary to resolve the issue.

For those investigators who are interested in the Asch situation for testing non-dynamic hypotheses, we believe our research has two very broad implications. One concerns viewing the phenomenon as a manifestation of individual behavior determined by individual characteristics in contrast to a phenomenon of individual behavior determined by the structure of social situations in which the behavior is elicited. We are not posing these as mutually exclusive approaches to conformity and influence phenomenon, but we believe the "individual differences approach" to the Asch situation has been too dominant. We approached the problems with the view that the Asch situation could be examined and utilized in the service of structural concerns. Clearly, our results support our initial conviction.

One of the major results of our experimental work is to show how manipulable the response process is in this experimental situation, whereas most of the previous research utilizing the Asch situation has focused upon the stability of the phenomenon. If one approaches the Asch situation with an individual differences orientation, then what is desired is stability of aggregate statistics coupled with variability of individual responses. With this orientation the ideal is to construct a test situation which reproduces treatment means from one experiment to another and at the same time allows some *a priori* measure to be correlated with the individual's response score. Thus replicability of a distribution of scores is also desirable. The fact that study after study has produced similar aggregate statistics coupled with a distribution of individual responses has reinforced the individual differences orientation. It reinforces the contention that the Asch situation is most suitably employed for investigating the consequences of characteristics of individuals. Since these characteristics vary in any given population, it is reasonable to assume that there are such individual characteristics that produce variability in conformity responses for any population. Hence, it is reasonable to search for the characteristic correlates of conformity responses.

The orientation with which we began argues that it is not necessary to postulate *a priori* differences in individual characteristics in order to account for individual differences in conformity response. As in our earlier work, we have again shown that behavioral differences can arise probabilistically even on the assumption that a population is initially homogeneous. More importantly though, we have shown that aggregate properties of the phenomenon will vary systematically with properties of the structure of the conformity situation. The orientation that has guided us demanded that we look for variations in aggregate properties of the conformity situation. The fact that we were able to find aggregate probabilities of conforming that range from 0.2 to 0.7 argues strongly that the Asch situation is at least as significant a tool for the study of structural properties as it is for the study of individual characteristics. We believe that our work has opened up the possibility of more precise formulation of propositions dealing with group determination of behavior because the Asch situation offers a highly controlled setting in which to evaluate such propositions.

It is clear from our work that the relationship between the individual and the group systematically affects the probability that an individual will conform to a group. This effect may occur in opposition to, or independently of, or superimposed upon, the effects of the trait makeup of the individual — his personality characteristics, for example — but what is reassuring is our demonstration that aggregate effects are not obscured by individual variation. We believe we have shown conclusively the utility of this experimental situation for hypotheses testing at other levels of analysis than the relationship between individual characteristics and individual probabilities of conformity, and we issue a call for the more structurally minded theorists to formulate hypotheses which can be tested using this situation. While there has been considerable discussion of the effects of the structure of the group and the individual's position in that structure on his propensity to conform, there has been a shortage of empirical testing of these effects. If our work calls attention to the possibilities inherent in using the Asch situation in the service of more "social" social-psychological formulations, we will have accomplished an important objective.

The second broad implication of our research concerns one's view of conformity phenomena as "rational attempts at problem solving" or non-rational expressions of underlying emotional states. In a sense, our results are quite supportive of those who would approach the phenomenon as an instance of rational problem solving. The strong relationship between relative ability status and equilibrium probabilities of conforming argues that a subject behaves rationally in the situation given his perceptions and definition of the situation. Since the task is defined as one requiring ability, it is quite reasonable that a subject who believes that the group has more of the requisite ability than he has, conforms to the group much more than a subject who believes that his ability is greater than the group's.

When Asch presented his work to a popular audience in the *Scientific American* in 1956, there was an underlying tone to his presentation which decried the fact that individuals could be made to contradict the judgment of their senses simply because other people disagreed with them. Asch's writing suggested that the ease with which subjects could be manipulated to contradict perceptions that were obvious when they were reporting orally was a cause for concern. It was almost as if many of his subjects had that "fatal flaw" which made them ripe for authoritarian control. Indeed, many other writers have approached this phenomenon in terms of a "good guy — bad guy" syndrome, the good guys being the ones who remain independent of the group throughout the experiment. The fact that perceived ability differentials provide such wide differences in behavioral response, however, seriously challenges such an approach. Would we consider as a "good guy" a person who acknowledges that others are better at a task than he is, but steadfastly resists any task suggestions that these others make? Many current views of the good guy require him to carefully assess a situation, to concur with other judgments when he thinks they are more likely to be right, and to stick to his own judgment when he has the basis for believing it to be right. Indeed, this is what we observe when we compare across our treatments.[1]

There is a fundamental problem in the typical approach to the Asch situation which we can discuss in terms other than "rational models" or "good—bad" dimensions. We believe that the conception of the phenomenon in the Asch situation in terms of invariant characteristics of individuals is inadequate; the view that subjects bring to this experiment varying amounts of a trait such as submissiveness or dependence which they then reveal in their behavior is a typical example. The position we take is that such an approach omits

---

[1] A similar point was made in a letter to the *Scientific American* shortly after Asch's article appeared. A chemist from Cal Tech questioned the underlying tone of distress in Asch's presentation, arguing that the training of scientists is deliberately aimed at making the individual skeptical of his own perceptions until they have been referred to an intersubjective test.

163

very significant, and perhaps the most significant, aspects of the phenomenon. The experiment is a social situation involving several kinds of social relationships and involving an orientation of the individual to the task. The naive subject's relationship to the confederates, his relationship to the experimenter, his commitment to work on the task, all operate to produce for him a definition of the situation. To be sure, his underlying personality makeup also contributes to that definition of the situation. But certainly the definition of the situation is not the simple function of some single personality trait that is implied by the relation: (number of conforming responses) = fn (amount of trait X). At the very least the social relationships interact with the individual's traits and under some circumstances it is conceivable that the social relationships are sufficiently powerful to overwhelm any effects of individual characteristics. Hence a major implication of this work is that the full potential of the Asch situation will be realized only if the constraints imposed by an individual differences approach are removed.

8.6 The use of our model for the analysis of experiments

We believe that the present model allows us to describe the situation, gives us tools by which to relate conformity and conflict resolution phenomenon to extrinsic variables, and also raises questions to be pursued in further research. Certainly we would encourage the formulation of alternative models, particularly models which did not involve such restrictive assumptions as, for example, constant transition probabilities. Nevertheless, we do believe that more can be gained from attempts to derive new quantities from the model and efforts to apply the model to other kinds of experimental situations. The basis for this position is the fact that the model incorporates some very general ideas with a great deal of intuitive appeal. Binary choice conflict situations form the kernel of a great many socially interesting phenomena. The fundamental idea that conflict resolution is an absorbing process is sufficient to justify further work on the model. To be sure, we would not claim that all conflict resolution can be characterized as an absorbing process, but there in itself is a theoretical problem: that of specifying those conflicts for which the equilibrium state is one of response absorption.

The fact that our model enables us to partition a behavioral

164

sequence into an initial starting point, a transition phase and an equilibrium phase, is also a very important achievement. The model provides a direct empirical test of the comparability of experimental treatments on the assumption that treatments with the same initial vector are comparable. This fact has very general implications for experimental research where initial measurements would be destructive, i.e., would contaminate the treatments we wish to compare. The development of models such as ours could greatly enhance experimental possibilities.

A second implication of the ability to partition the response sequence is that use of the model enables us to make inferences about equilibrium features of the process uncontaminated by variations in the way subjects reached equilibrium. For example, taking the model seriously tells us what the range of summation ought to be to compute the proportion of nonconforming responses for a treatment in equilibrium. In our present study, for example, the model suggests that proportion of nonconforming responses computed over the segment, Trials 40 to 60, represent a situation where more than 75% of our experimental subjects have reached equilibrium. This would suggest that comparisons of proportion of nonconforming responses would be more appropriately based on the last third of the experimental sequence rather than on the entire sequence. Such an analysis would be particularly appropriate for investigating experimental treatments that regardless of starting point arrive at the same equilibrium state. Although it is not applicable in this study (all of our treatments move at the same rate to equilibrium), the model provides the possibility of comparing treatments with regard to equilibrium properties where equilibrium is reached at very different time points. In other words, in place of arbitrary decisions to compare, for example, the last ten trials across experimental treatments, one compares equilibrium states, some of which begin at Trial 20 and some at Trial 40 or 50. These suggestions merely scratch the surface of analytic properties of employing the model. What we want to stress is that using the model substitutes a substantive rationale for arbitrariness in examining this type of experimental data.

There certainly are questions to be raised about the model. We have shown by simulation that there are no differences among our treatments in the speed of conflict resolution, yet our index, R/L, a function of the process, does discriminate among treatments. If we treat the relative referential power as analogous to a balance of forces acting on the individual, we can interpret our two results as suggesting that the speed of resolution of the conflict is independent of this balance of forces. This strikes us as counter-intuitive. If our intuitions are correct, we would expect that the more one-sided this balance of forces (that is, for very small values of the ratio or very large values), the quicker the conflict would be resolved. Applying the model to a situation where stimulus constancy was not a factor might produce such a result. On the other hand, it might be necessary to find more appropriate quantities to describe changes in the process, or to describe the relative balance of forces independently of the speed of resolution.

We have already indicated that the quantity R/L, while interesting and potentially related in a systematic way to structural features of the situation, omits one facet of the process. Namely, neither the numerator nor the denominator takes into account the probability of remaining in a non-absorbed state. It would be desirable to consider a quantity which deals with both movement and inertia, but such a quantity poses additional problems. R/L already represents a relatively complicated ratio of products of parameters; it is not an easy property about which to reason, thereby magnifying the difficulty of relating a process description to extrinsic variables. A more inclusive and hence more complicated quantity capturing both movement and inertia would be even more difficult to handle conceptually. While we do not argue that a name and verbal reasoning about the name is necessary for us to uncover systematic relationships, it is difficult to decide where to go next with a purely formal property. What basically needs to be done is to think about a modified R/L in such a way that it becomes embedded in lawful relationships; or, alternatively, to come up with a substitute that is sensitive to the unfolding process but is more manageable theoretically.

The model has possibilities for extension both by deriving new properties and by applying it to new situations. It also has problems to be resolved, but these are virtues because of which we regard our model as a tool to promote the development of social psychology.

It has long been argued that social-psychological experimentation will yield only very gross observations and very crude results until we have more sophisticated analytical and conceptual tools. We claim that our model with its ability to partition the experimental sequence is one such tool. Another aspect in which the model represents the possibility of increasingly sophisticated experimentation is that the model frees us from the constraints of

166

manifest data. The strategy of this study represents an alternative to the usual statistical design and statistical analysis of experiments. By postulating an underlying process and formulating quantities which describe this underlying process, we have a wider range of tools than means, variances or F ratios, as would be the case in studies that deal solely with statistics computed on manifest observations. Furthermore, with many of the quantities derived from the model, there is a substantive interpretation that can be used heuristically to guide the formulation of relationships containing those quantities. Most experimentalists are well aware that it is often very difficult to give a substantive interpretation to a statistical quantity like an F ratio.

What we call for here is the development of experimental programs around models like our own which will produce more meaningful empirical results. We use "meaningful" here in several ways: (1) in terms of theoretical significance of a particular empirical quantity examined in a set of data; (2) in the sense of opening up a wider range of empirical quantities to be examined; and (3) somewhat paradoxically, empirical quantities that are both closer to the phenomena and yet less constrained by the observations themselves. In short, the model imposes constraints by the nature of the substance of the phenomena rather than the statistical properties of the observations.

We have tried to demonstrate exactly how this model building orientation accomplishes such an objective and it is our hope that others will follow in this orientation either through employing and extending our own model or in developing new models that in their assumptions incorporate substantive considerations. It is unfortunately the first forgotten lesson of statistics training that every statistical analysis depends upon a model and a particular statistical model is not universally appropriate. While the statistician argues that the choice of statistical model is dictated by the substance of the phenomenon under investigation, the experimental practitioner in his rush to be quantitative often ignores this injunction. In our call for the formulation of substantive probability models, we hope at least to bring back into the awareness of social psychologists the necessary connection between what one assumes about the phenomena and how one analyzes experimental data.

8.7 The model as an emerging theory on conflict resolution

Throughout this monograph and particularly in the last two

chapters the way we have interpreted and used our model follows from a very particular conceptualization. Perhaps the best way to conclude our work is by recapitulating its key elements in very informal language. In reviewing our work we see emerging a theory of conflict resolution. This theory describes the response process of an actor who finds himself in a situation in which there are two contradictory sources of information — the visual stimulus presented by the slides showing the lines to be judged and the social stimulus presented by the other participants. On each and every trial the actor is forced to process this conflicting information and to indicate his own choice. Thus the actor has to choose between "call 'em as I see 'em" or "call 'em as I hear 'em" where "hear 'em" refers to responses of the other participants. But after the first trial, he also has another source of information to integrate into his decision making process — his own responses on previous trials. In several situations the actor has information of another sort — an estimate of his own ability and an estimate of the ability of the other participants in the situation. Further, in all situations the actor has another piece of information, a knowledge of the sex of all individuals in the situation.

As we conceive of it, the process of conflict resolution may be expressed in terms of the Cohen-Lee model as follows: using chalk, draw a straight line on the floor. Make it about six feet long. Then draw on the floor four circles each about one foot in diameter with the centers of each circle on the same straight line. Label one end of the line "left" and the other "right". Consecutively number the circles from one to four beginning by assigning the number one to the circle on the left. Then stand with your left foot in circle two and your right foot in circle three. Raise your left arm and extend it along the straight line to the left such that it is parallel to the floor. Similarly extend the right arm. Obviously, the four circles represent the four states of the Markov chain. Then a tug on the left hand would represent the force pulling the actor to "call 'em as I see 'em". A tug on the right hand would represent the force pulling the actor to "call 'em as I hear 'em". The weight on the feet represents the force to remain in a state once that response was made on the previous trial. Thus the actor is the center point of the tug of war. If a tug on either the left hand or the right hand is sufficiently strong and not counterbalanced by the other forces, the actor leans so far that he loses his balance and finds himself sitting down in either state one or state

168

four, respectively. Thus, sitting down represents the formal property of absorption.

The propositions which we have advanced further specify the evaluation function or the weighting function which may be thought of as operating upon these forces, and therefore are part of the interpretation of the model. When we point to the interpreted model as the emerging theory and claim that the model fits the data we are asserting: (1) that we are displaying the mechanism which produces the observed outcome (i.e., the sequence of responses of a subject in a binary choice situation) and (2) that the model is sufficient to generate the observed responses.

Instructions to Subjects and to Experimenter for Experiment 11

This is a study of perceptual ability. We have two different but related tests of your perceptual ability. These tests have been used throughout the country with considerable success. However, the tests have been given for the most part to younger people; we know a great deal about how the tests work for high school students and now we would like to know how they work for college students. The experiment, then, consists of these two tests of perceptual ability. The experiment will be run in two parts; the first part will be Test One and the second part will be Test Two. Instructions for each part of the experiment will be given separately.

As you probably already know, this room is equipped with special apparatus for listening to and recording your behavior. Behind the mirror in front of you are two observers who can see and hear you. The microphones in the ceiling carry sound to the observers who will record your behavior and tabulate your scores on the two tests. We will be happy to show you the special features of the laboratory as well as answer any questions you may have about the experiment at the end of today's session.

I will now give you the instructions for part one of the experiment.

The task for the first test requires each of you to judge whether or not a geometrical design flashed on the screen in front contains a particular pattern. Each one of you will be asked to make a total of twenty such judgments. At the beginning of the test you will each receive a card containing a single pattern. Since every card contains a different pattern, no two people will have the same pattern. You will be given thirty seconds in which to familiarize yourself with the pattern on your card, and then the cards will be collected. You should be careful not to show your card to any other member of the group. After the cards have been collected we will project a geometrical design on the screen in front of you. You will be given five seconds to look at this design. After the design has been taken off the screen, you will state orally whether or not the pattern which you were given appeared in that design. If you think your pattern appeared in the design say "yes"; if not say "no". Please do not make any other comments during the experiment. Because each person has been given a different pattern there is no necessary relation between the answers given by different persons. We will present five designs to you. After judgments have been made on each one of them, the cards containing the patterns will be redistributed. Each person will be given a pattern different from the one he had previously. After thirty seconds the cards will be collected, and the *same* five geometrical designs will again be projected on the screen. You will have to determine whether or not the new pattern can be found in each one of these designs. The cards will be redistributed and the process will be repeated four times so that each person will be given all four patterns. During the experiment each person will perform exactly the same total task, although order will differ from person to person. Before you begin, we will show you a sample slide illustrating the task in order to make certain that everyone understands what is required of him.

After the first test is over, we will have a short break while your scores are being computed. When the scores are totaled, they will be announced and then I will give the instructions for the second test.

CUE: May I have the sample slide, please?

The standard on this slide is similar to the pattern you will receive and study for thirty seconds. The other figures are like the designs we will project on the screen. You see that the top design contains the standard while the bottom design does not. Now, does anyone have any questions?

(PASS OUT STANDARDS): You now have thirty seconds to study your pattern.

(COLLECT STANDARDS): Each design will be projected on the screen for five seconds. Study the design carefully for the entire time it is on the screen. Please do not give your answers until the design has been taken off the screen. When the screen goes blank, would you give your answers in order beginning with NUMBER ONE.

(PROJECT SLIDES FOR FIVE SECONDS EACH. ALLOW SEVEN SECONDS BETWEEN BUTTON PUSHES AS IT TAKES TWO SECONDS FOR THE MACHINE TO CHANGE SLIDES.) (SLIDE FIVE OF EACH SERIES CONTAINS TWO "HATCHED RECTANGLES", ONE CROSSING THE OTHER DIAGONALLY.)

Before giving you your scores let me tell you something about the task which you have just completed. This task has been used widely and with considerable success in high schools, military organizations, and hospitals. It is known to be an excellent indicator of perceptual ability. This, however, is the first time it has been used for a college group. We are very curious about what the results will be.

The national average which has been calculated on the basis of thousands of applications is twelve. The highest score in this group was _____ achieved by person number _____. Next was person number _____ who scored _____. Person _____ scored _____, and person _____ scored _____.

Now we are ready for the second part of the experiment. We have found that people who do well on the first part of the experiment also do well on the second part although the task in the second test is somewhat different than that in the first.

For the second test, the task involves the discrimination of lengths of lines. A slide will appear on the screen, on one side will be a single line; on the other will be three lines differing in length. Each of the three lines will have a letter beneath it to identify it. One of the three lines will be exactly equal to the single line on the other card — you will decide in each case which is the equal line. You will state your judgment in terms of the letter identifying the line. The slide will remain on the screen while all of you announce your judgments.

As the number of comparisons is few and the group small, I will call upon each of you in turn to announce your judgments. Please be as accurate as possible. Suppose you give me your estimates in order starting at the left. Are there any questions?

172

Kemeny-Snell Estimation Procedure for the Conflict Model

The method of estimation proposed by Kemeny and Snell for the Conflict Model (i.e., the 4-state 4-parameter model) utilizes mathematical results for finite absorbing Markov chains. Such a chain is a model for describing a phenomenon that changes through time according to some probability law. Any model for describing events through time or space as governed by probability laws is known as a stochastic process. The phenomenon being described by the Markov chain is considered to be events which move in a sequence of steps through a set of states. The word finite indicates that there is a finite number, say r, of states. These states may be denoted by s_1, s_2, s_3, ..., s_r. When an event is in a state s_j, there is a probability, p_{jk}, that the next position will be state s_k. Such a Markov chain is completely specified when the values for P and the starting state(s) are given. The Conflict Model is a finite absorbing Markov chain.

To present the mathematical results, it is convenient to put the transition matrix in canonical form by listing the absorbing states first. Then we partition the transition matrix as follows:

$$P = \begin{array}{c} \\ \text{absorbing} \\ \text{nonabsorbing} \end{array} \begin{array}{cc} \text{absorbing} & \text{nonabsorbing} \\ \left(\begin{array}{c|c} I & O \\ \hline R & Q \end{array} \right) \end{array} \tag{B.1}$$

The matrix, $P = (p_{jk})$, called the transition matrix, contains as elements all the possible probabilities p_{jk} for describing the movement from s_j to s_k. The rows of P represent the state on the jth trial while the columns represent the state on the kth trial. The matrix P is square; that is, it has the same number of rows as it has columns. In fact, the number of rows, and hence the number of columns, equals the number of states in the chain. As each element of P is the value of a probability, each element must be non-negative. Each row of the matrix has the sum of 1. Because we listed the absorbing states first and we partitioned the matrix as we did, the resulting four components, I, O, R, and Q, will, in general, be matrices. Further, these matrices will have special features. I will be the identity matrix; that is, it will have 1's on the main diagonal and 0's elsewhere. This represents the fact that once you enter an absorbing state you remain there. 0 is a matrix of zeroes. This represents the fact that when you are in an absorbing state you cannot enter a nonabsorbing state. The elements of R and Q are non-negative; but the sum of the rows in either one is not, in general, identically 1.

The most basic result of the theory of such chains is that the process is sure to reach an absorbing state. However, additional results will be used to obtain the estimates. These may be presented by introducing two matrices, N and B. Let $N = (I - Q)^{-1}$. Then let the matrix N be called the *fundamental matrix* of the chain. Let $B = NR$. Let n_{jk} be the jk^{th} entry of N. Let b_{jm} be the jm^{th} entry of B. If s_j and s_k represent nonabsorbing states and s_m an absorbing state, then n_{jk} gives the mean number of times the process is in state s_k, when the chain is started in s_j, and b_{jm} gives the probability that the process is absorbed into the absorbing state s_m, given that the process started in the nonabsorbing state s_j (Kemeny, 1960, Theorems 3.2.4 and 3.3.7).

Let us introduce some preliminary definitions. The *terminal response* is the response made on the last trial of a response sequence. The *final segment* of a response sequence consists of all consecutive trials, ending at the terminal response, on which the response of the subject was the same as his terminal response and which occurred after the last alternation. That portion of the response sequences from the first trial up to the last alternation is the *initial segment* of the response sequence.

Figure B.1 presents an example of a response sequence indicating the initial segment and final segment. The entire row of 1's and 0's in Figure B.1 represents the sequence of responses made by a single subject on all critical trials of an Asch experiment. If the subject gave the correct response (thereby demonstrating "inde-

174

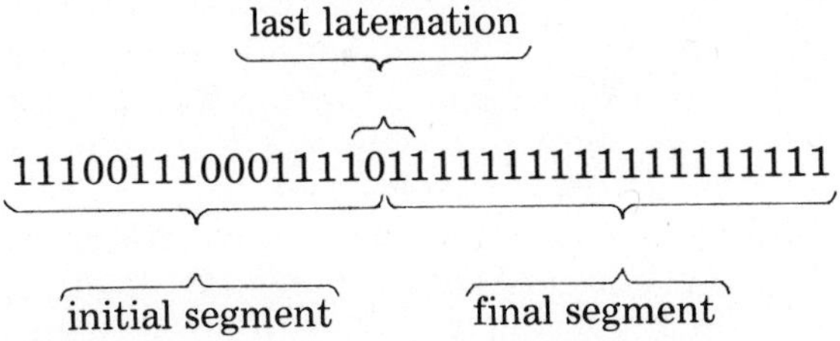

last laternation

111001110001111011111111111111111111

initial segment   final segment

Figure B.1. An example of a response sequence for one Asch subject. (Note: A"1" indicates a non-conforming response and a"0" indicates a conforming response.)

pendence" of influence atttempts) a code of 1 was assigned for that trial. If the subject gave either of the two incorrect responses (thereby manifesting "conformity" to the influence attemps of the other members of the group) a code of 0 was assigned for that trial. Thus, we may speak of a 1-response as representing non-conformity and a 0-response as representing conformity. In Figure B.1, Column 1 contains the coded response on Trial 1, Column 2 contains the coded response on Trial 2, and so on. Some Asch situation subjects gave sequences consisting entirely of 1-responses. Hence, these sequences had only a final segment.

Let i_{10} be the number of transitions from a 1-response to a 0-response and i_{01} be the number of transitions from a 0-response to a 1-response. The number of transitions from 1 to 1 in the initial segment will be i_{11} while the number of transitions from 0 to 0 in the initial segment will be i_{00}. As the Conflict Model hypothesizes, there is a Trial 0 on which all subjects are in State 2. Consequently, a 1-response should be considered to be prefixed to the initial segment. For a thus modified version of the example given in Figure B.1, we would have $i_{11} = 8$, $i_{10} = 3$, $i_{01} = 3$, $i_{00} = 3$. If i_1 is the total number of times a 1-response is made in the initial segment, and i_0 the total number of times a 0-response is made in the initial segment, then we have:

$$i_1 = i_{11} + i_{10}$$

$$i_0 = i_{01} + i_{00} \tag{B.2}$$

and the length of the initial segment = $i_1 + i_0$ \qquad (B.3)

Observe that if $i_{10} = i_{01}$ then the terminal response must be a

175

1-response, while if $i_{10} = i_{01} + 1$ the terminal response is a 0-response.

We will now extend the meaning of the notation we have introduced by considering it to be computed from the data on all of the subjects in the experiment, rather than upon the response sequence of a single subject. When we interpret the notation as applying to all subjects, we would have i_{11} represent the total number of transitions from a 1-response to a 1-response in the initial segments of all subjects. (Each initial segment is first modified by prefixing a 1-response.) In addition to an obvious extension of i_{10}, i_{01}, i_{00} to the entire set of subjects, we have to introduce the following: i_1, the total number of 1-responses in the initial segments of all subjects; i_0, the total number of 0-responses in the initial segments of all subjects; n, the number of subjects in the data set; t_1, the number of terminal 1-responses counted over all subjects; t_0, the number terminal 0-responses counted over all subjects. The terminal response is that single response given by a subject on the last trial of the experiment.

For Cohen's Experiment 1 (the moderate condition), it was found that

$$i_{11} = 196, i_{10} = 117, i_{01} = 106, i_{00} = 102,$$

$$i_1 = 313, i_0 = 208, t_1 = 22, t_0 = 11, \qquad (B.4)$$

$$n = 33$$

Implicit in the remaining mathematical development is the assumption that all subjects are absorbed within the number of trials for which the experiment was conducted. The transition matrix for the Cohen 4-state 4-parameter model (2.1) may be rewritten in the Kemeny-Snell notation as:

$$P = \begin{array}{c} \\ 1 \\ 2 \\ 3 \\ 4 \end{array} \begin{array}{cccc} 1 & 2 & 3 & 4 \\ \left(\begin{array}{cccc} 1 & 0 & 0 & 0 \\ p_{21} & p_{22} & p_{23} & 0 \\ 0 & p_{32} & p_{33} & p_{34} \\ 0 & 0 & 0 & 1 \end{array} \right) \end{array} \qquad (B.5)$$

Following the Kemeny-Snell treatment, this may be rewritten in canonical form by listing the absorbing states first:

$$P = \left(\begin{array}{c|c} I & O \\ \hline R & Q \end{array}\right) = \begin{array}{c} \\ 1 \\ 4 \\ 2 \\ 3 \end{array}\begin{array}{cc} \begin{array}{cccc} 1 & 4 & 2 & 3 \end{array} \\ \left(\begin{array}{cc|cc} 1 & 0 & 0 & 0 \\ 0 & 1 & 0 & 0 \\ \hline p_{21} & 0 & p_{22} & p_{23} \\ 0 & p_{34} & p_{32} & p_{33} \end{array}\right) \end{array} \qquad (B.6)$$

For this transition matrix, the fundamental matrix is:

$$N = (I - Q)^{-1} = \begin{pmatrix} 1 - p_{22} & -p_{23} \\ -p_{32} & 1 - p_{33} \end{pmatrix}^{-1} \qquad (B.7)$$

Let $\Delta = (1 - p_{22})(1 - p_{33}) - p_{23}p_{32}$ and invert N to obtain

$$N = \begin{array}{c} \\ 2 \\ 3 \end{array}\begin{array}{c} \begin{array}{cc} 2 & \quad\quad 3 \end{array} \\ \begin{pmatrix} \dfrac{1 - p_{33}}{\Delta} & \dfrac{p_{23}}{\Delta} \\ \\ \dfrac{p_{32}}{\Delta} & \dfrac{1 - p_{22}}{\Delta} \end{pmatrix} \end{array} \qquad (B.8)$$

From Markov chain theory it is known that the matrix of absorption probabilities, denoted here by B, is given by the matrix product NR; or, in equation form,

$$B = NR \qquad (B.9)$$

For the particular chain we are considering,

$$B = \begin{array}{c} \\ 2 \\ 3 \end{array}\begin{array}{c} \begin{array}{cc} 1 & \quad\quad\quad 4 \end{array} \\ \begin{pmatrix} \dfrac{p_{21}(1 - p_{33})}{\Delta} & \dfrac{p_{23}p_{34}}{\Delta} \\ \\ \dfrac{p_{32}p_{21}}{\Delta} & \dfrac{p_{34}(1 - p_{22})}{\Delta} \end{pmatrix} \end{array} \qquad (B.10)$$

The elements of B may be represented as follows:

$$B = \begin{array}{c} \\ 2 \\ 3 \end{array} \begin{array}{cc} 1 & 4 \\ \left(\begin{array}{cc} b_{21} & b_{24} \\ b_{31} & b_{34} \end{array}\right) \end{array} \qquad (B.11)$$

If we start in State 2, then the probability of absorption into State 4 (and hence, the probability of the subject's eventually giving conforming or 0-responses) is

$$b_{24} = \frac{p_{23} p_{34}}{\Delta} \qquad (B.12)$$

Also, if we start in State 2, then the probability of absorption into State 1 (and hence, the probability of the subject's eventually giving all 1-responses) is b_{21}, which is given by

$$b_{21} = 1 - b_{24} \qquad (B.13)$$

Since all subjects must be absorbed, we know that the rows of B must sum to 1.0.

The Cohen 4-state 4-parameter model (the Conflict Model) assumes that all subjects start in State 2. Consequently, the mean of the number of times that the subject is in State 3, given that he started in State 2, is n_{23}. As all subjects start in State 2, n_{23} unconditionally gives the mean of the number of times that the subject is in State 3. This mean is over the entire response sequence; that is, it is the mean over initial and final segments taken as a whole.

If we let f_{23} be the expected value of the number of times the subject is in State 3 in the final segment, then the expected number of 0-responses per subject in the initial segments, $E(i_0/n)$, may be obtained by subtraction; thus,

$$E(i_0/n) = n_{23} - f_{23} \qquad (B.14)$$

Notice that we cannot observe the number of times the subject is in State 3 in the final segment (except, of course, when that number is zero) because we do not know when the subject enters State 4.

Next, we will obtain an expression for the probability that there

178

are exactly m occurrences of State 3 in the final segment. Let q_m represent this probability. Obviously, we will have to resort to an indirect attack on the problem, as we do not know when the subject enters State 4. At this point we begin to appreciate the power and elegance of the analytical method developed by Kemeny and Snell to estimate the parameters of the model. If the terminal state is 1, then there will be no occurrence of State 3 in the final segment. Consequently, $q_0 = b_{21}$, which says that the probability of exactly zero occurrences of State 3 is given by b_{21}, the probability for absorption into State 1, given that the process started in State 2.

If we knew q_1, the probability that there is exactly one occurrence of State 3 in the final segment, then we could write

$$q_2 = p_{33} q_1$$
$$q_3 = p_{33} q_2$$
$$q_4 = p_{33} q_3$$
$$\cdots$$

(B.15)

These recursive equations can be written as

$$q_{m+1} = p_{33} q_m \text{ for } m > 0$$

(B.16)

This equation may also be written as

$$q_{m+1} = p_{33}^m q_1$$

(B.17)

or, in another form, as

$$q_m = p_{33}^{m-1} q_1$$

(B.18)

As the values of m from zero to infinity represent the total outcome space, we may invoke the fundamental axiom of probability theory that the sum of the probabilities of each outcome, summed over the entire outcome space, is identically 1; we can then write

$$\sum_{m=0}^{\infty} q_m = 1$$

(B.19)

By expanding a few terms of the sum as follows:

$$\sum_{m=0}^{\infty} q_m = q_0 + q_1 + q_2 + q_3 + \cdots$$

(B.20)

179

and rewriting terms with values of m greater than 1 as terms involving q_1 we obtain

$$\sum_{m=0}^{\infty} q_m = q_0 + q_1 + q_1 p_{33} + q_1 p_{33}^2 + \ldots \qquad \text{(B.21)}$$

By factoring q_1 from the sum, we obtain

$$\sum_{m=0}^{\infty} q_m = q_0 + q_1 (1 + p_{33} + p_{33}^2 + p_{33}^3 + \ldots) \qquad \text{(B.22)}$$

The portion within parentheses may be recognized as a geometric series whose sum is known to be

$$\frac{1}{1 - p_{33}}$$

Therefore, the sum may be rewritten as

$$\sum_{m=0}^{\infty} q_m = q_0 + q_1 \left(\frac{1}{1 - p_{33}} \right) \qquad \text{(B.23)}$$

Recalling that $q_0 = b_{21}$, we have

$$\sum_{m=0}^{\infty} q_m = b_{21} + \frac{q_1}{1 - p_{33}} \qquad \text{(B.24)}$$

Recalling the previous argument that $\sum_{m=0}^{\infty} q_m = 1$, we may write

$$b_{21} + \frac{q_1}{1 - p_{33}} = 1 \qquad \text{(B.25)}$$

which would produce

$$q_1 = (1 - b_{21})(1 - p_{33}) \qquad \text{(B.26)}$$

180

when solved for q_1. Again, by recalling a previous result, that $b_{21} = 1 - b_{24}$, and substituting, we obtain

$$q_1 = (1 - p_{33}) b_{24} \tag{B.27}$$

This expression for q_1 may be substituted into a previously stated form of the recursion,

$$q_m = p_{33}^{m-1} q_1$$

to obtain

$$q_m = p_{33}^{m-1} (1 - p_{33}) b_{24} \tag{B.28}$$

Now that we have an expression for q_m, we may obtain an expression for the mean number of times the subject was in State 3 in the final segment. This had been denoted by f_{23}. This quantity cannot be estimated directly because a direct estimation method would require knowledge of when the subject moved into State 4. By employing the definition of the expected value of a discrete random variable as the product of that variable times the probability that the variable takes on that value, summed over all possible values, we may write

$$f_{23} = \sum_{m=1}^{\infty} m \, p_{33}^{m-1} (1 - p_{33}) b_{24} \tag{B.29}$$

Recall, in the general result for series of the type

$$\sum_{m=0}^{\infty} m \, p^{m-1}$$

that the sum is given by $1/(1 - p)^2$.

Thus, after substitution and simplification, we may write

$$f_{23} = \frac{b_{24}}{1 - p_{33}} \tag{B.30}$$

Using the previously developed expression for b_{24}, ($b_{24} =$

$p_{23}p_{34}/\Delta$), we may write

$$f_{23} = \frac{p_{23}p_{34}}{\Delta(1 - p_{33})} \qquad (B.31)$$

By the substitution of this expression into that previously stated for the expected number of 0-responses in the initial segment,

$$\left[E\left(\frac{i_0}{n}\right) = n_{23} - f_{23} \right],$$

$$E\left(\frac{i_0}{n}\right) = n_{23} - \frac{p_{23}p_{34}}{\Delta(1 - p_{33})} \qquad (B.32)$$

This expression for $E(i_0/n)$ invites the substitution of p_{23}/Δ from the matrix, N, for n_{23}, which produces

$$E\left(\frac{i_0}{n}\right) = \frac{p_{23}}{\Delta} - \frac{p_{23}p_{34}}{\Delta(1 - p_{33})} \qquad (B.33)$$

This may be simplified as follows:

$$E\left(\frac{i_0}{n}\right) = \frac{p_{23}(1 - p_{33}) - p_{23}p_{34}}{\Delta(1 - p_{33})} \qquad (B.34)$$

$$E\left(\frac{i_0}{n}\right) = \frac{p_{23} - p_{23}p_{33} - p_{23}p_{34}}{\Delta(1 - p_{33})} \qquad (B.35)$$

$$E\left(\frac{i_0}{n}\right) = \frac{p_{23}(1 - p_{33} - p_{34})}{\Delta(1 - p_{33})} \qquad (B.36)$$

$$E\left(\frac{i_0}{n}\right) = \frac{p_{23}p_{32}}{\Delta(1 - p_{33})} \qquad (B.37)$$

by recognizing that $p_{32} + p_{33} + p_{34} = 1$ from the original transition matrix, P.

Finally, we have produced the first of four independent equations required to estimate the four parameters of the model. We may obtain the second independent equation by writing

$$E\left(\frac{i_1}{n}\right) = n_{22} - f_{22}$$

182

Then we apply the same reasoning as was just used to obtain

$$E\left(\frac{i_1}{n}\right) = \frac{p_{23}(1 - p_{33})}{\Delta(1 - p_{22})} \tag{B.38}$$

The third equation may be obtained from the matrix B as

$$E\left(\frac{t_0}{n}\right) = b_{24} = \frac{p_{23}p_{34}}{\Delta} \tag{B.39}$$

At a first glance, one might want to consider

$$E\left(\frac{t_1}{n}\right) = b_{21} \tag{B.40}$$

as a fourth independent equation. Unfortunately, this cannot be done because the equation is not independent of the others. That $E(t_1/n) = b_{21}$ follows from $E(t_0/n) = b_{24}$ and from $t_1 = n - t_0$, since $b_{21} + b_{24} = 1$. (The Conflict Model assumes that all subjects start in State 2. Given that a subject starts in State 2, he must be absorbed into State 1 or State 4. Hence, $b_{21} + b_{24} = 1$.)

To obtain a fourth equation independent of the previously developed equations, let us modify the original Markov chain. We shall assume that the chain is observed only when a change of state takes place. Consequently , in the modified chain, we count as a transition only a step from one state to a different state. This will produce another absorbing Markov chain, whose transition matrix will be denoted by $\hat{P}$. $\hat{P}$ may be obtained from P as follows:

$$p_{21} + p_{22} + p_{23} = 1$$
$$p_{21} + p_{23} = 1 - p_{22}$$

$$\frac{p_{21}}{1 - p_{22}} + \frac{p_{23}}{1 - p_{22}} = 1$$

and similarly for the third row of $\hat{P}$. This will produce the transition matrix

$$
\hat{P} =
\begin{array}{c}
 \\
1 \\
2 \\
3 \\
4
\end{array}
\begin{pmatrix}
\overset{1}{1} & \overset{2}{0} & \overset{3}{0} & \overset{4}{0} \\
\dfrac{p_{21}}{1 - p_{22}} & 0 & \dfrac{p_{23}}{1 - p_{22}} & 0 \\
0 & \dfrac{p_{32}}{1 - p_{33}} & 0 & \dfrac{p_{34}}{1 - p_{33}} \\
0 & 0 & 0 & 1
\end{pmatrix}
\tag{B.41}
$$

The fundamental matrix of this process, denoted by $\hat{N}$, is

$$
\hat{N} =
\begin{array}{c}
 \\
2 \\
\\
3
\end{array}
\begin{pmatrix}
\overset{2}{\dfrac{(1 - p_{22})(1 - p_{33})}{\Delta}} & \overset{3}{\dfrac{p_{23}(1 - p_{33})}{\Delta}} \\
\dfrac{p_{32}(1 - p_{22})}{\Delta} & \dfrac{(1 - p_{22})(1 - p_{33})}{\Delta}
\end{pmatrix}
\tag{B.42}
$$

For the modified process, $\hat{n}_{23}$ gives the expected value of the number of changes from State 2 to State 3. However, as a change from State 2 directly to State 4 is impossible, the expected value of the number of changes from State 2 to State 3 is the same as the expected value of the number of changes from a 1-response to a 0-response. Moreover, as a change from a 1-response to a 0-response is necessarily in the initial segment, the expected value of each of these two quantities is the same as the expected value of the number of such changes in the initial segment. Consequently, we may write

$$
E\left(\frac{i_{10}}{n}\right) = \hat{n}_{23} = \frac{p_{23}(1 - p_{33})}{\Delta}
\tag{B.43}
$$

At this point we now have four independent equations which will lead to the estimates of the transition probabilities. In the order in which they were developed, the four equations are repeated here:

$$
E\left(\frac{i_0}{n}\right) = \frac{p_{23}p_{32}}{\Delta(1 - p_{33})}
$$

$$
E\left(\frac{i_1}{n}\right) = \frac{p_{23}(1 - p_{33})}{\Delta(1 - p_{22})}
$$

184

$$E\left(\frac{t_0}{n}\right) = \frac{p_{23}p_{34}}{\Delta}$$

$$E\left(\frac{i_{10}}{n}\right) = \frac{p_{23}(1 - p_{33})}{\Delta}$$

Before we explicitly exhibit the theoretical expressions for the elements of P, we shall obtain the remaining expected values.

Using the previous results that

(a) $i_1 = i_{11} + i_{10}$

(b) $E\left(\frac{i_1}{n}\right) = \frac{p_{23}(1 - p_{33})}{\Delta(1 - p_{22})}$

(c) $E\left(\frac{i_{10}}{n}\right) = \frac{p_{23}(1 - p_{33})}{\Delta}$

we may obtain an expression for $E(i_{11}/n)$ as follows:

$$E\left(\frac{i_1}{n}\right) = E\left(\frac{i_{11}}{n}\right) + E\left(\frac{i_{10}}{n}\right)$$

$$E\left(\frac{i_{11}}{n}\right) = E\left(\frac{i_1}{n}\right) - E\left(\frac{i_{10}}{n}\right)$$

$$E\left(\frac{i_{11}}{n}\right) = \frac{p_{23}(1 - p_{33})}{\Delta(1 - p_{22})} - \frac{p_{23}(1 - p_{33})}{\Delta}$$

$$E\left(\frac{i_{11}}{n}\right) = \frac{p_{22}p_{23}(1 - p_{33})}{\Delta(1 - p_{22})} \tag{B.44}$$

In a similar manner, we may obtain $E(i_0/n)$. Using the previous results that

(a) $t_0 = i_{10} - i_{01}$

(b) $E\left(\frac{t_0}{n}\right) = \frac{p_{23}p_{34}}{\Delta}$

(c) $E\left(\frac{i_{10}}{n}\right) = \frac{p_{23}(1 - p_{33})}{\Delta}$

we proceed as follows:

$$E\left(\frac{t_0}{n}\right) = E\left(\frac{i_{10}}{n}\right) - E\left(\frac{i_{01}}{n}\right)$$

$$E\left(\frac{i_{01}}{n}\right) = E\left(\frac{i_{10}}{n}\right) - E\left(\frac{t_0}{n}\right)$$

$$E\left(\frac{i_{01}}{n}\right) = \frac{p_{23}(1 - p_{33})}{\Delta} - \frac{p_{23}p_{34}}{\Delta}$$

$$E\left(\frac{i_{01}}{n}\right) = \frac{p_{23}(1 - p_{33} - p_{34})}{\Delta}$$

$$E\left(\frac{i_{01}}{n}\right) = \frac{p_{23}p_{32}}{\Delta} \tag{B.45}$$

Finally, by using $i_0 = i_{01} + i_{00}$ to write

$$E\left(\frac{i_{00}}{n}\right) = E\left(\frac{i_0}{n}\right) - E\left(\frac{i_{01}}{n}\right)$$

and the previously obtained expressions for each term on the right-hand side of that equality, we obtain

$$E\left(\frac{i_{00}}{n}\right) = \frac{p_{23}p_{32}p_{33}}{\Delta(1 - p_{33})} \tag{B.46}$$

The four expectations, $E(i_{10}/n)$, $E(i_{00}/n)$, $E(i_{01}/n)$ and $E(i_{11}/n)$, may be shown to determine the transition probabilities contained in P. Recall that the sum of any row of P is identically 1. Then it may be shown that

$$p_{21} = \frac{\left[E\left(\frac{i_{10}}{n}\right)\right]\left[1 - E\left(\frac{i_{10}}{n}\right) + E\left(\frac{i_{01}}{n}\right)\right]}{\left[E\left(\frac{i_{11}}{n}\right) + E\left(\frac{i_{10}}{n}\right)\right]\left[1 + E\left(\frac{i_{01}}{n}\right)\right]} \tag{B.47}$$

$$p_{22} = \frac{E\left(\frac{i_{11}}{n}\right)}{E\left(\frac{i_{11}}{n}\right) + E\left(\frac{i_{10}}{n}\right)} \tag{B.48}$$

186

$$p_{23} = \frac{\left[E\left(\frac{i_{10}}{n}\right)\right]^2}{\left[E\left(\frac{i_{11}}{n}\right) + E\left(\frac{i_{10}}{n}\right)\right]\left[1 + E\left(\frac{i_{01}}{n}\right)\right]} \tag{B.49}$$

$$p_{32} = \frac{\left[E\left(\frac{i_{01}}{n}\right)\right]^2}{\left[E\left(\frac{i_{10}}{n}\right)\right]\left[E\left(\frac{i_{01}}{n}\right) + E\left(\frac{i_{00}}{n}\right)\right]} \tag{B.50}$$

$$p_{33} = \frac{E\left(\frac{i_{00}}{n}\right)}{E\left(\frac{i_{01}}{n}\right) + E\left(\frac{i_{00}}{n}\right)} \tag{B.51}$$

$$p_{34} = \frac{\left[E\left(\frac{i_{01}}{n}\right)\right]\left[E\left(\frac{i_{10}}{n}\right) - E\left(\frac{i_{01}}{n}\right)\right]}{\left[E\left(\frac{i_{10}}{n}\right)\right]\left[E\left(\frac{i_{01}}{n}\right) + E\left(\frac{i_{00}}{n}\right)\right]} \tag{B.52}$$

By appeal to the Law of Large Numbers, we obtain numerical estimates for the transition matrix by equating the expected value to the observed average values. From the data and the definitions of the expected values, we would write

$$E\left(\frac{i_{11}}{n}\right) = \frac{196}{33} \tag{B.53}$$

$$E\left(\frac{i_{10}}{n}\right) = \frac{117}{33} \tag{B.54}$$

$$E\left(\frac{i_{01}}{n}\right) = \frac{106}{33} \tag{B.55}$$

$$E\left(\frac{i_{00}}{n}\right) = \frac{102}{33} \tag{B.56}$$

We then would compute the estimates for the elements of the transition matrix to obtain

$$P = \begin{pmatrix} 1 & 0 & 0 & 0 \\ 0.06 & 0.63 & 0.31 & 0 \\ 0 & 0.46 & 0.49 & 0.05 \\ 0 & 0 & 0 & 1 \end{pmatrix}$$ (B.57)

At this point we have estimated the values of the transition matrix from the observed data.

When Kemeny and Snell used these estimates to predict other observed quantities not employed in the estimation of the model parameters, they rejected the hypothesis that the model was satisfactory. They pointed out that the basic deficiency is that the Conflict Model seriously underestimates the number of subjects who never make a 0-response. Kemeny and Snell then make the *ad hoc* assumption that 7 of the subjects are not described by the Conflict Model. (The response sequence of anyone of these subjects that the model fails to fit consists entirely of 1-responses.)

If a subject makes only 1-responses, his entire sequence consists only of a final segment. But the values of i_{11}, i_{10}, i_{01} and i_{00} remain the same for the remaining subjects, but the n is reduced to 26. This produces the modified expectations

$$E\left(\frac{i_{11}}{n}\right) = \frac{196}{26}$$ (B.58)

$$E\left(\frac{i_{10}}{n}\right) = \frac{117}{26}$$ (B.59)

$$E\left(\frac{i_{01}}{n}\right) = \frac{106}{26}$$ (B.60)

$$E\left(\frac{i_{00}}{n}\right) = \frac{102}{26}$$ (B.61)

which in turn produce the modified transition matrix, denoted by P', with values given by

$$P' = \begin{pmatrix} 1 & 0 & 0 & 0 \\ 0.04 & 0.63 & 0.33 & 0.0 \\ 0 & 0.46 & 0.49 & 0.05 \\ 0 & 0 & 0 & 1 \end{pmatrix}$$ (B.62)

When Kemeny and Snell tested this revised model, they concluded that it was in reasonable agreement with the observations.

The Kemeny-Snell method for parameter estimation is an elegant application of statistical theory to solve an exceedingly vexing problem. The problem existed because unobservable transitions took place. This fact prevented our obtaining observable quantities which could be equated to the transition probabilities. The very long development of the Kemeny-Snell estimates is an indirect attack on the problem of unobserved transitions. Their estimation procedure is one illustration of the power of formal analysis.

APPENDIX C

The Data

```
BPC E1    36 TRIALS   33 SUBJECTS
```

```
111111111111111111011111111111111111    B  P  COHEN    MODERATE  CONDITION    S202
100001000000000000001000000000000000    B  P  COHEN    MODERATE  CONDITION    S203
111100111000111011111111111111111111    B  P  COHEN    MODERATE  CONDITION    S205
110010000100000000010000000000000000    B  P  COHEN    MODERATE  CONDITION    S206
111111111111111111111111111111111111    B  P  COHEN    MODERATE  CONDITION    S207
110111010000000000000000000000000000    B  P  COHEN    MODERATE  CONDITION    S208
111111111111111111111111111111111111    B  P  COHEN    MODERATE  CONDITION    S209
100100000000000010000000000000000000    B  P  COHEN    MODERATE  CONDITION    S210
111111111111111101111111111111111111    B  P  COHEN    MODERATE  CONDITION    S211
111111101110111111111111111111111111    B  P  COHEN    MODERATE  CONDITION    S212
111101111111111111111111111111111111    B  P  COHEN    MODERATE  CONDITION    S213
101101011010101111010900010101110100    B  P  COHEN    MODERATE  CONDITION    S214
111111111101111111111011111111111111    B  P  COHEN    MODERATE  CONDITION    S215
111111111111111111111111111111111111    B  P  COHEN    MODERATE  CONDITION    S216
110101101111001100000011010000000000    B  P  COHEN    MODERATE  CONDITION    S217
110011011111010001101101130011110111    B  P  COHEN    MODERATE  CONDITION    S219
101101101110101110101111110101111011    B  P  COHEN    MODERATE  CONDITION    S220
111111100000111000100000000000000000    B  P  COHEN    MODERATE  CONDITION    S221
111111101111011011111111111111111111    B  P  COHEN    MODERATE  CONDITION    S222
101111001010001011110000011010111111    B  P  COHEN    MODERATE  CONDITION    S223
111111111111111111111111111111111111    B  P  COHEN    MODERATE  CONDITION    S224
111111111111111111111111111111111111    B  P  COHEN    MODERATE  CONDITION    S225
111101010100011000010010001000001000    B  P  COHEN    MODERATE  CONDITION    S226
111110011011011001110110001010000000    B  P  COHEN    MODERATE  CONDITION    S227
111111111111111111111111111111111111    B  P  COHEN    MODERATE  CONDITION    S228
101111010111011101011100010001111000    B  P  COHEN    MODERATE  CONDITION    S229
110000000000000000000000000000000000    B  P  COHEN    MODERATE  CONDITION    S230
111111111111111111111111111111111111    B  P  COHEN    MODERATE  CONDITION    S231
111111111111111111111111111111111111    B  P  COHEN    MODERATE  CONDITION    S232
101011100111100010110000010101100001    B  P  COHEN    MODERATE  CONDITION    S233
111111111111111111111111111111111111    B  P  COHEN    MODERATE  CONDITION    S234
111111111111111111111111111111111111    B  P  COHEN    MODERATE  CONDITION    S235
110011001110111010111101111111110111    B  P  COHEN    MODERATE  CONDITION    S236
```

```
100000010000000000000101010000000000   B P COHEN  EXTREME CONDITION    S301
111111111111111011001000101111111111   3 P COHEN  EXTREME CONDITION    S302
111001100011111111111111111111110111   B P COHEN  EXTREME CONDITION    S303
111111011101111111111111110111111111   B P COHEN  EXTREME CONDITION    S304
111111111111111111111111111111111111   3 P COHEN  EXTREME CONDITION    S305
101101110110100011011111111111111111   B P COHEN  EXTREME CONDITION    S306
111011111111111111111111111111111111   B P COHEN  EXTREME CONDITION    S307
001100101111011011111111111111111111   9 F COHEN  EXTREME CONDITION    S308
111111111111111111111111111111111111   B P COHEN  EXTREME CONDITION    S309
100101111111111111111111111111111111   B P COHEN  EXTREME CONDITION    S310
101100000010000101000011001001 10111   B F COHEN  EXTREME CONDITION    S311
111111111111111111111111111111111111   B P COHEN  EXTREME CONDITION    S312
101100111111101111111111111111111111   B F COHEN  EXTREME CONDITION    S313
110110111111111111111111111110111111   B F COHEN  EXTREME CONDITION    S314
111111111111111111111111111111111111   B P COHEN  EXTREME CONDITION    S315
111011001010111001111111111011111111   3 P COHEN  EXTREME CONDITION    S316
101000001010101000000000000000000000   B F COHEN  EXTREME CONDITION    S317
101000000000000000000000000000000000   B P COHEN  EXTREME CONDITION    S318
111111111111111011111101111111111111   3 P COHEN  EXTREME CONDITION    S320
111111111111111111111110111111111111   B P COHEN  EXTREME CONDITION    S321
100000000001000000000001000000000110   B P COHEN  EXTREME CONDITION    S323
111111111111111111111111111111111111   B P COHEN  EXTREME CONDITION    S324
111111111111111111110111111111111111   B F COHEN  EXTREME CONDITION    S325
111111111111111111111111111111111111   B P COHEN  EXTREME CONDITION    S326
001111001111111111111111111111111111   B P COHEN  EXTREME CONDITION    S327
111110111111111111111111111111111111   B P COHEN  EXTREME CONDITION    S328
001111111111111111111111111111111111   B P COHEN  EXTREME CONDITION    S330
```

```
11111110111111111111111111111111111111111111111111111111111111111111111111111111
11001011011101111111111111111111111111111111111111111111111111111111111111111111
11111110101101101100110111101111011110101101101111111110011101011111011110101011010
11111111111111111111111011010111111111111111100111111111111111111111111101111111111
11011110100010110110111101111011100011110111111111111111111101111111111111011111111
110000000000000000000000000000010010000000000000000000000000000000000000000000000
11111110110110110110111101111111000111110110111111111111111011111111111111110111111
110100110000110010101011101011100111111111111111111111111111111111111111111111111111
110100111111111111111111111011111111111111111111101111111111111111111111111111111111
11010100001100101110100111110000101010110110101111011101010001111111011111111111011
1111111111111111111111111111111111111111111111111111111111111111111111111111111111
1100000000000000100000000000000000000000000000000000000000000000000000000000000000
00000000300000000000000000000000000000000000000000000000000000000000000000000000
1100110000000000031000011001010000000000000000000000000000000010010000000000000000
11011110100010101010000000000000110001000001000000001000100000000001000000000000010
1011110100010101010030000000011001100000001011011010101011001010110110110110110111111
11110010000110010011000000011001100000000010110101010101101011011111111111111111111
11111111111111111111111111111111111111111111110110111011101011111111111111111111
10001010000101011001111111111111111111111111101111110111111111111111111111111111
11111111111111111111111111111111111111111111111111111111111111111111111111111111
11011111111111101101101111111111111111111111111111111111111111111011111111111111
11111111111111111111111111111111111111111111111111111111111111111111111111111111
11111111111111111111111111111111111111111111111111111111111111111111111111111111
11111110100110110111111111111111111111111111111111111111110111111111111111111101
10011101111111111111111111111111110111111111111111111111111111111111111111111111
11111111111111111111111111111111111111111111111111111111111111111111111111111111
11010111111111111111111111111111111111111111111111111111111111111111111111111111
11111111111111111111111111111111111111111111111111111111111111111100111111111111
11010110111111111111111111111111101111111111111111111111111111111111111111111111
1310000000000000000000000000003000000000000000000000000000000000000000000000000000
11111111111111111111111111111111111111111111111111111111111111111111111111111111
11001000000000000000000003000000000000000000000000000000000000000000000000000000
000000000000000000000000000000000000000000000000000000000000000000000000000000000
11111111111111111111111111111111111111111111111111111111111111111111111111111111
11111110110110110101011011111100100111011111111111111111011111111111111111111111
1000100000000000000000000000000000000000000000000000000000000000000000000000000000
11111110011111111111111111111110111111111111111111111011111111111011011111
10010010000110010111101111111111110111111111111111111111111111111111111111111111
11011111111111111111111111111111111111111111111111111111111111111111111111111111
10110111000110010101010011110100100101011010101110100010100101101101101 0111011
11011011000110010011011111101111011011111111011011111111011111011101101101111111
0100010000110000010000001000001010000000010101101000001100100000001001000000010001000
00000000000000000000000000000000000000000000011111111111111111111111111111111111
11110111111111111111111111111111111111111111111111111111111111111111111111111111
11111111111111001011100111110003001010111111111110110101111111011111011011011
11111101110111100100101111111111011101010100100110011011111011011111111111111111
1000001000000000000000000000000000000000000000000000000000000000000000000000000
11010100000110000000000011110000010001001011111110011111111111111111111111101111
11111111111111111111111111111111111111111111111111111111111111111111111111111111
11111111111111111111111111111111111111111111111111111111111111111111111111111111
```

191

```
111110011111111111111011111111110001010100101111011010101000101  *  EXP.  11  BPC   HH01
110011010101010101111011100101100011001010010101100111101101     *  EXP.  11  BPC   HH02
111111111111111111111111111111111111111111111111111111111111     *  EXP.  11  BPC   HH03
111110010101001010101000110000000000010000000000000000001000     *  EXP.  11  BPC   HH04
111111111111011101111111111111111111011111111111111000111111     *  EXP.  11  BPC   HH05
011011111111111101101111111111101011100000000001000001111111     *  EXP.  11  BPC   HH05
010010101001001010001000100000000000010000001000000           *  EXP.  11  BPC   HH06
111111111111111111111111111111110000000010000000010000000000     *  EXP.  11  BPC   HH07
111111111111111111111111111111111100101101110110101101011110     *  EXP.  11  BPC   HH08
111111111111111111111111111111111111111111111111111111101111     *  EXP.  11  BPC   HH09
100000000000000000000000000000000000000000000000000000000000     *  EXP.  11  BPC   HH10
111111111111011111111111111111111111111111111111111111111111     *  EXP.  11  BPC   HH11
111011111111111111111111111111111111111111111111111111111111     *  EXP.  11  BPC   HH12
111111101111111111111111111111111111111111111111111111111111     *  EXP.  11  BPC   HH13
111001000100100110010101000110011101011011000100100010110     *  EXP.  11  BPC   HH14
111111111111111111111111111111111111111111111111111111111111     *  EXP.  11  BPC   HH15
111111111111111111111111111111111111111111111111111111111111     *  EXP.  11  BPC   HH16
111111111111111111111111111111111111111111111111111111111111     *  EXP.  11  BPC   HH17
111111111111111111111111111111111111111111111111111111111111     *  EXP.  11  BPC   HH18
110101101011000011101101011111011101111101111110111101101111     *  EXP.  11  BPC   HH19
111111111111111111111111111111111111111111111111110110011111     *  EXP.  11  BPC   HH20
111111111111111111111111111111111111111111111111111111111111     *  EXP.  11  BPC   HH21
101101111111111111111111111111111111111111111111111111111111     *  EXP.  11  BPC   HH22
111111111111111111111111111111111111111111111111111111111111     *  EXP.  11  BPC   HH23
010101110111101011000111011011010011000100010101011011011101     *  EXP.  11  BPC   HH24
100101001010001000010010001001000100100100010010001000001     *  EXP.  11  BPC   HH25
111111111111111111111111111111111111111111111111111111111111     *  EXP.  11  BPC   HH26
010010010010001000000010000000000000000000000000000000000000     *  EXP.  11  BPC   HH27
111101111101111111111111111111111111111111111111111111111111     *  EXP.  11  BPC   HH28
111111111111111111111111111111111111111111111111111111111111     *  EXP.  11  BPC   HH29
                                                                 *  EXP.  11  BPC   HH30
```

```
111111111111111111111011111111111011111111111111111111111111     *  EXP.  11  BPC   HL01
111101111101111111101100100000100001000000000000000000000000     *  EXP.  11  BPC   HL02
111011101010010011101101010100110111110110101011101000000100     *  EXP.  11  BPC   HL03
101110110101110111111111111111111111010111111111111111111111     *  EXP.  11  BPC   HL04
110100100110101010110100110011010001010000000100010000001000     *  EXP.  11  BPC   HL05
010101101011010010110011000010010001000100011001001000           *  EXP.  11  BPC   HL05
111111111111111111111111111111111111111111111111111111111111     *  EXP.  11  BPC   HL06
111111111111111111111111111111111111111111111111111111111111     *  EXP.  11  BPC   HL07
111111111111111111111111111111111111111111111111111111111111     *  EXP.  11  BPC   HL08
111111111111111111111111111111111111111111111111111111111111     *  EXP.  11  BPC   HL09
111111111111111111111111111111111111111111111111111111111111     *  EXP.  11  BPC   HL10
111111111111111111111111111111111111111111111111111111111111     *  EXP.  11  BPC   HL11
111111111111111111111111111111111111111111111111111111111111     *  EXP.  11  BPC   HL12
101110010110010111011111110101011011011100101101101111111111     *  EXP.  11  BPC   HL13
111111111111111111111111111111111111111111111111111111111111     *  EXP.  11  BPC   HL14
101110111101011101101101101111111010101011110110011011111     *  EXP.  11  BPC   HL15
110010001010010100101000100010000101001011010111001011100101     *  EXP.  11  BPC   HL16
110101011110111111111111111111111111111111111111111111111     *  EXP.  11  BPC   HL17
101111111111111111111111111111111111111111111111111111111111     *  EXP.  11  BPC   HL18
111100000000000000000000000100000000000000000000000000001111     *  EXP.  11  BPC   HL19
101001100000110111011011111110011111111111111111111111111     *  EXP.  11  BPC   HL20
111111111111111111111111111111111111111111111111111111111111     *  EXP.  11  BPC   HL21
011111111111111111111111141111111111111111111111111111111111     *  EXP.  11  BPC   HL22
111111111111111111111111111111111111111111111111111111111111     *  EXP.  11  BPC   HL23
110011101001110111111110100100101101101111111111111111111     *  EXP.  11  BPC   HL24
101001101011111111111111111111111111111111111111111111111111     *  EXP.  11  BPC   HL25
111111111111111111111111111111111111111111111111111111111111     *  EXP.  11  BPC   HL26
100011010011111111111111111111111111111111111111111111111111     *  EXP.  11  BPC   HL27
101110011110001010100010000101011001000110010110010010011011     *  EXP.  11  BPC   HL28
110111111110001111001111111111111111111111111111111111111111     *  EXP.  11  BPC   HL29
                                                                 *  EXP.  11  BPC   HL30
```

192

BPC E11 LOW HIGH   60 TRIALS   30 SUBJECTS

```
110110001111111111111111111111111111111111111111111111111111 * EXP. 11 BPC  LH01
111111111111111111111111111111111011111111111111111111111111 * EXP. 11 BPC  LH02
101011010101111111111111111111111111111111111111111111111111 * EXP. 11 BPC  LH03
111111111111111111111111111111111111111111111111111111111111 * EXP. 11 BPC  LH04
110101111111010110110010111010110110100010010101000110010    * EXP. 11 BPC  LH05
111111111111111111111111111111111111111111111111111111111111 * EXP. 11 BPC  LH06
000000100000000000000000000000000000000001000000000000000    * EXP. 11 BPC  LH07
111111111111111111111111111111111111111111111111111111111111 * EXP. 11 BPC  LH08
010001011010101000100011001010101100100001100010000000100100 * EXP. 11 BPC  LH09
010000010100000000010001000011000000010010000001000000001100 * EXP. 11 BPC  LH10
110000111000000000000000000000000000000000000000000000000    * EXP. 11 BPC  LH11
001010001001010000000001010001100000000110000100000000001000 * EXP. 11 BPC  LH12
111111111111111111111111111111111111111111111111111111111111 * EXP. 11 BPC  LH13
111111111110011100111111110011111111111111111111111111111111 * EXP. 11 BPC  LH14
111110110101101101111111111111111111111111111111111111111111 * EXP. 11 BPC  LH15
010001000000000001000000000100100000010000000010000000000000 * EXP. 11 BPC  LH16
100010000001000010100001001010010011001000010111010010100100 * EXP. 11 BPC  LH17
111111111111111111111111111111111111111111111111111111111111 * EXP. 11 BPC  LH18
111111111111111111111111111111111011111111111111111111111111 * EXP. 11 BPC  LH19
010110001100101110100010010100100010000000100001000010100    * EXP. 11 BPC  LH20
100000000100010000010111011110001111111111111111111111111111 * EXP. 11 BPC  LH21
111011011011101101101111111111111111111111111111111111111111 * EXP. 11 BPC  LH22
110111111111111111111110111111111111111111111111111111111111 * EXP. 11 BPC  LH23
111111010110110111111111111101111111111111110111111111111111 * EXP. 11 BPC  LH24
100110000000000000000000000000000000000000000000000010000    * EXP. 11 BPC  LH25
101001010001000010110000000000000000010000000000000000000000 * EXP. 11 BPC  LH26
110110110111111111111111111111111111111111111111111111111111 * EXP. 11 BPC  LH27
100000010000000000000000000000000000000000000000000000000000 * EXP. 11 BPC  LH28
111011001100001000000000000000000000000000000000000000000000 * EXP. 11 BPC  LH29
111101010010000100000000000000000000000000000000000000000000 * EXP. 11 BPC  LH30
```

BPC E11 LOW LOW   60 TRIALS   30 SUBJECTS

```
110110010100011010000000000000000000000000000000010010000    * EXP. 11 BPC  LL01
110100111010010101011101111111111111111111111111111111111111 * EXP. 11 BPC  LL02
111111111111111111111111011111111111111111111111111011111111 * EXP. 11 BPC  LL03
110001001000000011010000001010000000000010101010001000100010 * EXP. 11 BPC  LL04
111111111111111111111111111111111111111111111111111111111111 * EXP. 11 BPC  LL05
110100100101101110111111111111111111111111111111111111111111 * EXP. 11 BPC  LL06
100010111000010100010001001001010000000001000100100111110000 * EXP. 11 BPC  LL07
111111111111111111111111111111111111111111111111111111111111 * EXP. 11 BPC  LL08
111111111111111111111111111111111111111111111111111111111111 * EXP. 11 BPC  LL09
110011101010110111110111111101100101001101111001111111111010 * EXP. 11 BPC  LL10
110110111111111111111111111111111111111011101111111111111111 * EXP. 11 BPC  LL11
111011111111111111111111111111111111111111111111111111111111 * EXP. 11 BPC  LL12
111101011011011111111111111111111111111111111111111111111111 * EXP. 11 BPC  LL13
111110011011010111111111111111111111111111111111111111111111 * EXP. 11 BPC  LL14
110001011001000000000001001000000000011000010100010001001011 * EXP. 11 BPC  LL15
111100110111111111101111111111111111111111111111111111111111 * EXP. 11 BPC  LL16
111100001110000101000000000000000000000001010000000000000010 * EXP. 11 BPC  LL17
111111111111111111111111111111111111111111111111111111111111 * EXP. 11 BPC  LL18
111111111111111111111111111111111111111111111111111111111111 * EXP. 11 BPC  LL19
111110111111111111111111111111111111111111111111111111111111 * EXP. 11 BPC  LL20
111111111111111111111111111111111111111111111111111111111111 * EXP. 11 BPC  LL21
111111111111111111111111111111111111111111111111111111111111 * EXP. 11 BPC  LL22
110110110111111011110111111111111111111110111111111111111    * EXP. 11 BPC  LL23
110011110101011011111111111011101111111111111111110111111111 * EXP. 11 BPC  LL24
101110110101011111111111111011101101111111111111110111111111 * EXP. 11 BPC  LL25
111111011011011010111111111111011111101111111011011011111111 * EXP. 11 BPC  LL26
111111111111111111111111111111111111111111111111111111111111 * EXP. 11 BPC  LL27
111111111111111111111111111111111111111111111111111111111111 * EXP. 11 BPC  LL28
111111101111101101111110110010110101011111101111110111010    * EXP. 11 BPC  LL29
010010100000000001000000010000000000000000000000000001000    * EXP. 11 BPC  LL30
```

```
100000100001000000000000000000010000000001000000000000000000   10JUN70 BPC 20LH 01
001101001001001001001100101101010000000113100101100110101101100010   10JUN70 BPC 20LH 02
111111111111111111111111111111111111111111111111111111111111   10JUN70 BPC 20LH 03
100100001000001001010010110000000000000000000000000000001000   10JUN70 BPC 20LH 04
010110010000010101001001000010010101001100000101010100001011   10JUN70 BPC 20LH 05
101010010001010000011001001001010001010100101001100101011010000   10JUN70 BPC 20LH 06
010000000000000000000000000000000000000000000000000000000000   10JUN70 BPC 20LH 07
010100000010010010010000010000000000000010000000000010000000   10JUN70 BPC 20LH 08
011111111111111111111111111111111111111111111111111111111111   10JUN70 BPC 20LH 09
111110111101011100100011001000111110001100000001000000000000   10JUN70 BPC 20LH 10
111111111111111111111111111111111111111111111111111111111111   10JUN70 BPC 20LH 11
100000000000000000000000000000000000000000000000000000000000   10JUN70 BPC 20LH 12
000111001010001000100000000000000000000000100000000000000000   10JUN70 BPC 20LH 13
000000000000000000000000000000000000000000000000000000000000   10JUN70 BPC 20LH 14
100010000000000000000000000000000000000000000000000000000000   10JUN70 BPC 20LH 15
110110111111111111111111111111111111111111111111111111111111   10JUN70 BPC 20LH 16
100100011011000011000000000010010010000000100000000001000000   10JUN70 BPC 20LH 17
000100100011111001111111111111111111111111111110110111111101   10JUN70 BPC 20LH 18
110001100001101010001000100000001001001001000001100100001000   10JUN70 BPC 20LH 19
111111111111111111111111101111111111111111111111111111111111   10JUN70 BPC 20LH 20
100000000100100000010100000000010000000000000000000000000000   10JUN70 BPC 20LH 22
001010000010110100001011001010011001010101010111111101011111   10JUN70 BPC 20LH 23
100000000100010101111111011111111110001001001010000011111001   10JUN70 BPC 20LH 24
100001100100100100100100000000000000000000000000000000000000   10JUN70 BPC 20LH 25
000010100101001100010000100000100001000000000000000000001100   10JUN70 BPC 20LH 26
100000000000000000000000000000000000000000000000000000000000   10JUN70 BPC 20LH 27
111011100111011111111111111111111111111111111111111111111111   10JUN70 BPC 20LH 28
111011110011001010011000010000010001011111010111101111111100   10JUN70 BPC 20LH 30
101000101010000000000000000000000000000000000000000000000000   10JUN70 BPC 20LH 31
100100100010000001000000000000000000000000000000000000000000   10JUN70 BPC 20LH 32
100011000010010000000000000000000000000000000000000000000000   10JUN70 BPC 20LH 33
110000000000000000000000000000000000000000000000000000000000   10JUN70 BPC 20LH 34
```

```
111111111111111111111111111111111111111111111111111111111111   10JUN70 BPC 20HL 01
111011111111111111111111111111111111111111111111111111111111   10JUN70 BPC 20HL 02
111111111111111111111111111111111111111111111111111111111111   10JUN70 BPC 20HL 03
111110111111111111111111111111111111111111111111111111111111   10JUN70 BPC 20HL 04
000000000000000000000000000000000000000000000000000000000000   10JUN70 BPC 20HL 05
111011001101101101311111011111111111111111111111111111111111   10JUN70 BPC 20HL 06
111011111101011111111111111111111111111111111111111111111111   10JUN70 BPC 20HL 07
011110101111011111101101111101111111111111101111111111111111   10JUN70 BPC 20HL 08
110001111111110011101111111111011111101011110110111111111111   10JUN70 BPC 20HL 09
101010101001000101000011000010110001101010101101101010100111   10JUN70 BPC 20HL 10
111111111111111111111111111111111111111111111111111111111111   10JUN70 BPC 20HL 11
111111111111111111111111111111111111111111111111111111111111   10JUN70 BPC 20HL 12
100000110010000000000001000000100000000000011000000000000000   10JUN70 BPC 20HL 13
110110001000011001111100000000000000001000001000000000000000   10JUN70 BPC 20HL 14
100001101101110101111101111111111111111111111111111111111111   10JUN70 BPC 20HL 15
101110000001001010000000000000000000000000000000000000000000   10JUN70 BPC 20HL 16
111111111111111111111111111111111111111111111111111111111111   10JUN70 BPC 20HL 17
101111111111111111111111111111111111111111111111111111111111   10JUN70 BPC 20HL 18
101000111011111111111111111111111111111111111111111111111111   10JUN70 BPC 20HL 19
110001000000110100000000000010100000110001100100000000000000   10JUN70 BPC 20HL 20
111111111111111111111111111111111111111111111111111111111111   10JUN70 BPC 20HL 22
111111001111111111111111111111111111111111111111111111111111   10JUN70 BPC 20HL 23
000000010011011100011101011000000000001000010000000000000000   10JUN70 BPC 20HL 24
010000010000000000000000000000000000100100000000000000000000   10JUN70 BPC 20HL 25
000100000010000000000000001000010000001000001011100001100010   10JUN70 BPC 20HL 26
110110111101010111111111111110011110110101111101011111111111   10JUN70 BPC 20HL 27
110100111111111111111111111111111111111111111111111111111111   10JUN70 BPC 20HL 29
111111111111111111111111111111111111111111111111111111111111   10JUN70 BPC 20HL 30
111111111111111111111111111111111111111111111111111111111111   10JUN70 BPC 20HL 31
001100101001001010010011100100011111111110111111101110111110   10JUN70 BPC 20HL 32
110010101010100000100010000000000001000000000100010010000000   10JUN70 BPC 20HL 33
111111111111111111111111111111111111111111111111111111111111   10JUN70 BPC 20HL 34
111111111111111111111111111111111111111111111111111111111111   10JUN70 BPC 20HL 35
```

194

BPC E21 HIGH LOW   60 TRIALS   28 SUBJECTS

```
110010101110101010110101101001100010011101101010100111111001  10JUN70 BPC 21HL 01
111111111111111110111111111101001110000101000110001111110010  10JUN70 BPC 21HL 02
010000010010101111111011111101110111111111111111111111111111  10JUN70 BPC 21HL 03
111111111111111111111111111111111111111111111111111111111111  10JUN70 BPC 21HL 04
111111111111111111111111111111111111111111111111111111111111  10JUN70 BPC 21HL 05
111111111111111111111111111111111111111111111111111111111111  10JUN70 BPC 21HL 06
111111111111111111111111111111111111111111111111111111111111  10JUN70 BPC 21HL 07
111111111111111111111111111111111111111111111111111111111111  10JUN70 BPC 21HL 08
111111101111111111111111111111111110110111001111101011111010110  10JUN70 BPC 21HL 09
111111111111111111111111111111111111111111111111111111111111  10JUN70 BPC 21HL 10
111111111111111111111111111111111111111111111111111111111111  10JUN70 BPC 21HL 11
111111111111111111111111111111111111111111111111111111111111  10JUN70 BPC 21HL 12
100010000000000000000000000000000000000000000000000000000000  10JUN70 BPC 21HL 13
100110110001101101111011111101110111111101111111111111111111  10JUN70 BPC 21HL 14
111111111111111111111111111111111111111111111111111111111111  10JUN70 BPC 21HL 15
111111111111111111111111111111111111111111111111111111111111  10JUN70 BPC 21HL 16
111111111111111111111111111111111111111111111111111111111111  10JUN70 BPC 21HL 17
111111111111111111111111111111111111111111111111111101111111  10JUN70 BPC 21HL 18
100110111111111111111111111111111111111111111111111111111111  10JUN70 BPC 21HL 19
000010101111010111111111111111010111010011001000010101001011  10JUN70 BPC 21HL 20
110111111111111111111111111111111111111111111111111111111111  10JUN70 BPC 21HL 21
111111111111111111111111111111111111111111111111111111111111  10JUN70 BPC 21HL 22
111111111111111111111111111111111111111111111111111111111111  10JUN70 BPC 21HL 23
111111111111111111111111111111111111111111111111111111111111  10JUN70 BPC 21HL 24
111101111111101111111111111111111111111111111111111111111111  10JUN70 BPC 21HL 25
000100000000000111111111110111111111100000000000100000000000  10JUN70 BPC 21HL 26
111111110111110000001111111111011100111011011111111111111111  10JUN70 BPC 21HL 27
100100000100101101111011100110110111110000110000010000000010000  10JUN70 BPC 21HL 28
```

BPC E21 LOW HIGH   60 TRIALS   28 SUBJECTS

```
100001000100101010001101110011001111011011011011101011010100  10JUN70 BPC 21LH 01
110000110001010000010000001000010000000100100000010000010001  10JUN70 BPC 21LH 02
111111111111111111111111111111111111111111111111111111111111  10JUN70 BPC 21LH 03
101101011111111111111111111111111111111111111111111111111111  10JUN70 BPC 21LH 04
111111111111111111111111111111111111111111111111111111111111  10JUN70 BPC 21LH 05
110010010101110001011001010100011110101001010111111110001  10JUN70 BPC 21LH 06
100000000000000000000000000000000000000000000000000000000000  10JUN70 BPC 21LH 07
010000001000000000000000000000000000010000000000000000000000  10JUN70 BPC 21LH 08
001000000000000000000000000000000000000000000000000000000000  10JUN70 BPC 21LH 09
010111001111111111111111111111111111111111111111111111111111  10JUN70 BPC 21LH 10
111111111111111111111111111111111111111111111111111111111111  10JUN70 BPC 21LH 11
110110101011110111011111101111011011111111111111111111111111  10JUN70 BPC 21LH 12
111110000000000001000000000110110111111111111011011001011010  10JUN70 BPC 21LH 13
110110010110110010101001010101000001010010001101100100011010  10JUN70 BPC 21LH 14
010001100110101101011011101011111101111101101111101111101111  10JUN70 BPC 21LH 15
101011010100101000110111111101111111111111111111111111111111  10JUN70 BPC 21LH 16
110111111111011101110101111001000000001010000100010010001111  10JUN70 BPC 21LH 17
110111111111111111111111111111111111111111111111111111111111  10JUN70 BPC 21LH 18
101001010100111011001010110010001110110110000110010110001000  10JUN70 BPC 21LH 19
110101101000110101101000011010010010101010000010100111000001  10JUN70 BPC 21LH 20
111111111111111111111111111111111111111111111111111111111111  10JUN70 BPC 21LH 21
100000000000000000000000000000000000000000000000000000000000  10JUN70 BPC 21LH 22
111111111111111111111111111111111111111111111111111111111111  10JUN70 BPC 21LH 23
100001000010000000000000000000000000000000000000000000000000  10JUN70 BPC 21LH 24
111111111111111111111110000000000000010000000000010000000000  10JUN70 BPC 21LH 25
100000000000000000000000000000000000000000000000000000000000  10JUN70 BPC 21LH 26
101001101001111111100100000100100100010000001100010000000010000  10JUN70 BPC 21LH 27
101010001011010100111111110011111111101011101111111111111111  10JUN70 BPC 21LH 28
```

References

Adler, I. Dimensional Analysis. Unpublished doctoral dissertation, Stanford University, 1971.

Allen, V.L. "Situational Factors in Conformity". *Advances in Experimental Social Psychology*. Edited by L. Berkowitz. New York: Academic Press, 1965.

Asch, S.E. "Studies of Independence and Conformity: I. A Minority of One Against a Unanimous Majority". *Psychological Monographs*, 1956, 70, No. 416, 1-70.

Back, K.W. "Influence through Social Communication". *Journal of Abnormal Social Psychology*, 1951, 46, 9-23.

Bales, R.F. *Interaction Process Analysis: A Method for the Study of Small Groups*. Cambridge, Massachusetts: Addison-Wesley, 1951.

Bales, R.F. "The Equilibrium Problem in Small Groups". In *Working Papers in the Theory of Action*. R.F. Bales, E.A. Shils and T. Parsons. Glencoe, Illinois: The Free Press of Glencoe, 1953.

Bales, R.F. and Slater, P.E. "Role Differentiation in Small Decision-Making Groups". In *Family, Socialization and Interaction Process*. T. Parsons and R.F. Bales. Glencoe, Illinois: The Free Press of Glencoe, 1955.

Bartholomew, D.J. *Stochastic Models for Social Processes*. New York: Wiley, 1967.

Berenda, R.W. *The Influence of the Group on the Judgements of Children*. New York: King's Crown Press, 1950.

Berger, J. and Snell, J.R. "A Stochastic Theory of Self-Other Expectations". Technical Report. Department of Sociology. Stanford, California: Stanford University, 1961.

Berger, J. and Conner, T.L. "Performance Expectations and Behavior in Small Groups". *Acta Sociologica*, 1969, 12, 186-198.

Berger, J., Connor, T.L. and Fisek, M.H. Expectation States Theory. Cambridge, Massachusetts: Winthrop Publishers, 1974.

Berger, J., Conner, T.L. and McKeown, W.L. "Evaluations and the Formation and Maintenance of Performance Expectations". *Human Relations*, 1969, 22, 481-502.

Berger, J., Cohen, B.P. and Zelditch, M. Jr. "Status Characteristics and Expectation States". In *Sociological Theories in Progress*. Vol. 1. Edited by J. Berger, M. Zelditch Jr. and B. Anderson. Boston: Houghton-Mifflin, 1966.

Berger, J. and Fisek, M.H. "Consistent and Inconsistent Status Characteristics

196

and the Determination of Power and Prestige Orders". *Sociometry*, 1970, 33, 287-307.

Berger, J., Cohen, B.P., Snell, J.L. and Zelditch, M. Jr. *Types of Formalization in Small Group Research*. Boston: Houghton-Mifflin, 1962.

Berkowitz, L. "Group Standards, Cohesiveness, and Productivity". *Human Relations*, 1954, 7, 509-519.

Blake, R.B. and Brehm, J.W. "The Use of Tape Recording to Simulate a Group Atmosphere". *Journal of Abnormal Psychology*, 1954, 49, 311-313.

Blake, R.R. and Mouton, J.S. "The Dynamics of Influence and Coercion". *International Journal of Social Psychiatry*, 1957, 2, 263-305.

Cohen, B.P. "The Process of Choosing a Reference Group". In *Mathematical Methods in Small Group Processes*. Edited by J.H. Criswell, H. Solomon and P. Suppes. Stanford, California: Stanford University Press, 1962.

Cohen, B.P. *Conflict and Conformity: A Probability Model and its Application*. Cambridge, Massachusetts: M.I.T. Press, 1963.

Cohen, B.P. "On the Construction of Sociological Explanations". *Synthese*, 1972, 24, 401-409.

Collins, B.E. and Raven, B.H. "Group Structure: Attraction, Coalitions, Communication, and Power". In *The Handbook of Social Psychology*, Vol. 4. 2d ed. Edited by G. Lindzey and E. Aronson. Reading, Massachusetts: Addison-Wesley, 1969.

Crutchfield, R.S. "Assessment of Persons Through a Quasi Group Interaction Technique". *Journal of Abnormal Psychology*, 1951, 46, 577-588.

Crutchfield, R.S. "Conformity and Character". *American Psychologist*, 1955, 10, 191-198.

Crutchfield, R.S. "Personal and Situational Factors in Conformity to Group Pressure". *Acta Psychologica*, 1959, 15, 386-388.

Darley, J. "Fear and Social Comparison as Determinants of Conformity Behavior". *Journal of Personality and Social Psychology*, 1966, 4, 73-78.

Deutsch, M. and Gerard, H.B. "A Study of Normative and Informational Social Influence upon Individual Judgement". *Journal of Abnormal Psychology*, 1955, 51, 629-636.

Festinger, L. "An Analysis of Compliant Behavior". In *Group Relations at the Crossroads*. Edited by M. Sherif and M.O. Wilson. New York: Harper, 1953.

Festinger, L., Gerard, H., Hymovitch, B., Kelley, H. and Raven, B.H. "The Influence Process in the Presence of Extreme Deviants". *Human Relations*, 1952, 5, 327-346.

Fiedler, F.E. "Assumed Similarity Measures as Predictors of Team Effectiveness". *Journal of Abnormal Social Psychology*, 1954, 49, 381-388.

Fisek, M.H. and Ofshe, R. "The Process of Status Evolution". *Sociometry*, 1970, 33, 327-346.

French, J.R.P. Jr. and Raven, B.H. "The Bases of Social Power". in *Studies in Social Power*. Edited by D. Cartwright. Ann Arbor, Michigan: University of Michigan Press, 1959.

Gerard, H.B. "The Anchorage of Opinions in Face-to-Face Groups". *Human Relations*, 1954, 313-325.

Gorfein, D., Kindrick, T., Leland, Q., McAvoy, M.E. and Barrows, J. "Cognitive Dissonance and Yielding Behavior". *Journal of Psychology*, 1960, 50, 205-208.

Hanna, J.R. "A New Approach to the Formulation and Testing of Learning Models". *Synthese*, 1966, 16, 344-380.

Harper, F.B.W. "The Sociometric Composition of the Groups as a Determinant of Yield to a Distorted Norm". Unpublished Ph. D. Dissertation, University of California (Berkeley), 1961.

Heinicke, C.M. and Bales, R.F. "Developmental Trends in the Structure of Small Groups". *Sociometry*, 1953, 16, 7-38.

Hicks, J.M., Monty, R.A. and Myers, T.I. "Group Consensus and Judgemental Accuracy: Extension of the Asch Effect". *Psychonomic Science*, 1966, 5, 159-160.

Hollander, R.P. "Conformity, Status, and Idiosyncrasy Credit". *Psychological Review*, 1958, 65, 117-127.

Hollander, R.P. "Competence and Conformity in the Acceptance of Influence". *Journal of Abnormal and Social Psychology*, 1960, 61, 365-369.

Homans, G.C. *The Human Group*. New York: Harcourt, Brace, and World, 1950.

Kemeny, J.G. and Snell J.L. *Mathematical Models in the Social Sciences*. New York: Blaisdell Publishing Company, 1962.

Kemeny, J.G. and Snell, J.L. *Finite Markov Chains*. Princeton, New Jersey: D. Van Nostrand, 1960.

Kemeny, J.G., Hazelton, M., Snell, J.L. and Thompson, G.L. *Finite Mathematical Structures*. Englewood Cliffs, New Jersey: Prentice-Hall, 1959.

Lott, A.J. and Lott, B.E. "Group Cohesiveness, Communication Level, and Conformity". *Journal of Abnormal Social Psychology*, 1961, 62, 408-412.

McFarland, D.D. "Intergenerational Social Mobility as a Markov Process: Including a Time-Stationary Markovian Model that Explains Observed Declines in Mobility Rates". *American Sociological Review*, 1970, 35, 463-476.

Meehan, E.J. *Explanation in Social Science: A System Paradigm*. Homewood, Illinois: The Dorsey Press, 1968.

Merton, R.K. *Social Theory and Social Structure*. Glencoe, Illinois: The Free Press of Glencoe, 1957.

Nagel, E. *The Structure of Science*. New York: Harcourt, Brace, and World, Inc., 1961.

Query, J.M. "The Influence of Group Pressure on the Judgements of Children and Adolescents: A Comparative Study". *Adolescence*, 1968, 3, 153-160.

Reitan, H.T. and Shaw, M.E. "Group Membership, Sex-Comparison of the Group, and Conformity Behavior". *Journal of Social Psychology*, 1964, 64, 45-51.

Roby, T.B. and Lanzetta, J.T. "Considerations in the Analysis of Group Tasks". *Psychological Bulletin*, 1958, 55, 88-101.

Rosenthal, R. *Experimenter Effects in Behavioral Research*. New York: Appleton-Century-Crofts, 1966.

Sable, J.A. Unpublished Honors Thesis. Stanford University: Department of Sociology, 1962.

Schachter, S. "Deviation, Rejection, and Communication". *Journal of Abnormal and Social Psychology*, 1951, 46, 190-207.

Schulman, G.I. "Asch Conformity Studies: Conformity to the Experimenter and/or to the Group?" *Sociometry*, 1967, 30, 26-40.

Sherif, M. *The Psychology of Social Norms*. New York: Harper, 1936.

Siegel, S. "Certain Determinants and Correlates of Authoritarianism". *Genetic Psychology Monographs*, 1954, 49, 187-229.

Stinchcombe, A.L. *Constructing Social Theories*. New York: Harcourt, Brace, and World, 1968.

Terry, C.W. Unpublished Honors Thesis. Stanford University: Department of Sociology, 1961.

Tuddenham, R.D. "The Influence of a Distorted Group Norm upon Individual Judgement". *Journal of Psychology*, 1958, 46, 243-251.

Tuddenham, R.D., Macbride, P. and Zahn, V. "The Influence of Sex Composition of the Group upon Yielding to a Distorted Norm". *Journal of Psychology*, 1958, 46, 243-251.

Tuddenham, R.D. "The Influence upon Judgement of the Apparent Discrepancy between Self and Others". *Journal of Social Psychology*, 1961, 53, 69-79.

Webster Jr., M. "Source of Evaluations and Expectations for Performance". *Sociometry*. 1969, 32, 243-258.

White, H.C. *Chains of Opportunity*. Cambridge, Massachusetts: Harvard University Press, 1970.

Wilson, R.S. "Personality Patterns, Source Attractiveness, and Conformity". *Journal of Personality*, 1960, 28, 186-199.

Zelditch Jr., M. Mimeographed class notes, Stanford University, 1969.

Index

"ad hoc" explanation, 6, 8
Allen, V.L., 5, 6, 8, 143, 144
Asch initial vector, see standardized
    initial distribution vector
Asch situation, 3, 11, 17-31 passim.,
    40, 49-56 passim., 60, 68, 82,
    115, 136-137, 146, 153, 157,
    158, 159-164
Asch situation, modifications of,
    17, 50, 62, 160
Asch situation, properties of, 44-49
Asch, S.E., 11, 27, 40, 45, 50, 61,
    62, 99, 152, 163
atomistic strategy, 3-4, 158-159

Back, K.W., 144
Bales, R.F., 44
Barrows, J., 45
Berenda, R.W., 44
Berger, J., 7, 24, 53, 55, 56, 145
Berkowitz, L., 5
bivariate analysis, 4, 10, 159
Blake, R.R., 11, 65
Brehm, J.W., 11, 65

Cohen, B.P., 1, 5n., 7, 9, 12, 14, 17,
    18, 23, 24, 26, 38, 39, 44, 48,
    49, 52, 53, 61, 62, 67, 69, 70,
    76, 101, 137, 145
Cohen-Lee Model, 22, 28, 43, 67-
    146, 153-157; changes from
    Conflict Model, 68-69; fit of
    model, 98, 113, 115-177; matrix
    of transition probabilities, A,
    69; see also parameters and

parameter estimation
Collins, B.E., 5, 9, 13
comparability, 11, 16; see also
    cumulative knowledge
comparison of treatments, see
    treatment comparisons
computer simulation, 47
conditional nature of science, 14
confederates, characteristics of:
    in Experiment 1, 100; in Exper-
    iment 2, 100; in Experiment 3,
    100; in Experiment 11, 64, 65;
    in Experiment 20, 105; in Exper-
    iment 22, 105
Conflict and Conformity, 1, 17, 23,
    27-31 passim., 40, 44, 46, 47,
    48, 50, 67, 69, 73, 100, 115,
    157; see also Conflict Model
Conflict Model, 17-20, 21, 23, 24-
    43, 47, 48, 67, 168; alternatives
    to Assumption 3 in, 28; assump-
    tions of, 25-26; constraints in
    applying, 39-41; criterion for
    goodness of fit of, 31; definition
    of, 25; matrix of transition prob-
    abilities, P, 26; problems in
    estimation, 67-68; properties of,
    29-41; purpose of, 24; states of,
    25; substantive meaning of
    parameters in, 19-20; see also
    parameters and parameter
    estimation
conflict resolution and conformity,
    relationship between, 137-139,
    146, 147, 149, 157, 164, 168

200